Y0-BGH-769

From Berlin to Bagdad; behind the scenes in the Near East

George Abel Schreiner

Nabu Public Domain Reprints:

You are holding a reproduction of an original work published before 1923 that is in the public domain in the United States of America, and possibly other countries. You may freely copy and distribute this work as no entity (individual or corporate) has a copyright on the body of the work. This book may contain prior copyright references, and library stamps (as most of these works were scanned from library copies). These have been scanned and retained as part of the historical artifact.

This book may have occasional imperfections such as missing or blurred pages, poor pictures, errant marks, etc. that were either part of the original artifact, or were introduced by the scanning process. We believe this work is culturally important, and despite the imperfections, have elected to bring it back into print as part of our continuing commitment to the preservation of printed works worldwide. We appreciate your understanding of the imperfections in the preservation process, and hope you enjoy this valuable book.

FROM BERLIN TO BAGDAD

Books by

GEORGE ABEL SCHREINER

THE IRON RATION
FROM BERLIN TO BAGDAD

————

HARPER & BROTHERS, NEW YORK
[Established 1817]

AT CONSTANTINOPLE

Reproduced from Vinegar Quay, Stamboul
under the limit of any-
from port by some of
tinople.

FROM BERLIN TO BAGDAD

Behind the Scenes in the Near East

BY

GEORGE ABEL SCHREINER

Author of
"THE IRON RATION"

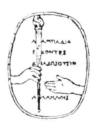

HARPER & BROTHERS PUBLISHERS

NEW YORK AND LONDON

From Berlin to Bagdad

Copyright, 1918, by Harper & Brothers
Printed in the United States of America
Published September, 1918

TO
MY DEAR FRIENDS
MARY AND MAX SMITH

CONTENTS

ILLUSTRATIONS

PREFACE

I SPENT nine months in warring Turkey as war and general correspondent of the Associated Press of America.

In that capacity I described, anonymously—for that is the policy of this news-gathering organization—the operations of the Allied naval and military forces against the Dardanelles and the peninsula of Gallipoli.

Later I had occasion to go toward Arabia. While on that trip I became an eye-witness to a part of what is now known as the Armenian crisis.

During my stay at Constantinople I had an audience with the Sultan and was received, as occasion required, by the leaders of the Young Turk government—Prince Saiid Halim Pasha, Grand Vizier; Enver Pasha, Minister of War and Vice-Generalissimo of the Ottoman army; Talaat Bey, then Minister of the Interior and now Grand Vizier and Pasha.

At the front I met Field-marshal Liman von Sanders Pasha, the man in charge of the defense of Gallipoli; Admiral-General von Usedom Pasha, who cared for the coast defense means along the Dardanelles; and many others.

But the social tastes of the newspaper-man must

PREFACE

be catholic He must meet, or should meet, everybody. True to this, I made it my business to cultivate as wide a circle of friends and acquaintances as was possible under the circumstances.

Among my friends in Constantinople, then, is Turkey's foremost writer and poet, feminist and reformer, educator and philanthropist, Halideh Edib Hannym Effendi.

I am deeply indebted to this brilliant woman. When I came to Turkey I was as ignorant of its life as most of us Westerners are. Turkey is of the East. We of the Occident say that it is hard to understand for that reason.

But the Orient is not so baffling as we have been pleased to maintain. Its people may be as well understood as any others, provided one sets out to understand them.

Halideh Hannym thought that I should make the attempt to understand the Turk. This I did under her guidance

But I have not attempted here to give the result of my observations in an academic form, for the reason that such an exposition might lack interest-holding qualities. Instead, I have given my own impressions as they reached me. Nearly all of them were recorded immediately afterward. To preserve their original flavor they are being reproduced in this book without material changes.

I picture here the Turkey at war and the Turkey at peace, and the life of those people who are still *in* the Ottoman Empire, instead of being *of* it, as once they and the Turks did hope. The revolution and the rehabilitation of the Ottoman Constitution have not removed the demo-political problems of the state. Turk, Greek, Armenian, Kurd, and Arab are as far apart to-day as they were when the Young Turks, the "Party of Union and Progress," announced that they would weld into a whole the races under the Star and Crescent.

Why this is so, I have set forth in this book. And here again I have avoided the strictly technical. It struck me that so much more could be said by leaving much unsaid. The picture tells often more than a description. It is the picture I have used.

Considerable attention has been given to the status of the Turkish woman. For that I had two reasons. In the first place, the West is woefully misinformed and uninformed on this subject. When we think of Turkey we think of the *hareem*, and when we think of that we think of women spending their lives as the plaything of brutal men. That is a fallacy. The other reason is that the Turkish woman has become a very progressive being in recent years; that in this respect she is by far the superior of the man.

During the last three years much has been heard of the "Berlin to Bagdad" scheme. In what state that enterprise is to-day is noted here as comprehensively as the fluctuations of the times permit. In the spring and summer of 1915 the naval and land forces of the British and French governments did their best to nip "Berlin to Bagdad" in the bud, by an attack upon the gate of Constantinople —the Dardanelles and Gallipoli. What the end of this undertaking was is well known.

PREFACE

It was my good fortune to be an eye-witness to the epoch-making events in the Strait of Dardanelles and on Gallipoli Peninsula. In describing them I present to the public the first authentic account of the Dardanelles-Gallipoli campaign as seen from the coast batteries and trenches of the Turks, to whose military forces I was then attached as war correspondent. I wish to say in this connection that I have not undertaken to view these operations critically in this volume. What I have to say of them is a simple and frank relation of facts—so constructed that general human interest rather than military science, and the like, occupies the attention of the reader.

S.

New York, *June, 1918.*

FROM BERLIN TO BAGDAD

FROM BERLIN TO BAGDAD

I

IN THE NATURE OF A PROLOGUE

SINCE the termination, by the Allies, of the Dardanelles-Gallipoli campaign it has been clear that the fate of Turkey would ultimately be settled on the European West Front. So long as Russia was in the war there was a chance, as some saw it, that the attack on the strait and the peninsula would be renewed. The collapse of Russia, however, made that possibility a very remote one.

But there were those who, even before the evacuation of the peninsula, were of the opinion that the West Front would in the end decide whether or no there was to be an Ottoman Empire in years to come. One of them was Field-marshal Liman von Sanders Pasha, commander of the Ottoman forces on Gallipoli.

Liman Pasha, with that fine objectivity that was his, always held that the operations of the British and French against the Dardanelles and on Gallipoli would serve no purpose. To take that stand, Liman Pasha had to feel, of course, that he could

keep the Allied troops from advancing to their objectives on the peninsula and in the strait—upon
Constantinople ultimately.

By the middle of June Liman Pasha was sure of
this. He referred to his ability to hold the Allied
forces in check on several occasions, and he did this
in a manner that could leave no doubt in the mind
of the hearer.

The opinion of the general interested me, naturally. I tested it several times in the manner we
newspaper-men acquire by dint of practice and
experience. Liman Pasha was sure of his ground.
If he had any misgivings they were due to the fact
that he never had enough ammunition for his artillery. I know that this worried him now and
then.

On the other hand, Liman Pasha understood that
the handicaps of the British and French were great.
Time and time again it had been shown that the
infantry of the Allies could not long hold ground
that lay below the topographical crest seen from
the sea—ground which, in other words, was not
visible from the battle-ships of the Allies, and
which, for this reason, could not be taken under
direct fire.

When trenches are close together, even if in plain
view of the artillerymen, there is always danger
that one may bombard one's own troops. The
slightest error in sighting may result in that
calamity. The difficulties become insurmountable
when such trenches are to be reached by indirect
fire from the ever-moving deck of a battle-ship.

There were other difficulties which the Allies

2

had to contend with. The climate was not suited for the men employed. Even the hardy and heroic Anzacs found Gallipoli insufferable. There was not enough water, of course, and, last but not least, there was lack of room and opportunity to give the Allied troops in reserve a chance to recuperate and recreate.

To show how fine a student Liman Pasha had been of the British troops let me cite that he always thought the lack of room in the Ariburnu terrain the worst hardship the Australians and New-Zealanders underwent.

The participation in the European war by Turkey has two phases. They are divided by the withdrawal of the Allied forces from the peninsula.

Without wishing to appear academic in a book that is to entertain as well as inform, I must, for the sake of clearness, devote a little space to these phases.

The phases of a campaign are determined and divided by the outcome of a series of operations. The reaching of an objective and the abandonment of a plan alike give periods to a phase. It was so on Gallipoli.

Since I propose to give elsewhere a more specific delineation of the objectives of the Allies, I will merely state here that the purpose of the naval operations was to open the way to Constantinople. These operations failed.

The next move of the Allies was to land troops at Kum Kaleh and on Gallipoli. The object to be attained in that case was to break down the Turkish coast-defense system along the Dardanelles, so that the British and French ships might then steam to Constantinople.

The British and French governments do not seem to have at any time seriously contemplated reaching the Ottoman capital overland. Such a plan could not be very inviting—for several good reasons. If Allied troops had been landed in the Gulf of Saros, in fighting their way toward Constantinople, they would have been obliged to take the Tchadaldja line of fortifications. That would not have been an easy task.

But success would have served in good stead on the Balkan. Bulgaria in that case would have never joined the camp of the Central Powers. On the contrary, she might have gone with the Entente. That contingency, however, could not be foreseen in the early spring of 1915.

As seen from the viewpoint of British policy the Dardanelles-Gallipoli campaign was well conducted, be it regarded from a military or from a political point of view. I know that the very opposite has been claimed in Great Britain and elsewhere. I also know that the British Dardanelles Campaign Commission differs from me, as its report plainly indicates.

It is the easiest thing in the world to criticize after the event. To belittle the plan of a military leader after that plan has miscarried is most inviting. All one has to do is to say that the leader should not have done the very things he did do.

Having made a close study of the Dardanelles and Gallipoli operations, I may be permitted to say that the critics of Sir Ian Hamilton, and the men

4

associated with him, have always appeared a little too eager to condemn. Many of them seem to have taken it for granted that the Ottoman soldier is not what the Allied troops found him to be—brave as a lion, as goes the saying. Others, with equal consistency, have overlooked the fact that in Liman Pasha, Admiral-General von Usedom Pasha, Admiral-General Merten, and other German officers in the Ottoman service, the British and French had to deal with antagonists of daring, training, and resourcefulness.

This world would look very different to-day had the Allied fleet reached Constantinople. The appearance of the fleet would have been the signal for the collapse of the Ottoman Empire. Never hung the fate of a state by so slender a thread. So long as such men as Enver Pasha and Talaat Pasha had the government in their hands a capitulation would have been out of the question. That these men intended to continue the fight is shown by the fact that the Ottoman government, on that fateful March 18th, was ready to go to Eski-Shehir in Anatolia, the cradle of Osmanli power. That government would have gone home to die.

While the powerful leaders of the Young Turk party were willing to carry on the fight, their intentions alone could not accomplish that resolve. They did not have the means in Anatolia to continue the struggle. After a few weeks they would have realized the futility of their effort. A Turkey might have existed after that—an Ottoman Empire, no.

Much has been taken for granted in the Dardanelles-Gallipoli campaign. The Russians especially were liberal in that respect. While the operations were in progress many of the Russian leading publications indulged in the fine anticipations of soon making Constantinople the southern capital of the Russian Empire.

There is no means of knowing whether or not Russian statesmen were equally sanguine. The best that had ever been promised Petrograd by the governments in London and Paris was the "internationalization" of Constantinople and its waterways.

But to bring this about in a manner befitting the times was not so easy. Critics have often found it hard to understand why the Allies did not synchronize the attack of the fleet with that of the troops, and with the landing of a large force of Russians on the Black Sea coast of Thrace—at Media, for example.

There can be no doubt that this would have been a bad blow for the Turks, but in the end it would have proved equally disastrous to the British.

It is the duty of British statesmen to preserve the influence of Great Britain in the Mediterranean—to hold, at any cost, the bridge-head of India, the Suez Canal.

That being the case, these men could not think of enthroning on the Dardanelles so imperialistic a power as Romanoff Russia was. Great Britain's two-power standard would have availed little in that event. The Sea of Marmora is the finest naval base in the world, and Eski-Hissarlik could be made a Gibraltar with three times the strength of the original. If the Dardanelles had never before been closed, they would have been hermetically sealed then, had Great Britain and France permitted the Russians to force through their wholly unfounded claims upon Constantinople.

With that day also would have passed into oblivion British control of the Eastern Mediterranean and the Suez Canal. In that event India would have been lost, or at least hard to keep. And what assurance is there that Russia, in order to fully enjoy the fruits of her good fortune, might not have decided then and there that, so far as she was concerned, the European war was over? Certainly so fine a morsel as the Bosphorus, Constantinople, Dardanelles Strait, Asia Minor, and the Balkans would have been worth a little political tacking, especially since Russia's plans in Western Europe could have been carried out at entire leisure. Who could or would have interfered?

These, then, were the contingencies that English statesmen had to bear in mind.

Thus it came that the taking of the Dardanelles and of Constantinople had to be made and kept a strictly British piece of business.

When it was seen that the Allied fleet could not force the Dardanelles the same thing was attempted *via* Gallipoli. From the Atchi Baba and Kodjatchemen Dagh, British artillery was to silence the forts along the strait, and then the ships were to steam through and make an end of Ottoman rule in Stamboul.

To synchronize with the naval operations in March a landing on the peninsula was a little risky for the reason that Russia would certainly have offered to co-operate with a landing on the Black Sea shore of Thrace. That was not desirable, for the reasons just given. Constantinople could be much easier internationalized if no Russian troops participated in its taking.

While the operations of the Allies on Gallipoli were in progress the Russians were rather busy holding the Germans and Austro-Hungarians back. The Allies were consequently spared a most inconvenient situation.

In August, while I was in Constantinople, Turkey consented to a border rectification in favor of Bulgaria. In September the rectification was actually made, and two weeks later Bulgaria joined the Central Powers. That was the beginning of the second phase of the campaign.

Sir Ian Hamilton on August 6th had landed his second expeditionary army. It made as little progress as the troops that had been set ashore on April 25th. In November the first German guns for the Turks and large shipments of ammunition passed over the Danube southward. The Serbs, who in the past had kept this line of communication between Germany and Turkey closed, had been thrown south by Mackensen.

So much war material and so many reinforcements were being rushed into Turkey by Germany and Austria-Hungary that the Allies finally decided to abandon Gallipoli. It might have been possible to continue holding on at Sid-il-Bahr and Ariburnu-Suvla Bay. But the sacrifices would have been heavy and there was no promise that progress would ever be made. The Allied troops were withdrawn in a masterly manner.

Since then it has been quiet at the Dardanelles.

The tragic end of the Russian Empire has made the Dardanelles, for the time being, an objective of secondary importance. The Turkish-German line of communication can no longer be cut at that point. To-day the Black Sea is open to the Germans and the Turks. The strait is fortified as it never before was fortified. The fate of the Ottoman Empire will be decided in Western Europe.

CONSTANTINOPLE, PERA, *February 9, 1915.*

Made my entry into the Ottoman capital at two o'clock this morning—train almost seven hours late. Seems that after all it was the bridge over the Maritza, near Adrianople, which caused the delay. Spring has set in suddenly in Thrace and on the southern slopes of the Balkan range. Snow having been plentiful throughout the winter, too much water came down the Maritza Valley in too short a time. The result was that the bridge gave way.

So at two this morning we pulled into the station of the *Sirkedchi Iskelessi*, Stamboul, had my passport once more examined by a sleepy officer, and then consigned myself into the hands and care of a hotel *portier*. Bade *au revoir* to the *espaniole* Jews with whom I had shared the *coupé* since Adrianople, and compared ancient and modern Spanish, the latter as spoken in Mexico; then tumbled, half asleep, into the *araba* (carriage);

noticed that we went across a good bridge; climbed a steep hill in what I concluded to be Pera; and finally brought up in front of a large, gloomy structure—the hotel.

In the morning called at the American embassy and met Ambassador Morgenthau, also his son, Henry, Jr., the Armenian *drogman* (interpreter), and the various diplomatic secretaries. Then registered at the Club de Constantinople—Le Petit Club, as they call it in contradistinction to the *Cercle d'Orient*, or Big Club. The bill of fare is good. Sampled some *yamourtas alla Turca*, *shish kebab*, and wound up with *yaourt* and *tchilek*.

"You might just as well get used to hearing some such mixture of Turkish and French from now on," said I to myself.

In Pera they speak a little of all languages. I haven't the heart to make a list of them. But they all speak French — Levantine French — and just now it is considered proper to air the few words of Turkish one has acquired—often after the residence here of a lifetime.

Have learned that when a Perote says "slaw" he does not mean cabbage in any form, but "c'la," a corruption of the French *cela*.

Made some inquiries relative to various massacres alleged to have occurred in Pera. Everybody smiled. Then they told me the name of the American correspondent who had disseminated these rumors from Salonika and Athens in the form of honest-to-goodness news despatches. Also the fact was mentioned that since then the Ottoman government had been rather severe toward all foreign news-

paper-men. As to the massacres—there had been no
such thing, of course. I was glad of that, but tried
to figure out what my chances would be working in
a place like this, where some dear colleague had
"fouled the nest."

After I heard what Mr. Theron Damon,
correspondent for the service, and Moschopulous,
Damon's reporter, had to say on this subject, and
the consequent attitude in Ottoman government
circles, I was certain that I should not stay long in
Constantinople and that my studies of conditions
in Turkey would be short and incomplete.

In the evening I met Bucknam Pasha, a good
Californian who some years ago brought a ship to
Turkey from the Cramp yards in Philadelphia,
and who then decided that he would enter the
Ottoman navy and become an admiral, or something
of the sort.

Well, it rained the greater part of the day. So
I watched them play poker and other games of
chance at the Petit Club, had long conferences
with Damon and Moschopulous, and learned
enough of intrigue and statesmanship on the
Bosphorus to feel that they were both intricate
and ruthless.

Back to the hotel, where I had a row concerning
the paucity of stove wood and the mental shortcomings of the *valet de chambre*.

So far my sphere is very limited. All of it lies
in Pera, in the rue Kabristan. Next to the hotel
is the American embassy, beyond that the Petit
Club, and across the street the editorial offices,
etc., of the Greek daily *Chronos*. At the embassy

11

I picked up a rumor to-day, at the club it grew, and at the hotel common sense killed it.

In Constantinople one meets two continents, two worlds, a score of races, a dozen languages, and half a score of religions. Here one picks up, without bending the back, so to speak, the fragments of ancient, and the tail-ends of present-day, civilizations, history, tradition, social laws, economic systems, and political fabrics. Constantinople lies on two great highways. Just now the water route is the most important. It runs from north to south—from the Black Sea, through the Bosphorus, Sea of Marmora, and the Dardanelles into the Mediterranean. The great turnpike travels from east to west. Over it have come many of the races whose descendants are now at war with one another in Western and Central Europe—over it have come all the impulses that gave rise to what we are pleased to call Western civilization.

This much at least I have known of Constantinople for some time. So far, I know little more of it. To-day I made my first trip to Stamboul—the Turkish part of Constantinople. Its streets are narrow, tolerably well paved, and clean. The houses generally have a stone *parterre*, while the upper story is of wood. Few of them are three stories high. The lower wall, as a rule, is pierced only by the door and a single small window beside it. To the second floor plenty of light is admitted. Generally there is a whole row of latticed windows, with a *shahnichin* or two—bay window—also latticed. Very few of the houses give the impression that they could be divided into two separate parts

—suites for the males and suites for the females of the family. The *selamlik* and *hareemlik* may still be found in Turkey, so my *drogman* informs me, but only in palaces.

"Monsieur," said the clever *espaniole* who acts as my guide and interpreter, "much of what I have read in books by European authors on Constantinople and Turkey is far removed from the reality of things. The *hareemlik* is one of the things they have dreamed about too much. The Turk of to-day is too poor to have more than one wife. He is satisfied when he can support one woman and her children. You will not find many Turks here who live in polygamy. I think I could name you most of them offhand."

It seems that the proud Osmanli finds it hard to get along in this modern world. He does not take kindly to trade and artisanship. He is far too honest to have much of a chance in competition with the Greeks and Armenians. But he must live, and since the Ottoman government is a thing peculiarly Turkish, even under the Young Turks, he has at least a chance to become a government official. But his pay is small. The result of this is that the Turk in the government service is not well off materially. Those sections of Stamboul in which he lives show this. The paint on the houses has been badly weathered, sun and rain have chipped it off, and somehow or other an aspect of genteel poverty hangs about the *shahnichins*.

Here and there a door would open in the quiet streets. A woman would emerge, wearing the *yashmak*, a heavy and impenetrable veil of black.

13

You can see that there is a face under the *yashmak*, but you have no means of telling whether it is pretty or not, young or not.

Most of the women I saw were rather slender and shapely. The *feredchch* they wear could not hide their pleasing figures. This garment, cut like a loose-fitting dress, is generally of silk, even among the poor classes. Somber colors prevail. The *feredchch* is black in a majority of cases, but I saw colors as well—dark tans, maroon, purple, violet, olive, lighter greens of a subdued hue, salmon reds, and, what seems to be a favorite with all young women at present, according to the *drogman*, a sort of slate color with a dash of violet in it. The rule is that the younger women may wear colors—youth leaning toward the gay. The lighter the color of the outer dress the younger its wearer is likely to be, though exceptions are not rare. Good shoes of European cut are generally worn by the women.

There was something in the graceful carriage of the *hannyms* that gave one an inkling of what the race has been in the past. I have no right to say that the Turks no longer possess these qualities, for it is certain, according to what authorities I have been able to consult, that the Osmanli race is still far from being a thing of the past. Too many of the fine qualities of this conqueror people show in their women to permit the snap judgment, given by so many, that the day of the Turk is gone.

Children always interest me. As subjects for study of the life of a people they have no equal. In the child the natural traits come out unreined.

14

The Turkish children, led by the hand of some *hannym*, were well behaved. They trotted alongside of their mothers with sturdy step, showing a keen interest in everything about them, as their lively chatter and the pointing of their little fingers indicated. Most of the children were dressed *alla Franca*—everything in Turkey having a European character is styled *alla Franca*: France is the one country of the Occident that the Turk really loves.

In the yard of a mosque I saw several children at play—boys and girls. Their cries and screams of delight rent the air. They were playing some sort of hide-and-seek, though the slim columns did not offer much cover for even their little bodies. The girls were the liveliest players.

One of them, with a tomboy face that needed washing, dancing brown eyes, and light-brown hair, seemed to be the leader of the game. Up and down the yard she rushed, yelling and gesticulating. Once she ran over a little two-year-old shaver. The youngster found contact with the stone pavement too much for him and set up a scream.

Of a sudden the game came to an end. The tomboy put the little one back to his feet, kissed away his tears, overwhelmed him with a flood of endearing terms, and then carried him off to a corner of the yard. Over a stick of candy, the little Turk quickly forgot his pains and troubles. The game proceeded, and soon the tomboy's torn brown skirt could be seen again all over the yard.

"Even the Turk who has only one wife sticks to the customs of his fathers, however," explained my *drogman*. "There may not be a *hareemlik* in his house, but you never see his wife and grown-up daughters. When there are male visitors the female members of their family stay in their rooms. Outside of that family life in Turkey is what it is elsewhere, I suppose."

I did not explain to the *drogman* how much of a difference even that would leave between Moslem and Western family life.

We came to a quarter where people seemed to be better off. The houses did not differ materially from those I had seen before, but they were larger, and had been painted within determinable periods. Here and there budding trees peeped over high garden walls. My *drogman* explained that in this section lived many of the higher government officials. Here also were to be found the town houses of the Turks owning large farms in Anatolia.

I saw some private carriages. Smart toilettes were not uncommon. While many of the women were still hidden behind the *yashmak*, I saw some who sought refuge only behind a thin veil of black, or of some color matching the *feredcheh*. My *drogman* explained that these veils were known as *burundchuk*—Broussa silk. The *burundchuk* does not hide much. It adds, however, to the attractiveness of the wearer, and that, as I understand it, is the prime purpose of this article everywhere.

I saw several remarkably handsome women and pretty girls in the space of two streets. Complexions ranged from peaches-and-cream to olive, and hair from blond to black. I suppose there was a similar range in eyes, but that I could not determine.

Some of the women were attended by eunuchs
—last of their kind. Most of them had a black
woman servant with them. Not a few were plainly
curious as to who this new *Franc* was—I really
seemed to be an object of interest.

The *drogman* explained that the ladies were going
to the shops to make their purchases. They bought
the best, he said. Since I saw only the *yashmak*,
burundchuk, silk *feredchehs*, lace petticoats, and
high-heeled shoes, I was not in a position to say to
what extent he was right. But even Stamboul has
department stores that would fit into any Western
city.

At the new bridge across the Golden Horn I
later watched the procession of Turkish women
going to and returning from Pera. That the Turk
should be jealous of his womankind I can well
understand now. Not alone is the Turkish woman
something which any man might wish to possess,
but she also does not mind flirting a little. She is
attractive and knows it, and that being the case,
craves admiration. She has my share of it, at any
rate.

Constantinople has two "sects" of women. I
say sects for the reason that religion divides them.
A woman of the City of the Golden Horn is either
a Moslem or a Levantine, the latter class including
both Christians and Jews.

The former class is easily distinguished from the
other, and *vice versa*. Women who wear the veil
are Moslems; while those who do not are Levantines
and in a few cases Europeans.

There are also several American ladies here. A

few of them are connected with the American
embassy and Roberts College, a few others belong to
the American Mission in Stamboul, a score or so
teach at the American School for Girls at Arnautkoi,
a baker's dozen have husbands and fathers in business at Constantinople, and three American ladies
are the wives of officers in the German naval and
military services.

But to continue with the ladies of native origin.
The veil, be it *yashmak* or *burundchuk*, does not
justify the conclusion that its wearer is a Turk
or Osmanli. She may be a Georgian, Tcherkess,
Turkoman, Syrian, Arab, Persian, Indian, or Egyptian. Now and then she is a Greek or Armenian who
chose to be the wife of a Moslem. Not a few are of
Balkan origin—Bulgar, Macedonian, and Albanian.

The slim and vivacious Levantine, more especially *la pérote*, as the non-Moslem woman of Constantinople is often called, has antecedents just
as varied. But the Greeks and Armenians form
the majority. Next in order come the women of
mixed blood, the Levantines proper. Some of her
forebears came from Italy and southern Russia,
the Balkan States and Rumania; and not infre-
quently one meets daughters of the *espaniole* Jews,
who fled from the cruel reign of Ferdinand and
Isabella when the Inquisition ravaged Spain.
Turkey in those days was the only enlightened
country in Europe. Its Sultan heard of the plight
of the Jews and offered them for a home the site
of what is now Salonika.

The men of Constantinople are rather a nonde-
script lot. The male Levantine runs to the highest

of collars and the oddest of shoes. His clothing is not bad, however. Generally it is made to order. His manners are good and directly related to the head-covering he uses. If the Levantine—Greek, Armenian, or Eastern mixture—is an Ottoman subject he must wear the dark-red fez that constitutes the badge of nationality and citizenship hereabout. In that case he *salaams* in the manner of the Turk. The Levantine who claims Italian, Greek, Swiss, French, British, or Austrian citizenship wears a hat made in Paris; this particular season it is of velour with a neat little bow in the back. His salutations are those of the Western world.

It is the head-covering, therefore, which in the near East prescribes how a man shall greet his friends and acquaintances. There is no rule for this. It is the red fez that does it. It is troublesome to take off the fez. The thing has no brim, of course. In most cases it is made of a single piece of felt, so that it is hard to put on correctly. Then, too, it is the Moslem custom to never uncover the head. The Turk keeps on his fez even before the Sultan.

The modern Turk of the better classes wears clothing cut by English tailors. He loves to be well dressed. Older men affect a sort of frock-coat with a collar of clerical cut. It is known as the *stamboul.* Dignitaries of the Ottoman government and the members of Parliament are never seen in anything else while in the city.

The man of the people still wears the *shalwarlar* (trousers). By the way, it is rather odd that this article of dress should also in Turkish be a single thing with a name in the plural. *Shalwar* would be

19

one trouser; *shalwarlar* is trousers. And Turkish trousers deserve their plural patronymic. There is enough of them, to be sure. One Turkish *shalwarlar* would make two pairs of ordinary pantaloons: four tubes of cloth joined into two units.

The *shalwarlar* are generally of heavy, brown stuff. They are said to last a lifetime. With them goes a colored shirt and short jacket, which latter is often blue. The dress is completed by a waist sash of loud coloring, reds and blues being preferred. There is the inevitable fez, of course. Most of the men wear heavy shoes of European pattern. Now and then some itinerant merchant, boatman, or porter prefers the Eastern *opanka* for the reason that he can make that article of footgear himself.

One wonders what the population of Constantinople lives on, especially now. In the Turkish capital and its many suburbs lives a population of about 1,135,000, of whom 540,000 are Turks, 280,000 Greeks, 180,000 Armenians, 65,000 Jews, and 70,000 of mixed European stock. And there is not a single smokestack. It almost seems as if the minarets of the mosques would not tolerate such intrusion upon their prerogative. From a landscape point of view this is an advantage. But from the angle of social economy the thing is an anachronism.

Constantinople is the metropolis without factories. It is a place of trading and home industry. The men all buy and sell something, and the poorer classes of women work themselves into blindness making lace and the like. That lace may be fine and all that, but it seems to me that it costs too much in poor eyesight and round shoulders. It also causes a great deal of tuberculosis of the lungs. Last, but not least, it causes many of the young women to cast about for greater and more easily earned incomes in the cabarets and other places.

With the Russians before the Bosphorus and the British and French at the Dardanelles there is no shipping business worth mention. Most of the steamers have been moored in the Golden Horn, between the old and new bridges. They are being fitted up for the transport service of the Ottoman army and navy. The only ships that come and go from the quays of Stamboul and Galata are the sailing *mahonies* that attend to trade in the Bosphorus, Sea of Marmora, and the Dardanelles Strait.

I understand that even in other days Constantinople was not a busy port and mart, despite the great tonnage cleared in and out annually. Most of the ships that passed Seraii Point did not even come to anchor. But they took on and discharged cargoes at other points of the Turkish coast, and Constantinople exacted its tribute. The merchandise exported belonged usually to some merchant prince in the capital, and the profit it brought was spent in the city in no niggardly fashion. Those who sold at Smyrna, Alexandrette, and a score of other ports bought eagerly at the shops of Stamboul and Pera. They kept many servants. That kept the money in circulation. There was also an active tourist trade, and, last but not least, the Ottoman government has many officials and employees.

Most of these are poorly paid, to be sure, but many of them steal enough, especially true of the days of Abdul Hamid, to make their employment or office worth while. That, too, keeps the *livre* going.

But Constantinople had considerable shore trade. The merchants of the bazaar did a fine business in Persian, Bokhara, Anatolian, and Syrian rugs and carpets. From the interior of Asia Minor they brought textiles, wool, and lace, and from south of the Sea of Marmora they obtained silks in large quantities. There was also a good trade in beaten copper and brass, leather goods, clothing, and shoes.

But the volume of trade was never and is not now what one would expect of so large a city. At best it is remarkable only for the fact that it keeps so many occupied. In Stamboul there are whole streets in which copper-beaters have their shops and make their infernal racket. In other streets the leather-workers hold forth. I saw several shops to-day in which men were fashioning horse-shoes by hand. In others they were making bridle-bits and stirrups for the Ottoman army. A gun-smith was busy turning out revolvers for the officers in the field. Near the Great Bazaar hundreds of tailors, three and four to a shop, were making uniforms; and near by, in a street inhabited largely by shoemakers, munition boots were being made for the army in the Caucasus.

The war has stimulated trade in Constantinople quite a bit, I am told. That is natural enough. The war has done that in other countries. I am wondering, though, who in this case is mulcting the government and the people. There are no great captains of industry to do it. These small producers have neither the ability nor the courage to fleece the army commissaries. The army commissaries themselves are said to be clean-handed. But I feel instinctively that somebody is squandering the taxes of the people. May be that sooner or later I will find out who is doing it. I would have to totally revise my opinion of the scheme eternal if it should turn out that Turkey was the one country in which the misfortune of the many was not being exploited profitably by the few.

February 12th (Friday).
To-day was the Sabbath of the Moslems. All the Stamboul shops were closed.

February 13th (Saturday).
To-day was the Sabbath of the Jews. Many of Pera's and Galata's shops were closed.

February 14th (Sunday).
To-day was the Sabbath of the Europeans, Greeks, and Armenians of Pera and Galata. Only a few shops were closed.

February 15th.
My studies of conditions in Turkey are making fairly good headway. I have written much copy for the mail, and in a few days hope to get at least one interview.

As seen from my present viewpoint, the entry of Turkey into the European war came about in this manner: The Ottoman government feared—and the German embassy succeeded in convincing it of this—that Turkey would have to engage in the war on the side of the Central States if she were not to be dismembered. The Entente governments, so runs the argument, would sooner or later have forced the Dardanelles for the purpose of making sure of Turkey. The waterway in question meant too much in the Entente scheme of things to have it remain in the sole control of the Turks during the duration of the war. The Turks feared that they would never again oust the Western powers from Constantinople, once they had been installed Though not enthusiastic adherents of the Central Powers, the Turks finally concluded that joining Germany and Austria-Hungary would be choosing the lesser of two evils.

I have found no real love for the Germans and Austrians in Constantinople. The Turks lean toward the French. The Greeks are ardent Francophiles. The Armenians incline toward anything that is anti-Turk. But the Turk is an ardent patriot, it seems, a man who is ready to make many sacrifices for the continuation of his rule over the Ottomans, Greek and Armenian, not to mention the Syrians, Arabs, and what not. The German is virtually disliked, and while his military qualities are held in high esteem, it is not for this reason that the Turk became his ally. It was entirely fear of the Entente, more especially fear of the Russians, whose openly avowed ambition to take and hold Constantinople has been the nightmare of the Osmanli for centuries.

IN THE NATURE OF A PROLOGUE

February 17th.

Had lunch to-day at the American embassy. Mrs. Morgenthau is a charming hostess. The company was good. It included among others Halideh Edib Hannym Effendi, foremost feminist of Turkey, poetess, novelist, teacher, reformer, and manager of a private school for girls maintained largely at her own expense. Present were also a deputy to the Ottoman Parliament from Bagdad, and Bustány Effendi, a former minister of something or other in Stamboul.

Embassy luncheons are not occasions for political discussions. So we talked of Turkish civilization, a subject which seemed nearest to the heart of Halideh Hannym. I learned, for instance, that the veil is not an Osmanli, but a general Oriental institution, more recently identified with the Persians and Arabs, though not unknown to the people of Byzantium.

"I suppose," said Halideh Hannym, "that the veil had its origin in social necessity. In the countries east of here, the countries which my ancestors traversed on their road to Europe, there was a time when a man who possessed a pretty wife had to hide her charms under the veil, so that he might not lose her to somebody stronger than he. Also in these countries a young girl found the veil her only protection. If she wanted to have for a mate a man at least reasonably acceptable, she could do nothing else but hide her allurements until the moment had come to employ them."

Halideh Hannym is a divorced woman, so I feel that she knows what she is talking about. She is a woman of great beauty, moreover—complexion the fairest one could imagine, eyes of a dreamy, soft brown, and hair that reminds one of bronze cooling from red-heat. Her face is noble in its regularity and of a distinctly Osmanli type, without too strong a contour, however. The nose is Turkish, yet not too Turkish, and in the mouth and chin passion and firmness have been blended into sublime balance.

Her soft voice—I heard her speaking in Turkish, French, English, and German, during and after the luncheon—is wonderful in its range. You hear it and you watch the *hannym's* eyes, feeling, meanwhile, that you are constantly being checked up, as it were. Halideh Edib Hannym wants you to understand. Whether you do understand or not her marvelous eyes quickly discern; the *descendo* of her voice demands your better attention—she repeats what she has said, you grasp the meaning of her words, and the conversation continues.

"I cannot say that I am an admirer of the Germans," she remarked in the *salon*, where we had coffee. "They are a little too heavy. They lack grace. They have peculiar notions as to what constitutes tact. But I must be fair to them. The fault may be mine. Though I have read the German classics, familiarized myself with German philosophy, studied their history and socio-economic tendencies, and found much good in them, I am never in harmony with their methods of thought. Some of their ideals are nightmares to me.

"I am more at home with the French and their ways. *Nos sommes en accord.* There is nothing

26

more delightful than French literature, nothing more acceptable than French philosophy, and nobody more charming than French people of culture.

"When it comes to efficiency, to capacity, to thoroughness, to all that makes for material progress, you cannot compete with the Germans, however. But I—well, I am not a materialist. In recent years I have come to realize that materialism is an essential in the social broth; it may even be the very beef needed to make this broth. I am one of those who think they are supplying the salt—merely a condiment."

I suggested that salt was very essential. Halideh Edib Hannym saw that I was aware of the value she had placed upon her own efforts. She smiled.

"I am doing what little there lies in my power," she explained, modestly. "I am not a materialist. We Ottomans have departed too far from idealism, and the effects of this change have not been such as to cause me to feel happy over it. We still hold the position of conquerors, without having the qualities of the conqueror. We still hold, but we do not hold to improve. We still rule, but we do not govern. We still assert our dominion, but we make too many compromises. We would give all Ottoman subjects, regardless of race or creed, their full share in the running of this country, but we lack the courage to really do so. We would have our fellow-citizens love us, but we show neither respect for them nor confidence in them.

"We are, in short, a people with no ideals, or with ideals that have fallen upon evil days. Our ideals have been tainted with materialism's worst phases. We look upon expediency and make-shifts as the things that will help us across the trials of the hour, without realizing that in the end this will foot up into a bill we cannot pay.

"Our government has been nerveless for almost centuries. The Osmanli who almost overran Europe became incompetent temporizers, who, to cajole fate into being kind to them, surrendered their sovereignty piecemeal in capitulations; who, to keep their government officials in bread and olives and pay the cost of a prodigal court, mortgaged their revenues until nearly all of them are in the control of foreign bank agents."

It struck me that what Halideh Hannym found lacking in her race, in the men of her race, was what is usually termed forcefulness. I was very much interested in the subject she had discussed, but it was time to leave.

February 20th.

I have with me now a peculiar person — one Raymond E. Swing, Berlin correspondent of the Chicago *Daily News*, who, like myself, has come to the Balkans and Turkey to study conditions here. To-night over a glass of something or other I had occasion to understand Swing. Most delightful chap—thinker, dreamer, radical, rationalist, opinionated, self-asserting, gentle and "cussed" at the same time; he dotes on philosophy, ancient and modern, and regrets missing the opera season at Berlin.

II

WHAT SOME TURKS THOUGHT OF THE SITUATION

WHEN one has been in a country only nine
days it is best to let the people of that
country speak for it.   That was my view in this
instance.

I set about to get a number of interviews with
prominent statesmen of Turkey.   They were on the
defensive, I found.   They had to be that.   The
Old Turks were still violently opposed to the war,
and there was division even among the Young
Turks.   In fact, the men who had led Turkey into
the war were a very small minority.   That they
had succeeded in their plan was due to their great
power.   Though Turkey had now again a Constitution and a Parliament it was still possible to proceed with arbitrariness, and Enver Pasha, Talaat
Bey, and Saiid Halim Pasha, the Grand Vizier,
had not overlooked their chances.

On February 18th I interviewed Talaat Bey,
Ottoman Minister of the Interior; a card from the
American ambassador introduced me.   The meeting
progressed satisfactorily after Talaat Bey had discovered that I was a lodge brother of his.

Talaat Bey is a European Turk of Albanian

origin. He is a large man. Upon broad shoulders and a thick neck sits a head of bold and strong lines.

In his youth Talaat was a poor boy. At the time of the Turkish revolution, in 1908, he was a telegraph-operator at Salonika. Something or other he did in those days caused him to get up high in the ranks of the Turkish "Party of Union and Progress." He has never relinquished the hold this gave him upon affairs in Constantinople.

I asked questions on Turkey's internal and external relations and politics. It is generally impossible to discuss foreign affairs with a minister of interior affairs, though that was the purpose of my visit. So we started by discussing the interior and ended, as I had designed, by reviewing the foreign relations of Turkey.

Talaat was certain that the entry of Turkey in the European war, on the side of the Central Powers, had been a national necessity.

"We Turks have felt the hand of European statesmen too often to give a fig for their promises," Talaat Bey said. "What they promise and what they do are very different things. The fact is that Turkey had to find, was forced to find, her place in the present constellation. That place for the time being is nothing more than an endeavor to weather this storm.

"The Turkish government happens to know what has been discussed in London, Paris, and Petrograd since the outbreak of the war in August. We knew that we were to be shorn once more and that the Entente would not temper the wind that would blow for us. So we decided to make war on the side of the Central Powers.

"That we shall emerge from this war victorious is not at all certain as yet. *Nous verrons!* Meanwhile we are doing what is obviously our duty, even if it be our last. We are fighting the Entente as best we can. We will fight the Entente so long as we can. If the issue goes against us we will have gone under as befits the Osmanli.

"Our nation has been bled white by the continuous wars it has engaged in. If this thing keeps up the day will come when there will be an Ottoman Empire without a real Turk in it—a day for which our friends are waiting, a day for which some of our fellow-citizens pray.,

"Well, we shall see! The Turk is yet here, and so long as he is here he must be reckoned with. We are going to fight to a standstill, and it may be our own standstill—our end. But they will not be able to say that the Turk laid down. Let them beware!"

That "Let them beware!" was uttered through set teeth. I left Talaat Bey with the impression that I would just as soon face an Andalusian arena bull unarmed as run counter to the man in charge of Turkey's interior. There was something so determined, almost savage, in the man's face that my picture of military Turkey underwent a decided change as I pondered over things in the *araba*.

Talaat Bey, now Pasha and Ottoman Minister of the Interior, had made a deep impression upon me. I felt that this man, should the occasion arise, could be hard as steel despite his genial exterior.

3   31

To gain his end he would not shrink from any measure, and since his ends were wrapped up in the welfare of a state, those measures were likely to be far-reaching.

The former telegraph-operator struck me as a romantic figure in the world's story. The man had once been poor and of no consequence. Now he held in his hands the destiny of a state with twenty-two million inhabitants. He was not only Minister of the Interior, but actually the ruler of the land. The Sultan and the Grand Vizier were said to be his tools, and Enver Pasha was at best his collaborator.

Three days later I again met Halideh Hannym and wrote a story about her. It was a pleasant task.

The lady seemed most "Occidental," despite her Turkish habilhment. We had tea together. To get her views on socio-political considerations in Turkey, I started to discuss the ballot.

"I do not consider politics within my province," she said, in reply to something I had said. "But I am interested in the subject. I am not so sure that limiting the right to vote to those considered qualified to vote would be an altogether unmixed blessing, as you seem to think. It would lead to two socio-political classes. I am not convinced that the voting class would look out for the interest of the non-voting class. Your scheme might result in better government, more intelligent government, more efficient government, if you please, but it would not be a representative government. The class not qualified to vote, by reason of not having the necessary education, might be lost sight of altogether, because the voting class might then be without incentive to educate the ignorant class. The situation might lead to helotism. I can understand why universal suffrage does not always result in the best government. It gives too much leeway to the demagogue, and passion rather than reason often determines the result of the ballot. If there were a guarantee that the educated and voting class would see to it that those less fortunately situated should in the end understand the principles and duties of government, then such a plan would be highly beneficial. But no such guarantee can be given, and, I am sure, if given it would not be always adhered to by those in power."

Halideh Hannym confessed herself in favor of universal suffrage, women included. I had made the remark that I had no prejudice against women voting, provided measures were employed to prevent the further augmentation of the class of voters who cast their ballots without knowing the why and wherefore.

We returned to Turkey. Halideh Hannym said that education for all was urgently needed. But education would have to move on a different plane. It would have to be more practical, get away from never-ending recitals from the *Qua'raan*, and instruct the young in the duties of citizenship. That education was to include women, of course.

"It has been said that the woman is the hope of Turkey to-day," said Halideh Hannym. "Maybe that is true. If it is true, then we have another reason why the Turkish woman must have a better education than she has had in the past, though, on the whole, her education has not been so far behind that of the men as is generally accepted. The fact is that the Turkish woman of the middle and better classes has had more time to read than the men. Her seclusion brings her more in contact with the books and reviews. It also causes her to think more, and, maybe, think deeper, than do the men."

She began to examine the position of the Turkish woman historically.

"The present feminist movement in Turkey is nothing new, after all," she began, settling back on the divan. "It is merely a renaissance, a re-development of a condition which once existed. There was a time when the Turkish woman had all the rights of her brother and husband. The mother of Ghengis Khan was the ruler of the Turks for many years after her husband died, leaving the country to a successor much too young to govern it.

"In those days the Turkish woman was on a parity with the man, in whose eyes she was really the life companion. It is no mere coincidence that the Turkish word for woman is in reality part of the word identifying the Supreme Deity.

"For many centuries this continued. Then the Turks, driven westward either by force of circumstances or following their own impulse, invaded Persia. Here they came in touch with Mohammedanism, which in Persia had already lowered the status of the woman to a low level. Following the force of bad example, our men divested them-

selves of the reverence in which they had held
their mothers, sisters, and wives and women generally.

"The Mohammedanism of the Arabs, which the
Turks were to encounter next, made things worse,
so that, within a short time, the Turkish women
became exactly what the women of these races
were—things of pleasure. Meanwhile the Turks
had subjugated these peoples and taken their
women to themselves, with the result, as always
happens in the case of an over-supply, that woman
in general was no longer esteemed. The Turkish
women paid a high price for the victories of their
men.

"This remained the status of the Turkish woman
for about five centuries. Since man is the son of
woman, the race deteriorated under the baneful
influence of polygamy and all that goes with it.

"Thirty-four years ago a change for the better
set in. Our poets began to once more sing of the
Turkish woman, who hitherto had been actually
thought too base to be mentioned in poetry. The
renaissance of Turkish literature now in progress
has done much to put the Turkish woman somewhere near the high place which was once hers.

"There is another cause. The Turkish public has
been reading French novels and other books for
many years now. Often it has been the sole
pleasure the Turkish girl and woman had in life.
Whether she asserted herself as the result of reading
these books, learning from them what the position
of woman was in the Occident, or whether the sense
of justice of the man was roused, I am not prepared

to say. At any rate, the emancipation of the Turkish woman is slowly but surely going on.

"But I feel justified in saying that the instincts of the race have much to do with the readmission to her former status of the Turkish woman. In our race still lives the memory, dormant but capable of being roused, of the glory of the days when the Turkish woman was the free and equal mate and companion of her husband."

Halideh Hannym's eyes sparkled as she thought of those days. The Turks had no capitulations and foreign managers of the public debt then.

"So our poets began to speak of women again—Turkish women—strange creatures at first, as they had to be—women of heroic, fantastic, and often bizarre qualities. The Turkish public, even the Turkish women, could not have taken kindly to a realistic portrayal of what the Turkish woman had been these many centuries."

But here our conversation ended, for Halideh Hannym had to catch the boat for Principo, where her little son lived on his grandfather's estate.

The interview-mill was running fine now. On the following afternoon I had a meeting with the Rev. Dr. Haim Nahoum, grand rabbi of Palestine.

His residence is a humble affair—a three-story building against the hillside in Pera. A few trees in front of the rabbinical "palace" distinguish it from all the other "tenements" in the narrow street.

The interview was short and cautious. The rabbi felt that he had to be very careful, despite the support which his friend, the American ambassador, might give him. We talked about much in general, and about little in particular, as is the case under such circumstances. The Jews under Turkish rule were not badly treated, the rabbi said. They had, in fact, been very liberally treated, on the whole, though this liberality was due more to the good nature of certain Ottoman government officials than to a policy of the government itself. There was nothing to complain of. The Jew in Palestine and Turkey was prosperous in the main, said the grand rabbi.

Doctor Nahoum is a tactful man. There is no doubt that he had more on his mind. But he was talking to a man who had come to Turkey to write. I might say things which, though true, would get his people into trouble. It was unlikely that he personally would suffer from anything he said. He was too big a figure for that. But in the East they have a habit of exacting vicarious sacrifices. What the grand rabbi said was likely to be slated against his race, and while the Jews in the Ottoman Empire were not being persecuted just then, it was still possible that criticism of the Ottoman government by Doctor Nahoum might have detrimental results for his race.

February 23d.

The city is full of all sorts of rumors. Some of them carry their absurdity on their face. Others seem to harmonize with the burden of the meager official *communiqués* that are issued daily for the reassurance of the populace.

37

FROM BERLIN TO BAGDAD

That populace is a peculiar one, to be sure. I am gauging it in the cafés of Pera, Galata, Taxim, and Stamboul. When news from the front is bad for the Turks it seems good to the Armenians. And *vice versa*. The Greeks don't seem to care who wins. To that extent they are true neutrals, as true as the flock of gipsies I interviewed near the Porta Aurelia in Stamboul to-day.

My information is that the Turkish coast batteries at Kum Kaleh, Orchanieh, and Sid-il-Bahr are no more. I learned to-day that the Allied ship guns outranged them hopelessly. If that keeps up the British and French will be here before long.

Meanwhile the population, regardless of race, lives under the severe strain of subdued excitement. The city may be shelled, they believe. There may be massacres in the eleventh hour. *Quien sabe?*

During the last few days there has been a decided falling-off of street traffic. The stores are not well attended. The Stamboul bazaar was nearly empty this afternoon. In the cafés men sit at the little round tables and talk in whispers. One group seems to be afraid of the other.

I suppose it would not go well with the gloating Armenian, or the Greek, who should happen to make a light remark concerning the affairs at the Dardanelles or out in the Caucasus. Distrust seems to have invaded every circle. Even the Turks feel that it is best to say nothing when enthusiasm fails to reach exuberance. One might be accused of being an ardent Old Turk—one of a class that swore by France and which has not yet embraced the German as warmly as the government desires.

Business everywhere is almost at a standstill. Nothing seems to matter very much now. Shopkeepers stand in front of their places of business and converse *sotto voce*, while looking furtively about them. When a stranger approaches, shopkeeper and passer-by enter the store and engage in the stage business of vending and buying. The political police has never been so feared. Bedri Bey, the head of this institution, has become the very embodiment of terror, though as a club member I find him congenial enough. But that might be different were I an Armenian or a Greek.

Everybody here suffers from the uncertainty of the situation. It is a most peculiar state of affairs. The Armenian fears massacre in case the Allied ships break in. He is sure that the Turk will visit his rage of defeat upon him in that case. The Turk, on the other hand, fears the same. There is no love lost between these two.

Though the Armenians have been very circumspect, everybody knows that they would welcome the Allies as their deliverers. Nobody expects the Armenian to regret the fall of the Ottoman Empire. *Ça va sans dire.* The Armenian could not love his Turkish *concitoyen* if he tried, and the Turk, on the principle that we hate none so well as those whom we have wronged, can find no cause in the military situation and its possibilities to change his feelings toward the Armenian.

There is much speculation as to what the attitude of the Greeks would be. It is unlikely that they would side with the Armenians. It is just as unlikely that they would help the Turks. The *Pérote* is still a Byzantian. He is that in a peculiar manner. If there is such a thing as a disemboweled nationalism, the Greek of Constantinople has it. His is a patriotism devoid of substance. He reminds me of the man who has married a second time and is still in love with his first wife. If a *Pérote* told me that he yearned to die so that he could join his Byzantian compatriots of yore, I would not be surprised.

The Turk understands the Greek full well and does not seem to mind. Toward the Armenian the Turk may be a ruthless master; toward the Greek he still feels the intruder—the man who took possession of property that was not his and who has not done well by that property. The thought is subconscious, but it is there, nevertheless. The splendid city of Constantine has sunk to the level of a pretty village with the monuments of a metropolis. Those monuments are largely Byzantian, and whatever metropolitan aspect the city now has is distinctly Greek. And I will say that this aspect is not mean. It still reveals the genius of the Hellenes.

Whether Constantinople falls into the hands of the Allies or remains in those of the Turks makes no difference to the majority of Greeks. There is only one prayer they have: God keep the Russians out of the city. Anybody but the Russians, even the Germans, would be more welcome visitors. If the city passed to the control of the French every Greek would celebrate. Toward any other

Copyright, by Underwood & Underwood

A STREET IN PERA

Pera is the Levantine (non-Moslem) quarter of Constantinople, being inhabited by Greeks, Armenians, Jews, and about 4,000 Europeans. The quarter lies on the left bank of the Golden Horn against a very steep hill-side and presents a most pleasing aspect.

authority the Greeks would be as indifferent as they are toward the Turks.

The Turks know this perfectly well, and since they themselves would prefer to be Frenchmen, if they cannot remain Ottoman, Turks and Greeks have a strong tendency in common. So they get along well together. Both feel that under French government they would be well off. They have agreed tacitly to pull together in that case, which means that the French would not have an easy time ruling on the Bosphorus. But, so far as I can learn, that would not prevent certain classes of Greeks from at least enjoying as spectators a well-run massacre of Turks by the Armenians, especially if, during that massacre, enough Armenians themselves perished. It is a peculiar frame of mind and one must be able to sense Constantinople to understand and appreciate it.

At the ministries in Stamboul there is much gloom. Nobody there knows what the next few days will bring. Even if allowance is made for the range handicaps of the Ottoman defense works at Kum Kaleh and Sid-il-Bahr—shortcomings which will not obtain inside the strait—the outlook is, nevertheless, none too good. The batteries along the outer Dardanelles may hold, will hold, for a time. But how long will they hold? That is the question everybody in official circles would ask, did one dare to ask.

The German coast artillery experts are none too sanguine. They are men of objectivity. They make no promises for the future. In their own grim way they merely reply that prognostication

41

in war is a most dangerous practice. They hold
that it is best to expect the worst, in which case
there will be no disappointment if the worst comes
to pass, while there will be occasion for rejoicing
if things should turn out well. I suppose that this
is a phase of their thoroughness. Don't expect
anything and you won't be disappointed. It is a
rather gloomy sort of philosophy, but it has its
rewards, I suppose.

The German officers put me in mind of physi-
cians handling a desperate case. The "Sick Man of
Europe" is really desperately ill. A major operation is about due. Luckily, the patient is no longer
conscious. The German diplomatists administered
the narcotic long ago. Saiid Halim Pasha, the
Grand Vizier; Talaat Bey, the Minister of the Interior; and Enver Pasha, Minister of War and
Vice-Generalissimo of the Ottoman army, hold the
etherizing cone.

It is hard to say how they feel about it now.
They reasoned, however, that this was the final
chance of the "Sick Man," and if I am rightly informed they will be the last to tremble while the
operation goes on. Desperate case, desperate
remedy, seems to be their motto.

Meanwhile, the former Sultan, Abdul Hamid,
has been transferred to the palace of Beylerbey.
I wonder whether the news of the great event at
the Dardanelles has come to him. It is said that
the present Sultan, Mohammed Réchad V, steals
of nights across the Bosphorus and consoles his
unfortunate brother. It would be an unusual case
of fraternal love, if this were true. Abdul Hamid

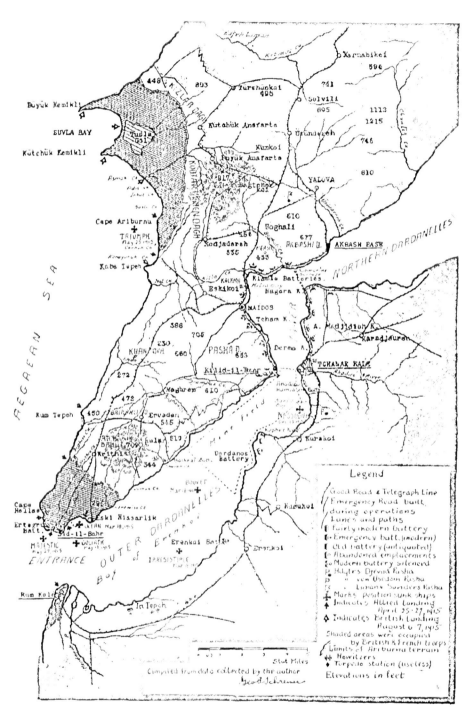

MAP OF THE DARDANELLES STRAIT AND GALLIPOLI PENINSULA,
SHOWING NAVAL AND MILITARY OPERATIONS OF ALLIED NAVAL
AND LANDED FORCES, 1915

took particular pains and great pleasure in keeping Mohammed Réchad in jail while he was ruler of the Ottoman Empire.

At any rate, if Mohammed visits Abdul the latter is bound to know something of what may come. Since Abdul Hamid was not unbeloved by the powers before the Dardanelles, it is quite possible that he may again rule over what Turkey there will be some other day.

February 25th.

Friend Swing and I negotiated an interview with Enver Pasha under peculiar and not altogether *auspicious* auspices late this evening. The occasion deserves mention for the reason that it shows what initiative has to be exercised by a poor correspondent now and then.

F. Swing and I have agreed to be good fellows to each other. He is not to "knife" me, and I am not to "knife" him—a sort of working alliance between two powers likely to make war upon each other.

The basis of this treaty of peace is that I do most of my work over the cable, while Swing does most of his by mail. There is no real competition between us, though I can see right now where there is likely to be. But let to-morrow take care of itself. I never pluck a quail until I have him.

F. Swing and I have been moving heaven and earth to interview Enver Pasha. We have the lever, but lack the fulcrum.

I was having a quiet cup of tea, all to myself,

at the Petit Club, when Swing rushed in, breathless, and hat at a rakish angle.

"What's the hurry?" I asked, setting down the cup.

"What's the hurry!" retorted Swing, with a look of disgust. "Smart question that. Enver Pasha is going to the Dardanelles to-night for a trip of inspection. May be away a week, I understand. So what's the hurry! I can't see how we are getting closer to meeting him, can you?"

In that "can you" there was all the irony, sarcasm, and wrath Swing can put into words, and that is not little. I felt almost ashamed that he had caught me drinking tea. He had run, it appeared. With a handkerchief he was swabbing the inside of his high collar.

"Have some tea and let's talk it over," I suggested, wishing to make Swing an accomplice.

I rang the bell, and without consulting my irate colleague ordered tea for him.

"When is Enver Pasha going?" I asked.

"Don't know," replied Swing, not yet in the best of humor. "Here I run around all day, and you sit in the club, taking it easy. Fine partner you are. Think you are putting it over, don't you?"

I told Swing remorsefully that I had no such intentions, that as a matter of fact I knew more than he did.

"If you would let me get in a word once in a while, Swing, you wouldn't have to shout so and use so much bad language," I said. "Now let me tell you a few things while you have your tea. Enver Pasha leaves aboard the Sultan's yacht for the Dardanelles at one *alla Turca*, which is to-night six o'clock and nine minutes by our time. He is about to go on a tour of inspection, all right, but not the sort you have in mind. There is something to the rumors that have been spread by the *Agence Tatavla* recently.

"The Allies have bombarded and silenced the forts at Sid-il-Bahr and Kum Kaleh. I verified this at the German naval base this afternoon. The thing started on the twentieth. There isn't much left of the Turkish batteries, I understand. What is more, the Allies have brought up reinforcements, among them, so the Germans say, the best thing in fighting-ships the English have, to wit, Her Majesty *Queen Elizabeth*. She was sighted two days ago by some advance agent wiring from Athens. Yesterday she was reported off Lemnos by another.

"The fleet of the Allies is a large one. So far it consists of about eight English and six French battle-ships of the line, several cruisers, a regular herd of torpedo-boat destroyers and torpedo-boats, not to mention mine-sweepers, submarines, supply-ships, hospital-ships, and what not.

"Drink your tea; we'll have to be off in a minute. The Turkish batteries at Kum Kaleh and Sid-il-Bahr are a memory. There isn't enough left of most of them to show you where they were. In Fort Orchanieh all the Germans were killed. Hell is loose and Enver Pasha is going down to see what the thing looks like. Do you think we can make that interview to-night?"

F. Swing drank his tea and consumed buttered

4   47

toast like a man who has been starved for a week. Swing, being a tall and lean sort of man, is always hungry.

"No, I don't think we can make that interview to-night," he said, with gloom written all over his face. Then he sweetened his disposition with a liberal lump of marmalade. "Why, the man will be too busy."

"We'll have to try, anyway," I remarked, not sure of the wisdom of my words. "We want to go to the Dardanelles, don't we? The Germans tell me that nothing can be done without Enver Pasha's consent. That consent we must get to-night."

Swing being willing, though none too anxious, to try so dangerous a game as waylaying a Turkish Minister of War about to go on so nasty an errand, we ordered an *araba* and embarked upon our weird-enough mission.

There was no telling what might happen. We might be grabbed up by some zealous sentry, and at least spend a night in some dirty *habyss*, the most uncomfortable variety of jail I can imagine.

The rain was coming down bucketwise as we bumped along the cobbled streets of Pera toward Galata Quai. Things looked gloomy enough. The few street lights had a hard struggle with the un-friendliness of the night.

"We stand a swell chance seeing Enver Pasha to-night," grumbled Swing. "We will be lucky if they do not pitch us overboard. I wish I were in Chicago."

"Can't help it. Got to try," I retorted, feeling

48

that all of my friend's sour remarks were directed at me.

It was deep night when we got to the quay at the head of the new bridge across the Golden Horn. I told the driver to turn to the left and be quick about it. Four blocks away lay a small steamer, well lighted and with the steam-valve blowing off. That boat was ready to sail; even now they might be casting off the hawsers.

There is a high iron fence between the street and the quay where the yacht was tied up. Through it I soon espied the white hull of the boat; further on I saw a gate, and a sentry pacing up and down.

When the *araba* drew up, the sentry stopped and showed more interest than we really cared for. We scrambled out of the conveyance, told the driver to wait, and then headed for the quay as if we really had business there.

That seemed to impress the German sailor on sentry. He had placed himself near the middle of the entrance by way of an invitation for us to address him. But he was as uncertain of his own position as we were of ours. We brushed past him without looking in his direction. That impressed the man wonderfully. He stepped back and took it for granted that we had business aboard the yacht. Well, so we had.

At the foot of the ladder another sentry was on duty. He was not so easily discounted. The factor of space was in his favor, moreover. The man stood in the center of the approach to the ladder, and evidently proposed to be spoken to.

I did speak to him. He inquired what my

49

name was and what the nature of our errand
could be.

I told him we had come to see Enver Pasha's
chief of staff, Colonel von Bronsart. That helped.
The sailor volunteered the information that the
colonel was already aboard, and then permitted
us to pass.

Up the ladder we went, losing no time. There
was no questioning by the sentry at the head of
the ladder, but I took good care not to stop near
him to find my bearings. To hesitate and look
around would have been courting the attention of
the man. He would have asked whom we wanted
to see, and that might have led to trouble.

So we walked on and stepped between two deck-
houses to make a hasty survey of our surroundings.

The deck was deserted, as it well might be in the
driving rain. The faint light given by the few
incandescent lamps that swung from their wires
in the wind broke in glistening streaks on the white,
wet paint of the cabin walls.

From a deck-house on the poop of the yacht
gleamed some lighted ports. We decided that we
might try our luck there. Our feet had just been
put in motion again when I noticed that the sentry
at the top of the ladder was wondering what had
become of us. He came around the corner of
the superstructure of the boiler-room just as we
meandered.

At the aft deck-house our search for somebody,
anybody, came abruptly to an end. As I was about
to open its door it moved by an impulse from within.
I stepped back to make room for the officer in

Ottoman army uniform who had one foot up for the purpose of stepping over the high sill.

That foot did not come down in regular time. As it poised in the air its owner looked me in the face with a great deal of astonishment. I was a stranger to him.

There was surprise in the officer's voice as he spoke. No doubt his mind operated somewhat along these lines: How in the name of all that is holy did these two strangers manage to get aboard the Sultan's yacht?

The officer said something to that effect when speech returned to him.

I overlooked his question and introduced myself and F. Swing. I was conscious of having shown considerable nonchalance in performing this ceremony. Then I proceeded to state our mission; in our business one must have his wits about him.

"But that is impossible," said Colonel von Bronsart, who had now introduced himself. His remark was polite but frigid. "It cannot be done! *Ausgeschlossen*—out of the question entirely! His Excellency is about to sail. He has no time. You will do me a favor, and save yourself some annoyance, by leaving this ship immediately."

The invitation was plain enough.

"But it is imperative that we speak to His Excellency," I interposed. "We have come to Turkey to view the military operations. We cannot get the necessary permission from Sefid Bey unless His Excellency interests himself in the matter."

Swing added a few words to the same effect.

He has a droll way of expressing himself in his Chicago-accented German. The chief of staff smiled. There is a strange appeal for some men in "broken" speech.

"Are all Americans as enterprising and persistent as you are?" asked the colonel, who felt the need of changing the subject.

We opined that quite a few were that and more. Just then Colonel Yansen, the German liaison officer, joined the group. Swing and I had met him before. That helped. His remarks were in our favor.

The colonel still hung in the wind. The fact was that he was in an embarrassment. He did not want to turn us down, but, as I knew well enough and admitted tactfully, it was awkward for him to introduce us to his commander at such a time and under such conditions.

An automobile came to our assistance. It stopped at the gate. The sentry saluted very smartly, and several officers stepped from the tonneau.

"Here is His Excellency now," said Colonel von Bronsart. There was a ring of annoyance in his voice.

The colonel hurried off, followed by Colonel Yansen and ourselves. I had made up my mind to see Enver Pasha that evening or land in jail or in the water. I sympathized with the chief of staff, but I also sympathized with myself.

We rushed along the wet deck, with the chief of staff in the lead and myself in the rear. Going down the ladder we had to slow up. The steps were slippery from the rain, and it certainly would not do to fall into the presence of Turkey's mighty war lord.

Enver Pasha must have waited for an invitation from his chief of staff to go aboard, or something of that sort. He was standing at the foot of the ladder, engaged in conversation with some of the officers who had come with him. The meeting between vice-generalissimo and chief of staff was cordial, almost effusive. Colonel Yansen also seemed to be very intimate with Enver.

We had decided not to get too near to the group, and so about five steps up the ladder we had halted. Above us swung an electric bulb. Enver Pasha seemed interested in the two civilians under it. Meanwhile I was making a survey of the dapper and smart young officer.

With the greetings over, the Ottoman Minister of War thought it proper to occupy himself with us. I did not hear what he said, but that he had asked a question concerning the two civilians was shown by the manner in which Colonel Yansen turned around and looked at us.

The psychological moment being good and in our favor, I hurried to the foot of the ladder and stepped in front of Enver Pasha. Swing did likewise. I introduced Swing first and then myself.

We did not there and then find favor in the eyes of His High Mightiness. For that I could not blame the pasha. I might feel the same way about it. The intruder is a most obnoxious sort of person.

I restated the purpose of our presence, watching intently the fine Tartar face to note the effect.

53

There was something like a scowl on Enver Pasha's handsome visage. I began to fear that we might have placed the two colonels in an awkward position. Having stood before displeased superior officers myself now and again, I had no difficulty realizing what the feelings of Colonels von Bronsart and Yansen might be.

It was a most awkward situation Finally Colonel von Bronsart took a hand. I will say for him that he proved a most astute strategist there and then. He explained his own part in our guest rôle adroitly.

Enver Pasha began to see the humor of the situation. He laughed.

"Always heard that these Americans stick at nothing," he said, good-naturedly. "Now I know this to be true." Military gallantry came to the front in him. "Gentlemen, I am at your service."

We proceeded to interview Enver Pasha there and then—in the driving rain. What did he think of the Allied fleet's chances of getting through?

"Well, they may get through," replied the vice-generalissimo. "But they will not get through easily. War is not a thing on which people should make prophecies. It is hard to say. That part of the situation I am not in a position to discuss."

Enver Pasha admitted that so far the Turkish batteries at the entrance to the strait had not fared any too well. But he hoped that those along the outer Dardanelles would do better. He intimated that he was in a hurry to get away.

But a minute or two did not matter to the interviewers. We had gone to too much trouble to have this personage slip out of our hands so easily.

"Just say," he went on, "that we Turks will defend the Dardanelles with the last man, if necessary. We realize that it will be hard work, that it will strain our resources, and that our losses will be heavy. But the British and French are not through yet. We Turks have never laid down and will not do it in this instance. We know that the hour has come."

I asked Enver Pasha for permission to go to the Dardanelles—in the morning, if it could be done. He thought it over for a second.

"You shall have that permission," he said, finally. Then he turned to his chief of staff. "I think we can trust them, eh, Colonel?"

"I think we can, Excellency!" was the colonel's remark.

"Very well, then," continued Enver Pasha. "You may go. I will give the necessary instructions."

I bowed in acknowledgment.

"But there is one thing I must tell you," continued Enver. "You know we are at war. Do you know what war is?"

I explained that Jupiter Mars and I were no strangers; that once, in fact, I had been in his service.

"Then you know what military law is, of course," continued the Minister of War. "If your friend does not know, do me the favor to explain it to him.

"You can go to the Dardanelles and see everything, provided you place yourself under Ottoman

military law and agree to abide by its provisions.
If your conduct at the front should warrant the
enforcement of any part of this law against you,
you will not in any way solicit the aid of your embassy here. Not even if it should become necessary for you to face a firing-squad. In return for
that you will get from me a general passport that
will take you anywhere you may wish to go.

"Agreed?"

F. Swing and I agreed. Enver Pasha shook
hands with us, to seal the agreement, and bid us
good-by. He was most genial now. As he climbed
up the ladder he turned around and saluted us with
a hearty *au revoir*.

We wished him *bon royage*, and Swing thought
that we had been foolish not to have gone with
him. I frowned upon this idea, and on the way
home we had a row in the *araba* over the eternal
fitness of things. It seemed to me that for one
evening we had exercised enterprise enough.

February 26th.

To-day F. Swing and I interviewed together the
Grand Vizier of the Ottoman Empire, Prince
Said Halim Pasha. The thing was a complete
success.

The Grand Vizier was very charming, our questions were happily selected and deftly put, and
the coffee and cigarettes of His Excellency were
excellent.

Well, things are coming our way. F. Swing is
satisfied. He is beginning to swear by me when he
is not swearing at me. He is a terrible taskmaster.

To let us know that the occasion of our visit to the Sublime Porte was no ordinary one, the Grand Vizier, meeting us at the door of his apartments, said that this was the first time in two years that he had met newspaper-men.

We confessed that it was the first time in our promising lives that we had the honor and pleasure of meeting a Grand Vizier. The prince said the happiness was all his; we insisted that this was not so. Swing especially showed up well in this; his *salon* manners are simply perfect.

We were still exchanging compliments as we seated ourselves at the desk of the Grand Vizier. The prince explained that he had never said anything for publication since this office had been intrusted to him, and we assured him that he had fallen into the hands of men who would treat him right.

I left it to Swing to put our victim at his ease. My colleague is the born diplomatist. Once in a while I would nail down, corroboratively, something he said, and meanwhile I was taking stock of our surroundings.

The room in which we were is of enormous proportions. It had been papered in a very simple manner, and there was but little furniture in it. Under the tall windows, overlooking the Bosphorus, lies a long divan, and against the wall back of us stood a score of chairs—all in a row. The desk of His Excellency, the simple swivel-chair upon which he sat, the two chairs we occupied, and a bookcase —these few objects seemed lost on the tremendous floor. The carpet was a beauty, I concluded.

57

F. Swing was making a drive for the interview already. I judged that the offensive came a little too soon. They are never in a hurry in Turkey, and when you show hurry yourself you make these people suspicious. They get the notion that you want to take something away from them.

"Your Highness believes in simplicity," I said, in pursuance of the objective I had in mind.

"My wants are not great," replied the prince, with an engaging smile. "I prefer lots of air and light to stuffy hangings and useless furniture. What is the use of having things around you do not need?"

All this in the purest English that one could wish to hear.

I noticed that His Highness was trying to cultivate the beard which tradition imposes upon the Grand Vizier. The result had not been a particularly happy one so far. The hair was altogether too thin and too light in color to make much of a showing. Oom Paul Kruger, last president of the South African Republic, had the same trouble. I did not comment upon that fact, naturally. Reference to this little tragedy might spoil his fine humor. The least it would do would be to remind him that much in life is vanity. *Vanitas, vanitatum vanitas!*

F. Swing had the lead again.

"So you have come to interview me," said the prince, with a laugh that showed he had not been in ignorance of the purpose of our visit. "What do you want to know? Ask any question, gentlemen, and I will take pleasure in answering."

The Grand Vizier was as good as his word. F. Swing put a leading question:

"The assertion made by the Entente press and governments that we went to war for the purpose of helping the Germans is absurd," replied the Grand Vizier.

Just then the servant entered with the coffee—three cups of Mocha *alla Turca*, done to the queen's taste. The prince handed us each a cigarette and lit a match. In Turkey one offers the box of cigarettes only to inferiors, so that they may take as many as they like.

While we sipped coffee and smoked the best *Kavala* tobacco, the Grand Vizier went over the situation in Turkey. Swing and I listened attentively.

"It is quite true that the Entente governments offered us a guarantee that for thirty years the integrity of the Ottoman Empire would be respected," said Prince Saiid Halim Pasha. "To be exact, that meant that if we stayed out of the war the Entente was not to touch our territory for the period named.

"But guarantees count for so little nowadays"—the Grand Vizier smiled wanly and as one who could see the funny side of a funeral—"and Turkey has had so many guarantees. When it comes to guarantees we Turks could tell a tale of woe that would bring tears to the eyes of a stone image. We have had our fill of guarantees. We really want no more of them. It is going to be a sad time for guarantees until this war is over. I have no faith in guarantees.

"And then what does a guarantee mean? **It** means that you admit that somebody has the right to—well, protect you. And this, in turn, means that you surrender your sovereignty, lock, stock, and barrel. It means that thereafter you ask permission of some other government if you want to do anything—perhaps the very thing that ought to be done. We have asked other governments long enough, and the Entente governments have been among them. We know what bargains they make.

"A protected Turkey means a dependent Turkey. We believe that we ought to be independent— more independent than we have been in the past. Others do not think so, of course. But we do. That is a matter of opinion which this war may settle forever. We are all entitled to our opinions. You are, I am, we are."

That naturally brought the Grand Vizier to the abolition of the capitulations—extra-territorial concessions wrung from the Turks by many of the governments of the world.

"Even the Germans opposed that step," explained the prince. "But that is a matter I do not care to go into now. At any rate, we have abolished the capitulations. Hereafter the foreigner who thinks Turkey good enough to live in must think our laws and courts good enough to conform to.

"We also propose to show more interest in the future in the foreign schools and missions in the empire. Some of these establishments have turned out young men who are not satisfied with our government. That will have to stop.

"That these institutions have been of great value to the state I will admit, but they would have been of greater value to all concerned had they borne in mind that we cannot make of Turkey an ultra-modern state overnight.

"The schools and missions, instead of enjoining their pupils to work for better government with the Turks, have fostered sedition. That must stop. We will stop it, if we have to close every foreign school and mission in the empire."

Saiid Halim Pasha then explained that foreign schools and missions throughout Turkey had already been placed under the supervision of the Ottoman Ministry of Education. There had been trouble when the inspectors of the Ministry appeared on the scene. There had been so much trouble, in fact, that the Ottoman government had for the time being withdrawn the inspectors. The prince also volunteered the information that these inspectors were not fitted for the work. Most of them were woefully ignorant.

"It has long been fashionable to look askance at anything the Turkish government does," continued the Grand Vizier. "We find it impossible to please anybody. We are to blame for that to quite an extent. Government in Turkey has been anything but good. It is not good even to-day.

"The Young Turks have been in power since the revolution. We have been running the state for five years now. That is not long. I wish that the world would be reasonable enough to see that we cannot make over the empire in five years. That will take decades. What the world expects from

61

us to-day we may have accomplished twenty years hence.

"We thought at first we could apply here some form of government that had been used with success in the Occident. We tried that, but found it to be a mistake. Before a Western form of government can be established in Turkey the attitude of the population toward government must be changed. We are somewhat in the position of the Latin American countries whose constitutions prescribe a democratic form of government, but whose heads are dictators at best.

"All we need is time and the recognition on the part of others that we are really doing our best to make a modern state of the Ottoman Empire. To get that time is the thing we are fighting for."

Saiid Halim Pasha is an Oxford man. His family is one of the oldest in Egypt. Orient and Occident are well mixed in him, though not merged. He is still of the East, and above all, he is an ardent Turk.

The interview lasted the greater part of an hour, and, as we left, the Grand Vizier was on the verge of forgetting that he was a Highness and all that. Swing and I found the pronoun *you* so very convenient that we lapsed into it at every turn. Saiid Halim Pasha never betrayed that he did not enjoy our informality. When he said that we were to call again he meant it.

III

AT THE SHELL-RAKED DARDANELLES

THE passport of which Enver Pasha spoke did not come—that sort of thing will happen in Turkey. The Minister of War had, indeed, given the instructions. But in the *harbiyeh nasaret* in Stamboul it was still the rule that what Enver Pasha did not attend to in person was sure to be overlooked.

Instead of the passports came word from Corvette-Captain Humann, commander of the German naval base at Constantinople, that we were expected at the front. Enver Pasha had informed the commander at the Dardanelles that he would have company. That worthy person had made arrangements for our transportation, and so it came about that we set out on nothing more than a letter from the naval-base commander.

That letter reached us at three o'clock in the morning. F. Swing and I had dined together, and then, just to kill time, as some people would put it, we had gone to the *Garten* Bar cabaret in Les Petits Champs. It was our intention to take a cup of coffee and then turn in. But the cabaret was good and lasted long. We had something else, and then some more. At the wee, small hour of three we decided to hunt the hay, but found the letter instead.

The good hotel *portier* had stuck that most important letter in the pigeon-hole, and had we followed our first impulse we would have gone to bed before the letter was delivered; in that event we would have gotten it next morning, when the destroyer on which we were to go to the Dardanelles had been under way for four or five hours. Newspaper-men are anything but early risers.

While I read the letter F. Swing was doing a sort of Highland fling on the marble floor of the hotel lobby. He was overjoyed, simply overjoyed.

As usual, there was a large fire that night. We heard the fire-fighters of Pera make an awful noise with brass horns. Swing, in that cocksure way of his, opined that the blowing of horns would not put out the fire. He always found it hard to understand some phases of life in the Orient. While we were packing our things for that momentous and fateful trip, I explained to him that it was quite within the bounds of possibility that this blare of brass did have a purpose. In the first place, the racket would rouse all the people in the neighborhood of the fire, and, secondly, it might remind others to see that all their fires were in bounds.

We had a fight then and there. I insisted that it was customary in the East to lock the barn after the horse was stolen. Swing, being much of an Orientophile, if there be such a noun, resented that,

64

and said that I could see no good in any people. One has to love humanity at large as Swing does to be utterly blind to racial faults.

When we stepped out into the street and began to cast about for an *araba* it was raining in streams again. Swing hunted in one direction for a hack, I in another, and the night porter in still another. In about ten minutes Swing returned with an *araba*, and the porter also had managed to find one.

In two minutes I had another row on my hands. Swing thought that one of the *arabadjis* should make himself absent, but the driver disagreed with him. Nor would Swing pay for service that had not been rendered. He is a stickler in some things. When I offered to pay the man my friend would not let me. There was quite a disturbance, and before long we had the editors of the Greek daily, *Chronos*, who labor in a somber building across the street from the hotel, sticking their heads out of the windows.

I ended the difficulty by suggesting that the baggage be carried in one *araba* and the war correspondents in another. That helped. Swing agreed with me that it was unseemly, anyway, to have real war correspondents travel together with their baggage.

Life is one subterfuge after another.

At six o'clock we were on the steamer *General*, headquarters of the German naval base. An obliging orderly made us a cup of coffee—which we needed after so strenuous a night of cabaret, packing, and hunting for carriages.

With the comforting fluid tucked away we made for the *mush* or tender. There was a high sea running in the Bosphorus, and as we tumbled down the ladder Swing almost landed in the funnel of the steam-cutter.

We enjoyed our matutinal ablutions while we were trying to get to the destroyer, the *Peik-i-Shefket*, that was to take us to the Dardanelles.

I must explain here that Swing was in fine civilian garb and that his outer raiment was a very expensive fur coat. He had shown up in the Ottoman capital to study the political situation, and had neglected to get himself clothing suitable for wear at a military front.

My friend had never been to a front in his life, and, being mostly a philosopher and a "fan" in the matter of classical music, he could not understand what military exigencies are. I had done all sorts of war for fifteen years and could no longer be caught in that manner.

The *mush* shipped several fine waves and Swing began to worry how the delicate fur in his coat would stand the soaking. Before very long he complained of finding it hard to carry the fur coat. It was licking up water like a sponge and Swing is not a very strong man.

We clambered aboard the *Peik* and were under way a minute later. As we rounded the Serai Point of Stamboul and raced into the Sea of Marmora, the little tub stuck her nose into a frightfully high mixture of headwind and sea. In a jiffy the deck was awash and we had to go below.

In the commander's cabin we had introductions

and breakfast. Most of the latter we caught on the wing, so to speak. The tail end of that little destroyer wagged in a most exasperating manner. When the *Peik* stuck her nose out of the water her bow went down with a speed that took the chair from under one, and when she reversed this maneuver one had the impression that the low ceiling of the cabin was about to raise a bump on one's cranium.

Swing struggled manfully with the food and liquids before him. He held his cup of tea and rum in the left hand, and with the right he tried to peel a soft-boiled egg. That he managed. But he was less successful when he tried to get away with a plate of pilaff and chicken liver with a fork. He had better luck with the spoon.

The Turkish and German naval officers who were running the *Peik* were hardened sinners. With breakfast stowed away, they began to smoke. That was a little too much for Swing. He began to criticize the smallness of the cabin and also found fault with the racing of the propellers directly under us. The fact was that Swing was being attacked by *mal de mer*.

So we ventured on deck again, where we found refuge in the gun-turret.

Toward noon the sea subsided a bit and the gun crews were set to drill. I watched the work with considerable interest, but first with little understanding. My artillery work had been done on *terra firma*.

How those chaps could hope to hit anything from that pitching deck was beyond me. I said

67

as much to the commander of the *Peik*. He thought that this was not so difficult as I thought. I was to try. I did try, but I was not convinced that I could hit the broadside of a barn at fifty yards when my trying was over.

There was ground for belief that Allied submarines were busy in the Sea of Marmora. Four sailors were set out to watch for them. In front of their stations were horizontal indicator disks with a hand on them. If a man saw a submarine he was to set that hand in its direction and give the alarm. The sentinels did fine work. They reported nothing.

There is no doubt that the Sea of Marmora can be as ugly a sheet of water as one may wish to sail in a small craft. The waves are short and choppy, and run high.

The *Peik* is built for speed, and for reasons best known to himself the commander was driving her as fast as he could. The least improvement in the weather caused him to add a knot or two to her speed. There were times when we were making well above twenty knots under forced draught. That meant, of course, that the fore of the steel shell was constantly under water.

Early in the afternoon we sighted the town of Gallipoli, and when the racket of the racing propeller and the swish of the sea subsided for an instant the noise of artillery fire from the south was distinctly audible. The great battle was on. I feared that, after all, I was too late.

Going through the Inner and Central Straits I had a chance to take a look at the country. It seemed as gray and desolate as the low clouds above—low hills and high hills with bare flanks; here and there a little valley with a few houses or a little *koi* (village) in it. That seemed to be all.

It was dark when we reached the town of Dardanelles, also known as Tchanak Kaleh and Kaleh Sultanieh. The Greeks have another name for the place, and the Armenians still another.

After the setting of the sun the wind had gained new fury. The heavenly sluices also again stood wide open.

With the Allied fleet at the entrance to the Dardanelles, all lights in the port were doused, of course. Inky blackness reigned, and the commander of the destroyer feared that he might set his craft on the rocks: The result of this was long floundering and steaming in circles. How the man kept his bearings I do not know. I was glad when finally the anchor splashed in the water.

Getting off the *Peik-i-Shefket* was no mean undertaking. First we had to wait for some sort of a lighter. When it came we thought that our troubles were over, at least in part. But that was not to be the case.

It was not easy to get into that lighter. As she bobbed up the destroyer flopped down. When we thought that now was come the moment for that fateful jump, the lighter would recede again and be lost in the dark.

The situation gave rise to much conversation and planning. The best thing would have been to make a light. But that was out of the question. The search-lights of the Allied ships reminded us of the reason.

After much ado in the Stygian darkness, F. Swing and I, together with a few other passengers whom we had not seen *en route*, found ourselves in the bottom of that lighter. There was already much water about our feet and more was coming over the gunwale.

My leather coat was doing fine service, and, naturally, Swing's fine fur coat was not. To ward off some of the water that was spilling over my friend, I stepped between him and the seas and hoped that something would happen soon.

Poor F. Swing! He sent a prayer into the darkness that the lighter be started on her way. He mentioned, as a matter of fact, that we were ready to go ashore. He cajoled, pleaded, suggested, forgod-saked, and finally cursed—damned things as any nice boy will do. What he said was really nothing very bad, since Swing is a philosopher and a musician.

What they were waiting for I have never discovered. Half a dozen times we were on the verge of departure, when somebody on the destroyer stopped us again. The ways of the sea have always been beyond me.

We were glad when finally the patience of the hawser gave way. The cable snapped with a bang. Somebody on the destroyer said, "*Eyi, eyi*," which is the Turkish for our "all right," and we drifted off—drifted off in the direction of the Allied fleet, which was still very busy cutting dashes into the black night with its projectors.

On the trip down I had heard something of a mine-field near Dardanelles. I thought of that and wondered what would happen in case the lighter drifted that far with the current. But there was still hope. On the little tug that was to tow us into the port—and Heaven only knew where that port was—there was a tiny red light. That little light was floating near us and from its direction came voices. Then a bell clanked a signal, sparks rose from somewhere in the dark, a propeller began to churn the sea, and a cable in front of us shook off much water as it squirmed under the stress.

Well, something was doing at last.

Next to me stood a man. I could not make out his face, but I thought it well to ask him where Dardanelles really was. It so happened that the man was an Ottoman naval officer who had intimate knowledge of the strait. He spoke English quite well.

"It is somewhere to the left of us, *effendim*," he said.

That was vague, but it was something, anyway.

Just then we bumped into an object that turned out to be a wooden pier.

The tug churned on a little more; we came into quiet water and struck a quay with full force. The timbers of the lighter groaned, and Swing fell from the heap of things he had been standing on—somebody's baggage, not his own.

By now we were chilled to the bone. The last day in February, even at the Dardanelles, is no voluptuous summer night. A cold wind was blowing over us from somewhere, *borea de sirocco*, who knew!

But we managed to get out of that lighter, made sure that nobody had decamped with our baggage, and then held council as to what we were to do. Where did we have to report? Where could we spend the night?

Those were great questions. I suggested that we go to the headquarters of Admiral-General von Usedom Pasha, inspector-general of the Turkish coast-defense scheme. But where were those headquarters?

We started out in search of them. The search was long and arduous.

A town expecting to be blown out of the ground every minute of the day and night does not indulge in street-lighting. Tchanak Kaleh was no exception to this. Not a ray of light could be seen. It was still so dark that we could not even tell how high the buildings were.

Somebody had told us that the major part of "Pot Castle"—for that is the meaning of "Tchanak Kaleh," lay to our right. That scant advice we had heeded. We walked on for about two city blocks. Some voices coming from the dark, I also lifted mine, and presently four Ottoman soldiers stood near us.

In the course of time I have learned how to talk with my hands. I graduated in that accomplishment on the South-African veldt, and later took a post-graduate course in Mexico, where I recorded the doings of a score of *insurrecto* leaders.

This I tried on the *askers*, after I had ascertained that they knew not one of the forms of speech with which I am acquainted. The *askers* were very sym-

Copyright, by Underwood & Underwood

GERMAN OFFICERS AT THE DARDANELLES

From right to left: Von Usedom Pasha, Inspector-General of Ottoman Coast Defenses; Merten Pasha, technical expert; Machmed Bey, Turkish liaison officer; Prince Henry of Reuss, XXXIX, in charge of the Dardanelles mine-fields.

Copyright, by Underwood & Underwood

ESSAD PASHA, TURKISH COMMANDER AT ARIBURNU

It was Essad Pasha's task to keep back at Ariburnu, the northern front on Gallipoli, the valiant and impetuous Anzacs. He once confessed to the author that the "job kept him very, very bus . . . he put in . . . d . . f . . or . . . h . . . der of J . . .ine.

pathetic, but at first dubious as to the meaning of my strange words and gesticulations. They held a long council among themselves and finally said "*ewwet*" a good many times. That word I knew to mean yes.

Just to show that they were good fellows, the four men took our baggage and started off.

We measured many a pool after that. It was a soggy night, indeed. My feet knew that they were on a pavement of cobblestones, but they could not guess that there were so many deep gutters about. At first that worried us a bit, but after we had stepped into a rushing stream that laved our knees it really did not matter how much wetter our feet got. Swing had long ago shipped water into his low shoes. But now the water had run into my boots. That was reassuring.

About midnight we finally got to the headquarters of von Usedom Pasha. Our reception was frigid, reserved, and not encouraging. A major by the euphonious name of Schneider gave us a hint that headquarters had more important things to do than charge itself with the care of civilians. I said that our claims upon his hospitality would not be heavy. All we wanted was a place to sleep that night. But the man was obdurate.

Fortunately, Admiral - General Merten Pasha showed up at the moment in which the major decided that his high-priced brains could not be employed in the interest of two war correspondents I addressed the pasha, stated our predicament, and found a sympathetic nature.

Merten Pasha went so far as to give Major

Schneider a sly little dig, and then instructed him that he should bestir himself in our service. Of a sudden the major recalled that there was room in the Hotel Stamboul on the water-front. We thanked Merten Pasha, made sure that our escort of soldiers was properly instructed, and then set out again.

The hostlery was a little better than I expected. When we arrived it was dank and dark, and deserted save for the *kamorote*—the steward who managed the place since his master, the proprietor, thought it best to get out of the way of the British and French shells.

But the *kamorote* had nothing to eat in the house. Being very hungry, I set out to find a meal, despite the protests of Swing, who has the stomach-destroying habit of eating preserved food when he can still get fresh things.

There was another long search. But in the end we found a hole-in-the-wall sort of eating-place, kept open for the benefit of the camel-train drivers. There we had some beans, broiled mutton, and, to warm us, several glasses of a stuff they call *sharrap* —alleged to be wine.

F. Swing and I are together in the same room, together with some whitewash on the wall and floor, two iron bedsteads furnished with thin mattresses and sheets, pillows and blankets, two chairs, a rickety old table, a candlestick with several inches of mutton tallow in it, and our soaked baggage, which will require days to dry. The shutters of the two windows are closed, and the rifts between the imperfectly closing slats are stuffed full of paper, an anti-bombardment measure directed against the Allied fleet.

On the floor is a *mangal* with a charcoal fire in it. The pan of sheet iron on legs diffuses a little heat and much smell of charcoal—oxide gas. The *mangal* reminds me of the suicide-pan of Paris. Though the dear *kamorote* found it unnecessary to warn his guests that they might be dead in the morning, I will take that *mangal* out of the room before retiring. Either that or I will open the transom above the door, seeing that the heat is needed to dry our things.

Meanwhile, F. Swing is sleeping the sleep of the dead. He has been on his feet since nine o'clock on February 27th, and this is 2 A.M. of March 1st.

March 1st (Evening).

When I got up this noon I was rather surprised that there was no bombardment in progress.

A peep out of the window showed that the weather was still bad, and that may account for it.

I also cogitated a bit on what would happen if a shell hit the Hotel Stamboul. We are on the third floor, and if the shell did us no harm personally, the fall to the street surely would.

But we might fly far enough to land in the water which splashes against the street revet fifteen feet away from the wall of the hotel. I hope the water along the quay is deep enough for a dive from such a height.

In the afternoon we paid our respects to the official world here—Admiral-General von Usedom Pasha, Merten Pasha, Colonel Wassidlow, Captain Herschel, and Prince Henry of Reuss, thirty-ninth of his line.

We also met a good many Turkish officers. But Turkish nomenclature is still a little too much for me. I find it impossible to say how many Ali, Ibrahim, Yussuf, Djevad, Djemal, Kemal, Kiamil, Sefid, Iben, Ben, Sen and other *beys* I was introduced to.

Even Major Schneider was agreeable to-day. A second survey of us seems to have melted down a little of the ice in this refrigerator. So long as Schneider is around Tchanak Kaleh the summer cannot be hot.

After that I had a peep at our surroundings. They are not uninteresting. Tchanak Kaleh is a nice little town at the mouth of the Rhodios River, which was not devoid of fame even in antiquity.

Most of the houses are two stories high and the upper story is invariably of wood. That will help some when the bombardment starts in real earnest. I can see that town go up in a roaring blaze right now.

Back of the town lie gardens, fields, meadows, and vineyards that must be good to look upon in the summer. I also saw some of the pits from which the potters of "Pot Castle" take the clay for their wares. Later I investigated their handiwork and found it decidedly mediocre.

The population of the place is largely Greek, as one might expect of towns along the Hellespont. There are also a good many Armenians, and some Kurds. The Turkish population forms about 12 per cent. of the whole, I was informed. In addition to making pots and clay toys, the people engage in agriculture, viticulture, silk production, and trade.

The better classes have gone to other parts. Their houses are empty and serve now as quarters for many of the Turkish and German officers active in coast defense. Here, as elsewhere, it is a case of the devil take the hindmost. The poor are still in town, and there is no telling how many of them will perish in the bombardment.

To the south of the town lie two coast batteries, Fort Tchemenlik and Fort Anadolu Hamidieh. The first of these lies to the west of Kaleh Sultanieh, an old tower and battlement erected by the Turks in 1462. The "fort" has four cannon of ancient vintage and large bore—35.5 centimeters.

About eight hundred yards south of Tchemenlik lies the *pièce de résistance* of the defense of the strait—Fort Anadolu Hamidieh. It is a more modern affair than its sister battery. The fort, if one may call it that, has twelve emplacements. Four of the guns, 35.5-cms., are of fairly modern origin; eight others, 25.5-cms., are of about the same age.

The emplacements are protected by an earth parapet and earth traverses. Of turrets and such there is not even a trace to be seen. That, I understand, is the state of affairs generally along the Dardanelles, with the exception of a battery on the site of the ancient city of Dardanos—five 15-cm. pieces in half-turrets.

I cannot say that the equipment of the Turks impressed me in the least. The guns are outclassed in range and lack many of the contrivances used nowadays to make artillery fire accurate and effective. The sights I inspected are poor, and the electric communication system in the batteries and to points beyond is exposed to the shells, being strung on poles in the most haphazard manner.

How the Turks and Germans hope to keep away, with guns of a maximum range of 14,500 meters, ships that have a maximum range of at least 18,000 meters, is more than I can understand. I discussed that with some of the officers, and found that they shared my views.

They have good reason to do that since the batteries at the entrance to the strait, Kum Kaleh and Sid-il-Bahr, have already been silenced through this discrepancy in range.

I was told that these batteries were lifted out of the ground by the Allied ships, and that to-day even the guns in them are mere fragments. All of which promises to make my stay here interesting.

One of the first things I did to-day was to cast about for a place of observation. The officers said that they would not mind having my friend and myself in the batteries with them when things came to happen. That was very kind of them, to be sure. But I am not minded to be blown to smithereens just yet. I am an observer of battles, not a fighter of them, having done my share of soldiering out in the Transvaal during the late Boer War.

But when in Rome one must do as the Romans do. It is fatal to have soldiers, with whom one must intimately associate, feel that one is not willing to take a chance. I felt that way myself when once I saw a crowd of war correspondents on the veldt show the white feather.

That being my position, I selected the platform of the old tower of Kaleh Sultanieh as my observation post.

Merten Pasha, who has such matters in hand, consented to that, but only after he had pointed out that the platform of the tower was almost sure to get some of the shells intended for Fort Tchemenlik, the battery at its base.

I took this into account, but discounted it again when I discovered how splendid a view of the coming actions we could get from the roof of the majestic stone pile.

There is a signal-station on the tower, and that also helped me make up my mind, or ours, for Swing has much to say in such things.

F. Swing fell in love with that tower forthwith. In a single day it has grown dear to his heart. He told me that next to Neoplatonic philosophy and Wagner opera he loved old walls and towers and ruins and such. Swing dotes on romance. The old tower veritably breathes romance.

Within its sixteen-foot walls lie many dungeons. On our way to the top we have to pass through them.

The keeps are now inhabited by bats and owls, and that makes them all the more interesting to my friend. He believes that once upon a time fair maidens and their lovers were imprisoned in the dungeons, like Aïda and Rameses. The proximity of the ford which Leander swam to see his fair Hero is beginning to tell on my friend.

With the matter of selecting a place of observation disposed of, we adjourned to a Turkish restaurant near the bazaar and ate more beans, more broiled mutton; for dessert we had an egg and some *sharrap*.

While thus occupied the Allied fleet made its début at the entrance of the Dardanelles, all unbeknown to us. About two in the afternoon the sky had cleared a little, the high wind had subsided, and the sea was tolerably calm. This was an invitation for the Allied ships to become aggressive. They steamed up close to the entrance, raked the remains of Kum Kaleh and Sid-il-Bahr once more, and then occupied themselves with something or other near the village of Erenkoi and on a hill known as In Tepeh.

The fire was too far off to rouse our interest, though Swing insisted upon going to the tower platform.

From up there the ships could be seen and the detonations were plain enough.

The flashes of the guns and exploding shells interested my friend very much, and I am afraid that a great deal of the kindergarten course in artillery I gave him was lost on him. This is the first time that my friend has seen such things. He seems torn between the curiosity of a child and the dread that things may happen, as I gathered when I gave him a lurid description of the effect of an exploding shell.

At 4.30 the Allied ships withdrew, that being tea-time for the British jackies. I was informed that the British adhere rigidly to their gastronomic habits.

In the evening there was much display of search-lightery. Allies and Turks alike engaged in it; the former anxious to gain an entrance to the Dardanelles, and the latter determined to keep them out. The effort reminded me of two Xantippes having unfriendly intercourse over the back-yard fence.

Still, the thing was beautiful. We watched the entertainment from the platform of Kaleh Sultanieh, while the owls were having a convention in the dungeon under us. F. Swing found the scene indescribably beautiful. He is a poet and does not know it.

March 2d.

The big event seems to be drawing nearer. To-day, for the first time, the ships of the Allies ventured well into Erenkoi Bay.

But the weather was not in their favor. Visibility was low. A forty-mile gale kept the white horses racing in the bay. That the Allies got busy at all shows that they really mean to force the Dardanelles. Such was the expert opinion of men who ought to know.

A little before noon appeared four of the British line ships, members of the *Majestic*, *Victoria*, and *Agamemnon* classes, accompanied by two cruisers and a herd of smaller fry. After a while the cruisers and most of the small vessels withdrew, and the bombardment began.

The four ships kept constantly in motion while they were firing. This is done in order that the Turkish gunners may not have too good a target.

Describing large circles about the bay, the ships kept the Turks guessing as to how they could be reached by the shells.

Each boat-length of progress means that the aim must be completely overhauled, and when the piece is fired the discovery is generally made that the ship is nowhere near the spot where the great column of water lifted by the shell rises heavenward.

The British ships were concerned with some objects further down the bay. They were not stingy with their ammunition. The same can be said of the Turkish howitzers on the Anatolian and Gallipoli hills. Things became rather hot in the lower stretch of the bay, and then for reasons not known to me the smaller of the four British ships withdrew and disappeared behind the cape of Eski-Hissarlik.

With the small ship out of the way, the British began a more serious bombardment, the battery at Dardanos, that on In Tepeh, and some howitzer emplacements getting all the attention.

The British gunners were working hard. Great tongues of yellow fire leaped from the turrets of the three ships. Huge clouds of reddish smoke seemed to spring out of nothing in the next instant, and seconds later a great geyser of earth and powder fumes would break into view somewhere on the Anatolian shore.

Fort Dardanos especially was severely punished, as the British must have thought. But that was a fallacy. From the tower I could see quite plainly that much of the British fire was far too high. It did not even hit on the venerable old rubbish-heap in which one of the Trojan cities still lies buried.

The majority of the shells sailed into the fields east of the battery and did no damage whatsoever.

The fire of the ships was very poor. I concluded that the high sea was responsible for that. After two hours' exercise the British ships withdrew.

Toward the last the Turks did not fire a single shell. I have not yet located all of their batteries, so that I cannot say whether it was a consideration of range or the desire to save ammunition that kept them quiet.

As the British ships neared the entrance to the strait some of the Turkish howitzers near Atchi Baba hill showed signs of life. There were three hits. But the British did not seem to mind this very much. After all, the howitzer shell is a puny affair so long as it meets armor. The case is rather different when it hits an unprotected deck.

With the day's labor done, Swing and I had the usual quota and bill of "eats." We had more beans, more *shish-kebab* and *sharrap*, and Swing nearly lost his teeth in a piece of sweets.

They have a habit here of sweetening honey with sugar. When that has been done, the mass is poured over a sort of pie-crust. Swing thought he would try a piece of this. He implanted his incisors firmly for the purpose of biting off a chunk.

That is as far as he got. The lower teeth went through the crust easily enough, and met the teeth from above half-ways. Dilemma! There sat my friend with his jaws glued together.

I could read in his eyes, and see by the working of his cheek muscles, that he wished to free 'himself of this incubus.

83

"Go slow!" I said, fearing that my friend would tear out his teeth by the roots. "That is usually done after gas has been administered."

Swing is rather ready with his words. But on this occasion I had the best of him. Not that Swing chose to remain silent. Though most effectively gagged, he tried to speak, but only inarticulate sounds came.

I suggested a sip of water. My friend looked at me in disdain. How could a man drink water when his teeth were cemented together! So I showed Swing how it could be done.

Well, after a while my friend was himself again.

I may mention here that the pastry in question is known as *helwa*, a name it may get from the fact that help is necessary when the uninitiated try it for the first time, though F. Swing connected the name to another root—one which identifies the abode of His Satanic Majesty.

Last night, by the way, we had the first night engagement here. Some Allied mine-sweepers ventured into the bay, were discovered, and were taken under fire by the batteries of field-artillery the Turks have brought here for that purpose.

The mine-sweepers were in very close before they were seen.

Friend Swing had given me a lecture on the wisdom of Alexandria, while the two of us quaffed a bottle of nepenthe—some special *sharrap* I have discovered.

I am a good *buscalero*. I use the Mexican word for the designation, because it was in that country that I learned to always find what I wanted.

At eleven the wisdom and the nepenthe had both run dry and so we turned in.

A sensation of great noise woke me some three hours later. I was still struggling for wakefulness when the racket came again.

Whommmmp!—zow! and close at hand, too'

"Night bombardment!" shouted F. Swing as he suddenly reached a sitting position in bed. "Get up! get up!"

Some of the nearby field-pieces began to fire, barking like angry dogs, and making the window-panes rattle. There could be no doubt, though, that the two shells which had exploded near us came from some Allied ships. I concluded that the hen of the mine-sweeping flock, a cruiser, had been rude enough to take a pop at us in the wee, small hours of the morning.

The racket increased. F. Swing and I slipped into some of our clothing and rushed down-stairs.

It was our intention to get to our post of observation, the old tower. But that was a good five minutes' run away, and before we had reached the middle of the barrack-yard north of Fort Tchemen-lik the night engagement ceased suddenly.

There is an old breakwater at the end of the yard. Thither we rushed to see what the cause of the trouble could be.

But it was too dark.

The only thing I saw, by the light of a Turkish projector, was a scout-boat making for the entrance as fast as steam could push her. The Turkish search-lights were lighting up beautifully her hull and heels so that some battery along the strait might take a shot at her. Many essayed the trial. All of them failed. The many water columns raised by the shells looked like great and wonderful pearls in the light of the projectors.

At any rate, we had seen something.

F. Swing and I stayed at the old sea-wall until the projectors of the Turks died out like sparks in a heap of ashes. We hung on for quite a bit even after that, but the cold got the best of us in the end.

March 4th.

The Allied fleet fooled about a bit outside the strait yesterday, but came into Erenkoi again this noon.

There were five line ships to-day. For a while they pelted away at something on some hillside above Erenkoi, the ancient Rhoiteion. What the British gunners thought they saw there is a little beyond me.

My field-glass is a very good one, but ply it as I might I could not see a thing at the spot the British ships had under fire.

The Turks have no battery there, that I know, except it be a decoy arrangement—stovepipes and water-mains in which some enterprising *asker* sets off several pounds of black powder now and then, to make the Allies believe that the shells that are falling near them do not come from some nest of howitzers in the hills above the Shavan Dereh. I can see that battery from the tower, but the men on the ships in the bay cannot.

The battery is one of many which the Germans

have stationed in the hills of Gallipoli. It fires indirectly and cannot be seen from below.

I am a little surprised, though, that the British, knowing that the Turks have some of Germany's best artillery and coast-defense experts in their service, should assume that there was so much as a single gun on the spot they kept under fire.

At 2.15 in the afternoon the activity of the Allies' ships increased. Some of the ships once more raked the ruins of Kum Kaleh, and one of them, a member of the *Majestic* class, took under vicious fire something near the mouth of the Mendereh River. What it was I don't know. But there was a certain eagerness in the *tempo* of the fire that causes me to believe that this time the ship had a real target.

It may have been the aftermath of the affair which occurred at Kum Kaleh, day before yesterday. The Allies landed a small party for the purpose of erasing Kum Kaleh entirely with dynamite.

But the Turks had been looking for that and had stationed some infantry in the wreckage of the batteries. When the British marines came ashore they were set upon and cut to pieces.

An Anatolian *onbashi* by name of Mustapha earned himself the "Iron Crescent," companion piece to the "Iron Cross," in that little affair. He is said to have killed ever so many men with his hands and a rock.

Well, maybe he did.

March 5th.

War drew appreciably closer to-day. Some of it came in the form of direct fire from the Bay of

Erenkoi, and more from across the peninsula of Gallipoli. The Allies stationed a few of their line ships and cruisers in the Ægean, off Ariburnu, and took under fire from there the batteries of Kilid-il-Bahr, across the strait from us.

It was a warm day in many respects. The sky was blue, the sun warm, the sea calm, and visibility very high. That meant that the Allied ships had a good day for their work.

F. Swing and I were on the platform of the tower, getting fully, or rather more fully, acquainted with one Fuad Réchad Bey Effendi, an Ottoman student officer who has been detailed to be of assistance to us.

The Turks are very obliging to their two American *harb mughbirs*, as we are called in red Arabic letters on the white bands on our right sleeves. So far they have not turned down a single request of ours. But then the word of Enver Pasha goes hereabout and everybody knows that we are under Ottoman military law.

Fuad Réchad Bey was attached to us to save us annoyance at the hands of zealous Turkish officers and soldiers who do not know us as yet.

Fuad is a droll youngster. Sometime he hopes to become a coast-artillery officer. Right now he belongs to nothing in particular so far as I can see. He speaks French well and English not so well. Paris he knows like a book.

When the war broke out he was still in the French capital, but being an ardent patriot, he made good his escape from *gai Paris*. He reached Switzerland in quite a roundabout way, and now hopes that he will be spared to take care of his sister Lahika and his mother.

Inshallah!

The three of us were discussing nothing in particular on the roof of the *kulle* Kaleh Sultanieh, when, *whommmp!*

The detonation was so close by that we scrambled to our feet in a hurry—we had been sitting behind the old parapet, smoking.

I had caught the direction from which the crash came, and, looking across the strait toward Kilid-il-Bahr, I saw a great cloud of smoke drift lazily in the sunny morning air.

F. Swing, true to his habit of looking immediately for the cause of things, just then mentioned that there were three ships in Erenkoi Bay. With "Weyer" and glass I established that two of them belonged to the *Victoria* and one to the *Agamemnon* type. I also saw that they were again firing their forward turret pieces.

Kilid-il-Bahr, exactly 1,400 yards away from us, got the benefit of that salvo. I had my glass on the batteries there when the British shells came

They were far too high, except one of them. It landed in a garden to the rear of Rumeli Medjidieh battery and caused the gunners in that emplacement to show real signs of life. The men in brown scampered for cover in all directions. They had reached it before the next salvo arrived.

Thirty shells were planted in the Kilid-il-Bahr works. Nine of them were reasonably close. None of them hit the works themselves.

After this the British ships took under fire again

the batteries of Dardanos and Erenkoi—their whipping boys and *bêtes noires*.

There was no telling when the British ships might try their luck on Anadolu Hamidieh and Tehemenlik. In that case it might be best not to be on the platform of the tower, nor even in the town itself. A shell intended for Hamidieh, but aimed too high, was bound to get us; a shell for Tehemenlik, aimed a little to the right, would have the same effect.

The advisability of undertaking a dignified, albeit diligent, retreat was considered. Swing thought that soon it might be too late. He spoke with some emotion every time the line ships in the bay fired.

Fuad struggled manfully to be impartial. When Swing suggested that he should side against me, the student officer said that he could not do that, because as our adjutant he had no vote.

I persuaded my friend that as yet there was really nothing to fear. It was against all law of probability that the first shell of the Allied ships would hit so comparatively small a target as the platform of the tower. We could still retreat when it became certain that the batteries near us were to be bombarded.

Meanwhile I learned that other guns than those on the ships in the bay were belaboring the works at Kilid-il-Bahr. I saw shells explode in the works that did not come from the bay.

A shell from where the Allied ships were would require about twenty-eight seconds to land in Kilid-il-Bahr, as I had established by count. Often these shells exploded near Rumeli Medjidieh within five seconds after I had seen the flashes out on the bay; again it would require no more than one second.

That was odd enough. There was only one explanation, however. The shells that were falling into Kilid-il-Bahr were coming from some other part. I surmised that the Allies had ships in the Ægean, and later I learned that such was indeed the case.

At about 3.45 an Allied hydroplane hove into view above Kilid-il-Bahr. The observer was to report on the damage done. What he reported I don't know, of course. I hope he told the truth —that the effect so far had been *nil*, as it was.

He had not been gone very long before the bombardment took on a new spurt. Soon it reached its maximum intensity. Crash fell upon crash. Before long Kilid-il-Bahr, batteries and town alike, were enveloped in a dense cloud of powder fumes, which my field-glasses could not penetrate.

The explosions which flared in the cloud, like lightning, showed that the Allies had made up their minds to put Kilid-il-Bahr out of the running.

A little later, when a fire began to show through the fumes, it seemed that this plan was making good headway.

It was now impossible to say what was the effect of the shells in the batteries across the narrow strait from us. The entire site lay under a thick bank of vapors. There was no breeze to carry off the fumes and smoke.

The many earth columns that rose, the vivid flashes of the explosions, and the ever-gaining blaze made an impressive picture. Fuad Bey was sure that no stone was left on top of another in Kilid-il-Bahr. I told him that he was very much mistaken. Once I got my vision into a rift of the vapor bank. I caught the rear of the Medjidieh emplacement. It was intact, but deserted of man.

The ships out in the Bay of Erenkoi were once more concentrating their fire upon the Kilid-il-Bahr works. They were pumping shells at a rate that was imposing.

The bombardment of the works was at its full height when something sailed over us with the wail of a lost soul. The sound was not pleasant. We ducked behind the parapet.

Swing and Fuad agreed that it was a shell. Perhaps it was. To me it did not make the sound of a shell. Then, plupp! somewhere. No explosion!

Later I discovered that the thing was the huge fragment of a 38.1-cms. shell. It had struck the front of the bazaar building and had crushed it like an egg-shell.

In the Tchemenlik battery at our feet men stood by their guns. The officers were at their posts; pieces were loaded. A chaplain (*hodja*) was circulating among the men and saying words of encouragement. Now and then he would spread his prayer-rug, kneel on it, *salaam* innumerable times, and invoke the blessing of Allah.

The tall, gaunt form in brown *burnus*, scarlet sash, and green turban did his best to be a comfort to the gunners. He addressed one after the other, and patted some of them on the shoulder. Maybe he was picking out for this special attention those who seemed to need it.

Verily, death was not far off. Across the strait, 1,400 yards away, it was reaping its harvest, maybe, and every moment the Allied gunners might shift their aim a bit, with dire results to Tchemenlik. A single good hit might snuff out scores of lives in that cramped emplacement at the foot of the tower.

But at 4.25 the Allies retired—tea-time, as the Turks put it.

I was anxious to know what effect the bombardment had on the population of Tchanak Kaleh. But in the East they have splendid nerves. There had been no panic even after the bazaar had been hit. The water-front throughout the day had been crowded with curious men, women, and children.

After a bite to eat, F. Swing, Fuad, and I paid a visit to Fort Anadolu Hamidieh, to ascertain, if possible, the sum total of the day's event. The Turkish losses in men and munitions were slight, I was informed. In the opinion of the officers nothing had transpired during the day to cause them uneasiness.

The Allied ships had kept up their fire diligently, but were standing well out of range of the Turkish guns, especially those in Hamidieh. They had also betrayed a great respect for the mine-fields in the Dardanelles. Such was the consensus of opinions. I tried to get the conversation directed upon the question of ammunition. In that I failed. Nobody deigned to notice my intimations. Yet I know that this is where the shoe pinches.

The German artillery experts held the view that the ammunition used by the Allies was not suited for the work in hand. The shells were made to do their best in armor-penetration.

But there is no armor worth mention along the Dardanelles. The parapets and traverses are of sand. The shells of the Allies do not go far in that. Each little grain acts as a brake upon the side of the projectile, whose progress is in that manner quickly checked.

When the retarded action fuse finally springs the fulminating charge the shell has not penetrated deep enough to have the explosion do much damage. Shells that would go through steel armor as through a piece of cheese are nearly worthless against the sand protecting the emplacements.

When we got to the Hotel Stamboul its poor *kamorote* was on the verge of distraction. He is a Levantine and not used to battle. From the roof of the building he had seen the bombardment of Kilid-il-Bahr, and now he was certain that in the morning it would be the turn of Tchanak Kaleh. What had he better do in that case? Would we not move out and persuade two other guests to do likewise, in which case he could close up the hotel and go into the hills back of the town?

We told him that while we were people willing to oblige others, we could not go to that extreme. On the other hand, he could leave the hotel in our charge. But as the man looked into the great blaze across the strait the thought came to his mind that in his absence the *han* in his care might burn down. He is a conscientious being, I will say.

After that we went to our room, I to dash off some cable despatches, Swing to write something for the mail. When other people rest from battle we have to sit down and describe it, so that the good people at home may have it at the expenditure of two cents with their breakfast and without giving us poor devils so much as a thought.

March 6th.

Bombardment from 9.30 to 4.30—breakfast to tea, with a short pause for lunch.

Four British vessels of pre-dreadnaught types steamed boldly into Erenkoi Bay, milled for position, and took under desultory fire the batteries of Erenkoi, Dardanos, and those at Kilid-il-Bahr. The effect of the bombardment was *nil* again.

In the afternoon we had the most unusual, indeed unique, spectacle of seeing battle-ships bombard one another by indirect aim.

During the night the Turks had brought into the Central Strait the line ships *Haiireddin Barbaruss* and *Torgut Reiss.* The purpose of this move was to make it interesting for the Allied line ships which have been bombarding the works at Kilid-il-Bahr from across the peninsula. It is reported that one of the line ships, allegedly the *Bouvet,* was hit.

Fort Anadolu Hamidieh drew fire to-day for the first time. We were on the tower platform at the time. Half a dozen shells buried themselves in the yard of the battery. The British ships in Erenkoi Bay let it go at that.

The shells fell not more than eight hundred yards

7   95

away from us, and some of their splinters hit the wall and platform of the venerable pile on which we roost in the day. We put up a brave front to the signal-men who share the platform with us, but were not sorry when the British withdrew.

I have the impression that the British sent the shells into Hamidieh for the sole purpose of serving sarcastic notice that in the near future there would be more where those came from.

Well, the great event cannot be far off. I understand that the Allied fleet is growing with each day. The German aviators in the Ottoman service go nightly on patrol to Tenedos, Imbros, and Lemnos. Their reports are not very encouraging to the men in charge of the defense of the Dardanelles and the city that lies beyond them.

March 7th.
To-day's bombardment lasted from 12.15 to 4.10 P.M.

It was a short session, but a hot one.

Five ships participated: One *Lord Nelson* type, two *Agamemnons*, and two French line ships, one of them of the *Gaulois* class, the other unidentified for the reason that part of her superstructure has been disguised in some manner—canvas, I suppose.

The Allies took under fire Erenkoi, Dardanos, Rumeli Medjidieh, and Anadolu Hamidieh.

I must record that the fire of the Allied ships is improving. Much damage would have been done the Turkish emplacements to-day were it not that all of them lie on "soft" land—meadow soil of a light, loamy character.

From 1.10 to 2.30 the cannonade was terrific Shot followed shot. The air was rent with the roar of explosions, echoing and reverberating from the steep hills of Gallipoli to the mountains of Anatolia. I wonder if the spirits of Agamemnon and Priam attended? If they did they will have some notion as to what progress has been made since their nearby Troy fell.

Some shells fell close to Troy to-day. Were I facetious enough I could have written a lead for my despatch that to-day Troy was bombarded. But this is serious business and no occasion for flippancy.

The Turks husbanded well their ammunition. They have none too much of it. Fort Anadolu Hamidieh loosed sixteen large armor-piercing shells. Three hits were registered by the Turks as the day's total. One of the British ships withdrew with a list to port, after a large sheaf of red sparks had announced that the steel of shell had struck the steel of armor.

We were glad when the sun set—in an angry red—behind Cape Eski-Hissarlik.

There is no doubt that we are living here on a volcano. The Turks and Germans are beginning to realize the situation, and it is worrying them. The *kaimmakam*, incidentally, has ordered the population of Tchanak Kaleh to move on, stating that those who remain must do so with the knowledge that the town may be bombarded any day.

Well, we had to abandon the old tower; much as we love its old walls and sunny parapet. The signal-men have it all to themselves now. They are sorry. We were good company, they said. And well they may say that, for many are the *extra*, *première*, and *deuxième* cigarettes they have smoked with us. It was a treat to them.

The poor devils smoke *sixièmes*.

Admiral-General Merten Pasha is to some extent responsible for our change of station. He thought we ought not to go to the tower any more.

"You know what will happen when a 38.1-er gets it," he said. "It 'll crumble into crushed rock. Let me warn you!"

Thus dispossessed, we hunted for another point of vantage to-day, but found none. The result of our hunt was that we were caught on the bare beach between Forts Tchemenlik and Anadolu Hamidieh during the hottest part of the bombardment.

We had followed the bombardment from the beach when suddenly the Allied ships took the two forts named under fire, without so much as "by your leave." In a second our retreat was cut off. With the strait before us, the Rhodios River in our rear, and the Allied fire in our flanks, we could do nothing but crawl behind a small heap of sand.

It was a very ticklish situation indeed. The Allied shells were thick and fast, going over us with the noise of a thousand wheels in a tunnel full of bridges.

In Anadolu Hamidieh, on our left the roof of the barracks had been long a thing of memory and the shells of the Allies were turning the barrack-yard upside down. In Tchemenlik things were no better.

But there was enough ammunition coming the

98

Turks' way that some of it spilled beyond the emplacements. The field back of us was for quite a while a favorite spot for the explosions, and things grew decidedly worse when all the short shells intended for Tchemenlik struck on the beach. Each moment one of them might strike into that little heap of sand and send us to kingdom come.

My poor friends felt that keenly. Swing had never been under artillery fire in just that manner before, and Fuad was by no means enthusiastic. He thought that before a man could be a good coast-artillery officer he had much to learn. I agreed with him.

Meanwhile the Turks were not firing a shot. The Allied ships were out of range and stayed out persistently. I hoped that it would be tea-time soon.

But it seemed as if the Allied commander had made up his mind to at least put a bad dent in the Dardanelles coast-defense system to-day. He was most persistent. His ships came in closer.

Our sand-heap was not far from the Hamidieh battery, on which I had my field-glasses all the time. I felt that something would happen there before long.

It did happen.

A leather-lunged German officer shouted something through a megaphone. Men began to tumble out of the casemates. I knew what that meant; my heart went into my boots. If Hamidieh replied to the fire there was bound to be more in return, and we would get our share of that.

I recognized the officer as Captain Herschel.

When next I heard the staccato rap and snap of his great voice he was giving the range—13,400 meters. It seemed that he had his eye on a ship of the *Agamemnon* type, which was furthest in and just then about to present broadside in a maneuver.

Four flashes of fire, four clouds of smoke, and then came a long crash as the four shells left the main battery of the emplacement. The screeching of the shells was soon over, then a column of water rose ahead of the ship, another a little short of amidships, the third astern, and the fourth again amidships—all of them off the mark.

What I had feared came soon to pass. Within the space of two minutes the Allied ships had brought their forward turrets face to face with Hamidich and forthwith the shell rain started.

Of that we got our share; more than our share. The fire of the Allies was not good this time. It was high and the shells landed around us. Great columns of water and huge geysers of earth and mud, flame and vapor rose and fell. For several seconds the air teemed with shell fragments. Some of them landed within a few feet of the sand-heap—one of these being the third of a shell and more than four feet long.

Well, we were not the only ones who were caught on that beach.

I saw von Usedom Pasha and one of his adjutants, Major Schneider, and an orderly draw nigh in good order on the road that runs from Tchemenlik to Hamidich.

When von Usedom came to our sand-heap he

stopped. "You are not a good risk for a life-insurance company to-day," he remarked, lightly—too lightly.

"Very true, Your Excellency!" I returned. "It doesn't look as if we were."

"Can't you find better cover than that?" he inquired, quite unmindful of a huge geyser that rose behind him that instant.

"Not and see anything," I explained, getting to my feet.

"You had better get down again. You haven't much cover there against shells, but it will help keep off some of the pieces," said the pasha as he turned on his heels and walked on.

Before the party got to the little bridge over the Rhodios River the pasha had a very close call. A large piece of shell buried itself at his heels. Von Usedom looked around to see what had happened and went on.

There was no doubt that the Allies were riled at the temerity of the Turks. They started to hammer their antagonists in the most merciless fashion, without knowing, no doubt, how futile their efforts really were.

In that meadowland around us a shell could have no more than minimum effect—a large crater from which the steel fragments sped skyward—to come down again in most perturbing fashion. It was not long before this was quite plain to Swing and Fuad. They no longer minded the shells; the thing that worried them was the after-effect.

More and more savage grew the bombardment. The Allies worked their guns as hard as they could without melting them down, and the Turks kept under fire whatever was in range.

I was wondering what the Turks in Tchemenlik were doing. I hoped that they at least would not get mixed up in this thing. If they did we on the beach would get all the short shells aimed at them. While the Allies had already taken the battery under fire, they had now been diverted to Hamidieh.

But I had hardly finished taking in that part of the situation when several shells reached Tchemenlik simultaneously.

I was looking at the tower of Kaleh Sultanieh, when I saw a great cloud of smoke rise over its parapet. The next instant the tower was withdrawn from view by the blue fumes of the shell and the white vapor ribbons which the catapulted rocks drew after them. I thought that the old friend had surely come down, but when the smoke had drifted off I saw him rear his proud, gray head as haughtily as before.

We had by that time large wads of cotton in our ears. But the stuff did not keep much of the explosion-shock from our tympanums. Swing began to complain of headache and wished that he were in Chicago, or at least Constantinople, and Fuad had been thoroughly disillusioned. Would that bombardment never cease? That was the question.

Hamidieh was now at it again, drawing more fire for us. Fort Rumeli Medjidieh joined, as did Fort Rumeli Hamidieh. Dardanos was barking now. Erenkoi mixed in; the howitzer batteries coughed away.

I began to think that this general mêlée had been ordered by the Turks in order to call the dogs off Anadolu Hamidieh. If this was the intention, it failed.

The Allied fleet, not minding much of anything for the first time, was sending salvo after salvo into Hamidieh. Its temper was roused and high, but rather impotent, I thought, so far as the battery was concerned. From my position I could see every shell that fell near the battery; so far the parapet and traverses had not been hit a single time. The fire of the Allies was good, but not effective.

At three o'clock my friends could stand the infernal racket no longer. Swing and Fuad both were anxious to leave the beach, and as I had seen enough of the bombardment for a good despatch, there was no reason why we should remain exposed to danger any longer.

Before starting I warned them that there was great danger getting through the Tchemenlik battery. It might be taken under fire again any moment. I wanted to have them understand that they were venturing into a center of fire.

But they were willing to risk it.

Just as we had gotten across the little bridge over the Rhodios River a shell exploded fifty feet away from us on the beach, near a water-logged beam which it sent rolling in our direction. Happily, the spread of the steel fragments lay forward of us. While we were in the yard south of the battery a shell crashed into a one-story building on our right. The force of the explosion almost threw us to the ground. We stopped and held our arms over our faces to avoid having our eyes cut out by the flying pieces of glass.

Traversing the yard of the battery, I cast a look at the old tower. It was still there, but at its southwest corner there was a large crater.

North of the tower there is a sort of tunnel gate. I concluded that that might shelter us effectively. Before a shell could reach the tunnel itself it would have to penetrate the old tower through and through, and that was not likely. Only a high-angle shell could reach the tunnel and the Allies were using no guns of that sort.

The place was also an excellent storage for spare ammunition, and the Turks were using it as such. When Swing and Fuad saw the hundreds of shells that stood in and near the tunnel they decided that it was best to move on a little further.

We were now in the large barrack-yard north of Tchemenlik, and from that point nothing at all could be seen but the exploding shells in the Kilid-il-Bahr works. After hugging the old wall of the *kaleh* for a few minutes, the three of us wanted to have another look at the bay from near the old breakwater.

That came near being our undoing forever. A large shell exploded in the shallow water inside of the breakwater and the load of rock and splintered steel rushed past us. When I had wiped the sea-water out of my eyes I saw that Swing and Fuad were still alive, but swaying about in the manner of groggy prize-fighters.

By that time we felt the need of something wet and

refreshing. I knew of a little Turkish café, standing on piles well out in the street. I had been there once before and had noticed that from the windows one gained a splendid view of the Bay of Erenkoi, though a headland south of Kilid-il-Bahr shut off all view of the entrance to the strait.

We made up our minds to go there. We had gone only a few paces when another shell hit in the shallow water to our right and a little behind us. There was another avalanche of rock, steel, and copper shreds, mud and water. We fell prone to let it pass over us after it was already gone. Luck was with us that moment.

By this time we were ready to run. That we did not run is due to the fact that we were too tired and fatigued. We had been under intense, if subdued, excitement the greater part of the noon and afternoon, and were so thirsty that we could have gulped down sea-water.

To my surprise, the little coffee-house was filled with inhabitants of Tchanak Kaleh. Wet and dirty as we were, we caused no small sensation as we stepped into the place.

Some Turks at a table near one of the windows overlooking Erenkoi Bay made room for us at their table.

We began to gulp down hot tea as fast as the waiter in high boots could serve it. The cups were not large, but Swing had ten of them. I did away with six or seven, and Fuad had enough with four. This done, I got a bootblack to occupy himself with me, and in a few minutes I was again presentable.

Soon thereafter the bombardment ceased. One of the last shells sent a great fragment of steel through a cookshop adjoining the little café.

The calm of the men in the coffee-shop was remarkable. They were in imminent danger, but did not mind it. It may have been the fatalism of the East that held their nerves in check.

Well, it was tea-time again. The Allied ships withdrew, and everybody felt, no doubt, that a good day's work had been done.

IV

WHEN THE ALLIED FLEET FOOZLED

March 8th.

THE bombardment of March 7th seems to have persuaded the population of Tchanak Kaleh that it would be best to go to other regions. The demolition of the bazaar and the cookshop by fragments of shell had given these people an inkling of what the effect of a square hit would be.

There had been little response to the proclamation of the *kaimmakam* and Djevad Pasha, the commander of the Dardanelles. Much more was accomplished by the shells.

F. Swing and I were hauled out of our beds at three o'clock in the morning by a tremendous babble under our windows. It was dark yet. A great crowd was surging about on the quay, however. Everybody was trying to get into the *mahonies* ahead of some one else. It seemed that of a sudden the population was gone mad. The stoical indifference of yesterday had disappeared.

Most of the noise was being made by those about to embark, and much of it concerned the little baggage that could be taken along. It seemed hard to tell the bundles apart. Somebody would seize what did not belong to him or her and screams and expostulations would ensue.

Knowing well enough that there would be no more sleep for us that morning, F. Swing and I got up, dressed, took breakfast, and then watched the migration.

It was a motley crowd—Greeks, Turks, Armenians, and what not. Most of the women, regardless of race, wore pantaloons tied at the ankles and belt, a sort of blouse, also a shawl in case of the Christians; *yashmak* and *feredcheh* in the case of Moslems.

There was an unkempt look about the women. I concluded that it was largely due to the circumstances under which they were leaving home, having had ample opportunity to observe that usually these women were rather tidy.

The men made a better appearance. They were a picturesque lot. Their loose trousers, high boots, richly colored waistbands, colored shirts, and embroidered jackets were of good material and contrasted sharply with the garb of the women.

Some soldiers and gendarmes arrived to keep order in the crowd. At least this had been somebody's intention. But nothing of the sort happened. The minions of law and order began shortly to increase the babble and bedlam. The Turk has to do just so much scolding, no matter what he is about.

Every now and then a *mahonie*, loaded to overflowing with men, women, children, and baggage, would set sail for the Central Dardanelles. We learned that off Nagara several steamers were waiting for the refugees. Everybody had to pay passage, of course. Those who wanted to go to Constantinople could do that, though the advice was being given that it might be best to visit relatives in the interior.

I wondered what would become of many of the pretty Greek girls when they got to the capital. *Qui vivra verra!*

There is no crowd so poor as to be without class distinction. It was so in this case. People with a little ready cash on hand had hired *mahonies* to take them to their destination. They were taking along much of their furnishings, which in the case of the Turks consisted almost entirely of taborets, large brass trays, some china, and bales of carpets. Each family of this "better class" had a large number of pet animals, dogs, cats, parrots, rabbits, and the like.

For them the start of the hegira was something of a holiday. Father saw to it that his own were made comfortable in the sailboat, and mother acted very much like a hen taking care of a playful flock of hatchlings. The children were having a great time of it. To them it meant an outing and nothing more.

On the fringes of the vast crowd were the very poor. They were timid. How to get the fare that would take them to Constantinople or some other place was a problem they had not been able to solve. Some of them were offering their belongings for sale. But in a crowd that was leaving behind many much better things than these poor devils were willing to sell nobody bought, of course.

109

FROM BERLIN TO BAGDAD

As the last *mahonies* pulled away for the steamers, whose smoke could be seen rising behind Cape Nagara, these unfortunates became frantic. They appealed to the gendarmes and to some officers. But that was of no avail. By noon many of them had returned to their homes in town.

In the afternoon my friend and I took a *mahonic* to go to the works of Kilid-il-Bahr. We wanted to see what damage the bombardment had done. No British ships were in sight, though the weather was good. The fact that we had to sail around the mine-field made the trip agreeably long.

The commander of the Kilid-il-Bahr batteries received us very pleasantly. We made it a point to impress him with the fact that we had come to pay our respects. Of course, we would not object being taken around the works to see how "little" damage there really had been done.

We had the usual coffee and cigarettes and talked to the commandant with the aid of our inimitable and indispensable Fuad Réchad Bey.

The old commander was one of the few Turkish officers of the old school who had been allowed to stay in the service when Enver Pasha came to the helm. He had never been out of Turkey in his life.

That under these circumstances he should be left in command of so important a point as Kilid-il-Bahr surprised me greatly for a time—until I was taken over the batteries. The commander might be a home-product officer, but I doubt if a more efficient man could be found along the entire strait, the Germans included. The effort of the

110

organizer and disciplinarian was discernible everywhere.

The effect of the Allies' fire was not great by any means. The damage done was small—ridiculously small. Not a single gun had been damaged. A small barracks, several sheds, three living-houses and a number of outhouses had been destroyed. A large barracks and five other buildings were slightly damaged. Two gunners dead and seven wounded were the total of the casualties.

It was rather different beyond the precincts of the coast-defense establishment. The southern part of the town of Kilid-il-Bahr had suffered severely. Shells had set the buildings afire, and an inspection of the burned-over area showed that most of the shells of the Allies' guns had struck there.

The old commander was highly pleased, naturally. He concluded that there was so much room about his batteries that the Allies would have to hammer away a long time before they could hope to steam past his bailiwick. When I saw the shells of the *Queen Elizabeth*, which had not exploded, I felt that the old man was not far from being right.

After the commandant, a score of his officers, and the chaplain, *hodja*, and we had been photographed behind one of the shells of *Queen Bess*, Swing and I concluded to take a look at a real Turkish town—Kilid-il-Bahr. There would be no war that day from the look of things. The *sirocco* was blowing gently into the Dardanelles and with it came just enough haze to make visibility low.

We found Kilid-il-Bahr a most interesting place. Any place becomes that when Swing is along. His

poetic soul finds romance and picturesqueness anywhere. But Kilid-il-Bahr is beautiful.

It was still in the narrow streets. The houses
had been deserted. Through the latticed windows
and *shahnichins* showed dainty scrim curtains.
Here and there they would blow from a window that
had been left open.

Over the garden walls peeped cherry, plum,
almond, and apple trees with more bloom than
foliage on them. The green of the willows was
very fresh. White, slender minarets reached into
the blue sky. The old gray walls of the castle
erected by Sultan Mohammed II were set off by
heaven-reaching cypresses of somber green. At the
end of the alleys one caught glimpses of the delicate water tints of the Dardanelles.

Swing and I invited ourselves into a Turkish
home. We got Fuad to simulate the owner thereof.
The door was open.

The front room of the ground floor, lighted by
a single small window high up, had been used for
storage purposes. To one side of this was a narrow
hall with the stairs leading to the story above.
Back of the storeroom was another room with a
high window looking toward the garden. Then
came the kitchen. It had an open hearth, and the
walls and ceilings were thickly covered with soot.

The yard was very tidy and screened off from
the houses in the rear by a hedge of cypresses.

All sorts of tender green things peeped out of
the beds in the garden. The dwarf fruit-trees
along the garden wall were in bloom. There were
green berries on the strawberry-plants under the

stunted fruit-trees. In the corner nearest the street was a sort of rose garden. The gravel paths and stone borders of the beds indicated that somebody had bestowed much care and love upon this little spot.

We re-entered the house and went up-stairs. The Turk never lives on the ground floor when he can avoid it. It was so in this case. The entire lower story had been given over to other than living purposes. Fuad explained that his people do not care to live within stone walls. He assigned this as reason why most houses in Turkey have a stone understructure, while wood only is used on the story above.

The upper floor remained in much the same condition as when tenanted. The Turks do not care much for furniture, and when the carpets and rugs have been taken up and baled one is ready to move. It had been so in this case.

Around the room ran the wooden part of the divan—a mere box with here and there a drawer in it. The mattresses had been taken away, as had the covers and pillows. An old carpet and two threadbare and frayed rugs were all that remained of that part of the *ménage*.

Whether that family had been rich or not so rich was hard to say. The bare floors, white-washed walls and ceilings, left that a mooted question. Swing discovered an empty perfume-bottle in the corner of one of the rear rooms. We did our best to establish the quality of the perfume, but failed. Finally Fuad took a sniff. He, too, was unable to arrive at a conclusion. As a clue to

113

the family's endowment with the good things of this earth the little bottle was a failure.

We left the house and ascended the mountain back of the town. There was a large wireless station there which we wanted to see. On the way up we passed a Turkish shepherd who was minding some threescore of sheep to the tune of his *kaval*.

The wireless station was a very modern, and to Swing a very banal, affair. Swing hates the things that are modern. He says that civilization as the real thing is not being helped by this tremendous mechanical progress.

This inspection over, we scaled a crag, and from up there looked into the alleys of Kilid-il-Bahr and the inclosures of Mohammed's castle. That was my friend's great opportunity. Up there one's vision was unhampered.

Before long Swing was spouting the history of the Hellespont. Dorians, Athenians, and Spartans, Pericles, Themistocles, Pausanius and Cleonice, Alcibiades, not to mention the heroes of Troy and the lovers of Abydos and Sestos, and such plebes as Cyrus, Alexander the Great, and Pompey, came to the mind of Swing like reels of a moving-picture before the eyes of the crowd.

Indeed, from the crag upon which we were perched one could see the *locales* of the most heroic exploits of antiquity.

To the south of us, in a bend of the Mendereh Valley, we spotted with our glasses the hill upon which lie the remains of Troy. A little to the north of that we spied a peak, Mount Ida, the "couch of flowers" of which Homer sings in the Iliad.

Down on the Anatolian shore we saw the hill of Dardanos, in whose bowels rest the remains of a city, perhaps older than Troy; and to our right lay glistening in the sunshine the Heptastadion Ford made famous by the alleged feats as a swimmer of one Leander and his love for Hero.

We concluded that any good swimmer could get across the strait of Nagara, provided he started far enough upstream. Swing there and then decided that he would repeat the exploit of Leander and Lord Byron—provided he was accompanied by a boat.

In the evening we were the guests, at dinner, of a Turkish general-staff officer. Our host proved to be a most modern sort of Islamite.

The teachings of Mohammed, the great prophet, were largely philosophy to him, he said with frankness and in the presence of a score of other Turkish officers. It was poor philosophy at that. He thought that Moses made a much better job of it, especially from a legal and moral point of view.

But as he progressed our host found fault even with Moses. That personage, he insisted, was somewhat of a plagiarizer. The laws of Moses were things not unknown to the Chaldeans and Sumerians, as recent finds in cuneiform tablets had demonstrated *ad libitum.*

There was not, and there could not be, anything new under the sun. Civilization was a thing of indefinable qualities and dimensions, he said. What proof had we that the ancient Sumerian, in his boat of wicker-work and pitch, did not travel just as fast to his liking as did we who crossed the Atlantic in a steamer making twenty knots an hour?

What people did not know did not worry them. We were mistaking mechanical improvements for human progress, thought our host.

The man is well informed. Oriental history is at his finger-tips. The customs of the East he recounts with the greatest facility. He named for me a string of Armenian kings that took my breath away. The rulers of Old Byzantium might have been his next-door neighbors; Queen Hatsheput his aunt.

She may have been so far as looks go.

That meant, of course, that Swing was in his element. He helped to maintain as fine a line of philosophy as I have heard in a long while.

Soon the two became too abstract, with the result that Fuad and myself dropped out and consumed all the coffee and the cigarettes. While Ibrahim Bey and Swing were tearing the cosmic scheme to pieces and putting it under the microscope, Fuad and I exchanged confidences on Paris and agreed that the city on the Seine was a lovely place.

March 11th.

F. Swing and I surrendered ourselves to the attendants of the Turkish bath—a real Turkish bath—to-day. It was quite an experience.

Not that we have not bathed since Pera. We have done that o' nights in the chilly waters of the Dardanelles. But there cometh a time when one feels the need of a good steaming. We got that. Later we had our epidermis saturated with perfumed alcohol, and since then we have risen one hundred per cent. in our own opinions.

This afternoon I had a long talk with Admiral-General von Usedom Pasha, the purpose of which was to get some information on relations between the Turks and Germans here.

I learned that these relations are not entirely frictionless. The Germans say that they are doing all the work. The Turks claim all the credit. Von Usedom Pasha said that he did not mind this, but that some of the officers under him were less liberal in that respect. He was content with being of account to his fatherland anywhere. Whether that was at the Dardanelles or in the North Sea would never worry him.

There were one or two things which the Turks and Germans had overlooked so far. The white minarets and houses, the great towers of the *kalehs* at Tchanak Kaleh and Kilid-il-Bahr, and the white stone revets of some of the batteries, have in the past made excellent targets for the Allied gunners. That having been ascertained, these surfaces are now being cross-hatched with black paint.

Old Kaleh Sultanieh has a comical look now. It is undignified treatment that has been given the old pile. But there was no help for it. The white minarets about town look just as crazy. Some of the more prominent trees are being chopped down, among them several of the stately willows on the Rhodios River back of Anadolu Hamidieh.

Just now Dardanelles is peaceful enough. The

117

air is balmy with the scents of spring. The trees bloom and the foliage is making good headway. The hedges are green, and such fields as were tilled before the exodus are doing well enough.

F. Swing and I spend much time under the great elm-tree in front of a little café to one side of the triangular plaza on the rue Saat Hissarlik—Street of the Clock Tower. The proprietor has moved the tables there so that the patrons may sun themselves.

So we watch the traffic by the hours. It is entirely a military traffic. Regiments of infantry tramp past us all day long, some of them going south toward Kum Kaleh, others returning. Artillery is being trundled back and forth. Engineer equipment is taken one way or another, and there seems to be no end to the supply columns. Great strings of camel-trains amble along—ten animals to the string, with a little burro at their head as leader.

"Mosyu Sweng" and I—there is no reason why I should perpetuate the cognomen by which I am known hereabout — are great favorites. Everybody buys coffee and tea for us, offers cigarettes, and invites us to the mess. Well, there is no reason why we should not enjoy life while we can. It may be different very soon.

There are a great number of Allied ships in the Bay of Mudros. Others are steaming toward the Dardanelles, according to "inside" sources. Since the weather is entirely favorable for a continuation of the bombardments, we have been wondering why the Allies left off so suddenly on April

7th. Putting two and two together means in this case that the British and French are preparing for an operation on a scale larger than what has yet been attempted. I fear, Swing fears, they all fear, that there will be a grand concert one of these days. Little may be left of us when that concert is over.

We would like to be back in Pera. But that cannot be. If something big should come to pass in my absence somebody in New York would raise all sorts of a row, and Swing says that we will get scant thanks if we emerge crippled for life. There are times when Swing is inclined to be gloomy.

March 13th.

It is night.

The wind from the Mediterranean has blown low-hanging clouds over the Dardanelles Strait, which now precipitate in cold rain.

The hill masses above the shores of the waterway and the Bay of Erenkoi are enveloped in impenetrable gloom, since the starlit sky, at first still visible in purple patches, was blotted out.

Around the battlements of the old tower of Kaleh Sultanieh howls a tempestuous wind in dismal tones. Even the many owls who inhabit the old pile seem to find the situation unpleasant and flutter about, with their screeches fitting well into the picture.

The good Dardanellians, who have not yet taken to flight, are within doors and are glad of it, or ought to be.

Over the parapets and traverses of the batteries

119

of Fort Anadolu Hamidieh the rain sweeps in cold sheets. Men in oilskins are on post.

The search-lights along the Bay of Erenkoi have been traveling over the waters lazily, revealing nothing that would excite interest. The men in the batteries and at the search-lights are guarding the goal of the Allied fleet—Constantinople.

It is war!

For a while the lights continue to wander about aimlessly. So it seems. Their bright rays illume the wave-crests in the bay and occasionally light up parts of the shore. One gets the impression that the men directing the lights play with them in this manner so that the weary night may pass the quicker.

Of a sudden one of the projected rays fixes itself on some object near the Gate of the Dardanelles. In the same moment the object emits a yellow flash—and then another.

Fifteen seconds elapse and then two red flames leap from the ground where the bright glow of the search-light is seen. Simultaneously the carbons of the search-light show red and then die, while from some other point a new ray appears.

The Allies are at their nightly task of shelling the search-lights, preparatory to sending a large mine-sweeping fleet into Erenkoi Bay. The vigilance of the Turks and Germans has made this task dangerous and tedious, but it must not be neglected if the Allied ships are to go to the Ottoman capital.

Other flashes come from the ships, and near the

Turkish projectors more red sheets of fire leap into the night.

Soon a night engagement is on.

Guided by their search-lights, the Turkish gunners take the Allied vessels under fire. The black hollow between the Gallipoli and Anatolian heights begins to echo and reverberate the crash of artillery and exploding shells.

Every projector is in play now.

The almost circular shores of the bay spit fire at many points and the Allied light war craft which is now over the entrance replies industriously. Through the night air sing shells of the small bores with plaintive whines. Steel fragments shriek and whistle in all directions.

From nearby coast batteries the word of command is heard. Four flashes follow soon afterward, and out in the bay, a few seconds later, rise as many opalescent water columns in the path of a search-light. A Turkish howitzer battery answers the call from its lofty perch.

But, altogether undismayed, the British destroyer nosed its way across the waters of Erenkoi. It finally came within range of the night-glass.

The Turkish search-lights showed its low and glistening hull, three funnels, two masts, turrets, and gun-barrels, like high-lights in a smudge drawing. Now and then the flashes of the ship's own guns would reveal some other details. Its gunners were not saving ammunition. They were sending it to the sites of the Turkish projectors as fast as it was possible to serve the pieces.

These are the essential details of an attack made

night before last on the Turkish mine-field; they
are typical of all the other attempts that have been
made by the Allies to rid the fairway of the Dardanelles of this sort of obstacle. Generally, the
performance on this night stage begins at eleven
o'clock and ends when dawn creeps over the Anatolian hills.

The mine-sweepers of the Allies are in many
cases sailing-boats manned by Greeks from the
adjacent islands. Night before last one of them
sailed a little too far north. A Turkish search-
light kept its sail illumined. Several small water-
spouts had risen around it.

The undaunted master of the ship kept on. Suddenly a vivid flash sprang up where the sail had
been seen, and when it died away the search-light
showed no more than bits of wreckage—the *mahonie* had struck a mine.

Later three steam mine-sweepers were sunk by
Turkish artillery fire.

It had been a costly night for the Allies, and
they decided to give up another one of their attempts to rid the channel of mines.

Last night the Allied mine-sweeping department
returned in full force under the protection of a
heavy thunder-storm and rain. For a while the
fleet kept near the mouth of the Menderch
River.

Later a cruiser advanced and began to bombard
the Turkish projectors, whose lights served better
in the heavy atmosphere to reveal their location
than to illumine the waters of Erenkoi. A lively
cannonade ensued between ship and anti-mine-

sweeper battery. It ended another attempt to get rid of the mines.

So far the Allies have made five serious attempts to sweep the channel. None of them has been a success. The few mines they have been able to get have been replaced by the Turks with Russian mines which have floated into the Bosphorus after having been liberated with malice aforethought by the Russians near the entrance to that strait.

March 16th.

There was much ado here to-day. A party of Ottoman government officials and members of the Parliament came down from Constantinople to convince themselves that as yet there was no occasion for anxiety.

The gentlemen seemed very much relieved when they saw that the Dardanelles were still on the old spot. There was much talking and gesticulation. The Turkish "l's" worked overtime in fervent *"mashallah, inshallah, bismillah,"* and other *"allahs."* The Moslem seems to invoke the Deity quite as much as other people when he becomes excited and interested.

The American ambassador to Turkey was a member of that party, and seemed to enjoy the novel outing very much. It is not often that a peace-loving diplomatist gets so close to the scene of death and destruction.

Mr. Morgenthau was taken to Dardanos, Anadolu Hamidieh, Tchemenlik, and the Kilid-il-Bahr batteries. He seemed much impressed by what he had seen.

FROM BERLIN TO BAGDAD

Swing and I had an invitation to trail along. But there was nothing to be seen so far as we were concerned. Instead we spent the time under the large elm, watching the lovelorn sparrows and the stupid camels over many a glass of *tchai* (tea).

In the afternoon I boarded the yacht that had brought the party to the Dardanelles. Mr. Morgenthau was asked what he thought of it. I gathered that he had been highly skeptical of the official *communiqués* of the Ottoman government, and my own despatches, which generally come to his notice.

Of course, His Excellency could not say much. But he said this much for publication:

"There is nothing much for me to say. I found the forts undamaged and the situation good. The spirit of the officers and men is one of tranquillity and confidence."

One has to be careful when one quotes an ambassador. So I jotted down the few words.

That done, I relieved the ambassador of twenty Turkish pounds, which I need in my business.

When the yacht was off I accepted an invitation from Prince Henry of Reuss, thirty-ninth of his line, to go mine-fishing. He warned me that it was a most dangerous form of sport.

While the *mush* was skirting the western limits of the mine-field I learned that the mine had gotten away from its mooring and that it was drifting toward the entrance of the strait. There it might sink one of the Allied ships in a most unexpected manner.

My impression that Prince Henry wanted to

prevent this contingency caused me to wonder, Why should he, of all people, be so concerned? He is the mine expert hereabout and makes usually a specialty of setting mines adrift. Why this sudden compassion?

As we hunted the waters near the Gallipoli shore I learned more of the prince's intentions. That particular sort of mine he wanted to keep in a fixed position. He had none too many of that sort. It was a large affair with enough explosives in it to cut any dreadnaught in two like a lump of cheese.

We hunted and hunted—and found nothing. It seems that the pesky critter had too much of a start on us.

Near the entrance to the strait an Allied scout-boat was fooling around, and since we had no gun on the steam-cutter it was decided not to press the point. The scout might see us and announce that fact with a salvo from her rapid-fire pieces. That would be disagreeable.

So we pulled back. Prince Henry regretted that we had not been more successful. But I was fully satisfied with the trip.

We had skirted the boundaries of the mine-field, marked by small barrels painted gray and having a red band around the belly. I had also established the density of the mines in the field, so that now I had a good idea of how many of these death-dealing giant pears—for such is the shape of these mines—the Allies would have to take up before the strait was clear.

I wondered how welcome that and some other exclusive information would be to the Entente governments. But then, I am under Ottoman military law, and, what is far more important, I have never yet violated that of hospitality.

March 19th.

Ye gods and little fishes! I am still alive and so overjoyed that it is hard to bring my feet back to earth.

They were much in the air yesterday.

March the eighteenth will always be an anniversary with F. Swing and myself; also with poor Fuad.

The British came back yesterday, accompanied by the French. It was to be a great day. They were perfectly willing to make it that. This was to be no puny affair.

With nineteen battleships of the line and thirty cruisers, and with an imposing entourage of destroyers, torpedo-boats, and mine-sweepers, they paraded into Erenkoi Bay at 11 A.M. They limped out again at five in the afternoon without the *Bouvet*, *Irresistible*, and *Ocean*, and two smaller vessels. Five of their line ships had been disabled. The super-dreadnaught cruiser, *Queen Elizabeth*, terror of the Dardanelles gunners, was worsted by the Turkish howitzers and hobbled out of action as best she might.

But between the arrival and departure of the Allied fleet lies a day that would give new shivers even to a Dante. What can Inferno be to any of us after yesterday?

It all happened in this manner:

F. Swing was to meet me at the little café in the

rue Saat Hissarlik at 11 A.M. Fuad Réchad was to do the same thing.

It was our intention to finally pay Djevad Pasha, commander of the Dardanelles defenses, that long-delayed official visit. We had postponed that call for the reason that the pasha has selected a most outlandish site for his headquarters—a little building near the top of a high mountain. Some say that he has done this to have a free view at all times of the strait he defends; others say that his motive is to get away from the Germans.

My friend showed up promptly—to report that he had found Fuad Réchad in the act of shaving. The bey would be with us in about twenty minutes, said F. Swing, as he sat down to have a glass of tea.

It was a perfect day in spring, and I remarked that it would be a shame to waste it in climbing up that mountain when the willows along the Rhodios River were so inviting.

"Well, old top," came Swing's casual remark, "you are right again. But what can we do? We have been here almost three weeks and haven't paid our respects to the chief guy of this layout. First thing you know he will suspect us of standing in too close with the Germans here. That would be fatal to our" . . .

Zow—whommp!

Swing stopped there and then.

The two of us began to stare around wildly.

What the dickens was that—double explosion?

I looked around in time to see several wooden houses go in the air almost bodily. Up there they

9

rested a bit on the pressure of the explosion that had started them, then they divided into parts.

The roof tiles began to rain down around us. Swing and I jumped under the protecting branches of the tree. The *cafédji* gathered in his long, white apron and made for the door of his shop. Fuad Réchad was coming around the street corner with his arms over his face.

It took a seemingly interminable time before the rain of brick subsided. Swing dodged a huge tile that was making for his head. A piece of a tile struck me in the back. Fuad Réchad could not be seen for a moment in the cloud of pulverized stucco that was coming down around him. For a moment he stood still and then made a wild dash for the tree.

"What's the matter?" he gasped.

I looked at the place where the houses had been and shrugged my shoulders.

"Bom - bom - bom - bombardment!" said Swing. "Should-should say so."

"We should!" I said.

"What are we going to do?" was the next question.

I didn't know.

There was an ominous silence now. Through it grated the noise of the iron roll shutters of the few shops that had been opened since March 7th. I caught sight of the boss of a camel-train moving down the rue Saat Hissarlik. The man seemed in a hurry; not so the camels and the little donkey that was leading them.

The *cafédji* was straining away at his own shutters. I really don't know why he wanted to close them. They would not keep the shells out of his shop.

"*Bordchum ne kedar!*" I shouted, being anxious to pay my bill. The man might never get the few paras I owed him if he did not collect them forthwith.

But the *cafédji* was not interested in money. I threw the required number of paras on the table, and then started off—up the Street of the Clock Tower.

Shells were still coming in. But they were not close enough to worry us. The bombardment seemed to have drifted to another part of the strait. I concluded that the British had fired that turret to give the people of the town warning that it was time to move.

At the gate to the barrack-yard north of Fort Tchemenlik I suggested that for the time being we seek shelter under the traverse of the battery. That advice was well received by my friends.

On the way there we called at the telegraph and telephone central near the administration building to see what was going on. The operators did not know yet. The shells that had landed in town had been thrown by a large ship lying directly in the entrance. But there was much smoke behind Cape Eski-Hissarlik. The Allies were coming in force.

The bombardment was now down the bay— Dardanos and Erenkoi, no doubt.

I suggested going to the tower. Swing almost fainted when he heard that. He doubted my sanity.

Fuad, poor boy, pleaded with his eyes that I was not to attempt such a foolhardy move.

"But we can't see a thing from here," I protested. "We can't miss this."

My suggestion that we go to the old breakwater was better received. If things grew too hot there we could always dart behind the battery traverse and wait for better times.

As we walked toward the water's edge, I saw that the shell warning had been effective.

A great crowd of men, women, and children, accompanied by donkeys, goats, and dogs, was streaming down Clock Tower Street. Just then two shells crashed into the bazaar quarter, adding to the speed of the refugees. Two more of them came. One of them took off the upper part of a minaret, as far as the balcony. That also helped the crowd to find its legs.

The bombardment was already very active. It seemed that the Allies were really coming in force. Most of the shells were striking far away, but they came in such salvos that no other conclusion was possible.

But I had trouble believing my eyes when I got to the old sea-wall and began to survey the bay with my glasses. I counted nine ships of the line. They were just going into milling position. Back of the nine were others. The smoke prevented my counting them. The ships were on a level with my eyes and formed a solid wall of steel. Their superstructures were hidden in a dense cloud of smoke and powder fumes.

Turkish shells were already exploding among the

ships. Great water columns danced about like mad. Forts Rumeli Medjidieh, Dardanos, and the battery at Erenkoi seemed to be in a frantic hurry about something. The howitzers on the Anatolian and Gallipolian hills were also much excited.

"That looks ugly," remarked Friend Swing, with a mixture of frown and dismay on his face. "How many can you see?"

I trained my glasses again and counted. Nine of the ships were in position just then. Behind them appeared a forest of funnels and masts. Above them a smoke signal appeared as I looked —a ring with a globe in it.

That signal seemed to break up the tangle. The line shifted toward the middle of the bay, and gradually dissolved—into another nine ships. That made eighteen ships of the line. In the entrance hovered the *Queen Elizabeth* belching fire and smoke like an engine made expressly for that purpose.

F. Swing had also counted. He, too, made it nineteen.

"Well, old top," he remarked, dryly, without taking his field-glass from the scene, "it's all over! The Turks won't stand that, of course."

This seemed reasonable even to Fuad.

"Our batteries are not equal to that," he remarked, mournfully. "That is the end of us." With that he let his hands fall to his side, like a man who knows that all is lost.

I cheered the boy up as best I could. There was the mine-field. That might help.

The Turkish fire had not lasted long. Was it possible that the men in the batteries along the bay were as dumfounded as we were? The British and French ships, too, were silent for a few minutes.

To our left, on the parapet of Tchemenlik, two Turkish officers were talking excitedly. The man behind the range-finder was telling his comrade what the strong glass showed him.

Well, the actors of the great spectacle were marching up. It would be a case of thumbs down throughout the day. No mercy would be shown and none expected.

The Allies were ready for the clean-up—the *coup de grâce.* The large ships were attended by all the craft one needs to steam on hostile waters— cruisers, destroyers, torpedo-boats, and mine-sweepers. They meant business this time.

The first salvo from nineteen turrets hit various points along the Dardanelles like a tornado, as you might put it, though I am sure that a tornado is but a pitiful imitation of the effect produced by the forty-odd shells that crashed almost simultaneously.

I thought that the earth would be torn asunder.

A dozen of the shells went over our heads and mowed down the first row of houses behind the administration building of Fort Tchemenlik. Whole floors, entire walls, doors, furniture, and several human bodies, were hurled high in the air. The sight was sickening.

An awe-inspiring stillness fell over the landscape after this salvo. It was pierced, presently, by the crash of a collapsing house. Then it was stiller yet. The voices of the officers on the parapet could be plainly heard, as also the gentle lapping of the water against the sea-wall. Some birds, thoroughly frightened, fluttered past us so close that we might have caught them with our hands.

Another salvo came. It was of the same character. Evidently, the Allies were playing for moral effect.

I was greatly interested in what that effect would be. I watched the officers on the parapet. One of them was still behind the range-finder. He went about his business coolly enough, I thought. The other was toying with the huge megaphone through which he expected to bellow fire orders shortly. His seeming indifference may have been simulated. But even if it was not, I am sure that his heart was beating a little faster than usual. I know that mine was.

The second salvo did as much damage to the town as did the first. This time the shells were a little higher. We could not see the houses that were hit, but we saw their wreckage go up and heard the walls collapse a second later.

From the scene of the first crash smoke was now coming. Some soldiers, with a hand-pump carried by four of them, were rushing toward the fire.

The Turkish guns were now silent. I surmised that they fired at first only because some of the Allied ships, while steaming into the bay, had passed within range. I looked at my watch When the first shells surprised us near the café it was 11.20, now it was 11.33.

"It is likely to be a long day," I remarked to my friends after Fuad had asked me what time it was.

Just then a shell struck the road that runs between the glacis of Tchemenlik and the shore. Tons of macadam started in our direction. We ducked behind the sea-wall and let the avalanche pass. Another shell exploded in the shallow water directly in front of us. We were almost swept off our feet as the tons of water descended.

It was now plain that we could not remain behind the sea-wall. That was clear also to the Turkish officers on the parapet. They motioned to us to get behind the traverse. It was the best we could do under the circumstances.

But from behind the traverse we could see nothing. Yet it was our business to see.

With that in mind I crept up the glacis on all-fours, with the intention of joining the officers on the parapet.

But they did not want company just then and said so. It was their opinion that there would be dead men on that parapet and in the emplacement before long, and they did not want to have me among them. I protested that I could not see anything behind the traverse, and assured them that I did not mind running a little risk. But the two men were obdurate. If anything did happen to me they might be held responsible. I would do them a favor—by leaving them.

So I slid down the grassy slope and joined my companions behind the traverse.

But we were not to stay there long. A shell hit the parapet at its junction with the traverse. Tons of earth fell around us, and in side-stepping some of that I noticed that where I had been a minute ago, where the observation officers had stood, there was a large gash in the greensward.

I did not have time to make a closer investigation. In that very instant another shell struck the old wall where it joins the modern revet of the traverse. A rock weighing half a ton missed Swing by a foot as it toppled over and fell.

Fort Tchemenlik was under a very serious bombardment for the first time and was getting enough of it.

I surveyed the situation and surmised that the old tunnel gate, with the solid walls of *kulle* Kaleh Sultanieh between it and the fire direction of the Allies, would, for the time being, give us the best cover. It was not likely that both the tower and the old rampart would be brought down at the same time.

There was no occasion to lose words.

"Come!" I said to my friends, and rushed off.

Into the court of the battery shells were falling thick and fast now. One explosion followed on the heel of another, and every time the earth trembled under us.

I looked up at the old rampart. It was high. There was no telling when its battlemented crown would come down upon us. Directly over the tunnel gate stands a minaret. That, too, might tumble.

A shell hit the old rampart a little to our left. A rain of rock was started by it. Some of the stones rolled around on the ground, and a little pup, quite unmindful of the things that were going on, began to race after them.

Happy little dog!

I was curious how that yard behind me looked now. Very gingerly I made my way to the far entrance of the tunnel gate and peeped into the battery.

The guns of Tehemenlik had not yet fired a single shot; it looked as though they never would. The yard was strewn with heaps of wrecked masonry. Some fifty tons of this had been torn from one of the corners of the old tower.

Where the officers had been standing there was now, as seen from the rear, a crater from which the wreck of a brick wall protruded. The nearby gun was out of action. Its ammunition-derrick was gone. Over the platform of the gun sprawled the lifeless form of a man—possibly one of the officers who had insisted that I should leave them.

A Turkish soldier stumbled into my arms. I don't know where the man came from. He was covered with pulverized mortar from head to foot. He seemed half stunned.

He was not wounded, he said. He had been buried under the debris in the yard and had just freed himself. Was I a doctor? He had frightful pains in his chest and abdomen.

I helped the man through the tunnel and told him that near the far gate there was a dressing-station. He limped off, each step a painful effort.

Great was our predicament. We were running all the risks without seeing anything at all worth while. Some observation post would have to be found. But where?

It was Swing who thought of the little hill on which the military hospital is located. From there we could get an excellent view of the bay and the Turkish batteries.

Our minds were quickly made up, despite the fact that we had to cross the northern yard of Tchemenlik, into which all the "high" shells for the battery fell. The administration building had already been hit several times, and before we could reach the gate all sorts of things might happen.

Swing was off at a pace that took my breath away presently. Fuad was a close second to my friend.

When I got to the middle of the yard I pictured to myself how undignified it would be to run, and slowed down. To be known as an ex-soldier is very awkward at times. Everybody expects so much more from such a person.

Not a single shell came near us while we crossed the yard. We had reached the street in which the bazaar stands before we ran into trouble.

That unfortunate thoroughfare was paying a heavy price for the miscalculations in aim of the Allied officers. Whatever went high over Tchemenlik crashed into the street.

Fifty paces away from the intersection of the street with the rue Saat Hissarlık another street runs into the bazaar street at a sharp angle. The building occupying that "flatiron" corner had a bakeshop on the ground floor. As I stepped across the street I cast a look in that direction to see whether there were people around.

I saw none, with the exception of the old *ckmckdji* in the bakery. He was taking bread out of the oven. Knowing the man by sight, as a customer, I wondered at his grit.

But I did not wonder long. Of a sudden a vivid flash sprang from the large opening in the wall behind which the old man was working. Then came a deafening report. The building sailed away.

When the smoke cleared the bakery was gone. Poor *ckmckdji!* He had baked his last bread.

Swing was waiting for me in the lee of a building close by. When he saw me looking up the street he came back. He reached the corner just as a large stone from the wrecked bakery catapulted past the corner. My friend gave the projectile a dazed look and then retreated again.

To go down the rue Saat Hissarlik became a trying experience. Above us a roof took wings presently. We stepped into a doorway until the tiles had settled down. Just as we came to the little triangular plaza another house near by was blown up. At one side of the clock tower lay a dead civilian.

Some of the braver of the townspeople had collected on the hillside. They seemed greatly interested in the terrible spectacle which this measuring of strength between battle-ship and coast battery offered.

That they would be seen there by the Allied observers, who at that range might mistake them for soldiers, had not occurred to the crowd until a shell exploded a little to the rear of them. After that they scampered off like a nest of field-mice.

There was no cover on the hill. Swing thought that we might get some spades and dig ourselves a trench. That would have been the logical thing to do. On the other hand, we did not have the time for it. The progress of the action had to be carefully watched. Then, too, the observers on the ships might see us digging, misunderstand us, and take us under fire.

In the course of our search for some cover we came to a little ridge between two fields, not more than two feet high. Behind that we took position.

Our observation post was an excellent one, we agreed. It would remain that until the battery of Anadolu Medjidieh, right in front and only two hundred sloping feet away from us, should be taken under fire. Since the Allies were shooting frightfully "high," it was a certainty that in such an event we would get the first shells.

The bombardment was a regular routine affair by this time. The Allied ships distributed their fire evenly. It was their intention, evidently, to wear down the Turks along the entire outer strait.

From In Tepeh to Tchanak Kaleh, on the Anatolian shore; from the heights south of the Shavan Dereh to Kilid-il-Bahr, on the Gallipoli shore, everything was under fire.

Earth-geysers and water columns rose in and near every Turkish emplacement. The noise was ear-splitting. It resembled the effect of a dozen thunder-storms in a pocket in the mountains. The crashes were reverberated from hillside to mountainside, starting with the discordant notes of a giant Chinese gong and ending with a low rumble.

Over Erenkoi Bay hung low a bank of smoke and powder fumes. The bright sunlight rested on the top of this, leaving the ships of the Allies in deep purple shadows. Out of this leaped the flames of the propelling charges.

It was a glorious spectacle—and an expensive one. And Swing and I were the only spectators. There were others who saw this thing, but they had stakes in it. We had not.

Little activity was being shown by the Turkish emplacements. Erenkoi would fire a few shots now and then, and Dardanos would do the same. But their fire was short. The Turks were anxious to get at their tormentors, but their guns did not have the necessary range.

The thing began to look very one-sided. The Allies had in the strait thirty-nine ships that could hammer away at the Turks. Of the nineteen battle-ships of the line each was as good, at least in armament, as any two Turkish forts.

It was hard to see, under these circumstances, how the Turks could hold their own. Their emplacements might all meet the fate of the batteries at Kum Kaleh and Sid-il-Bahr. Even if the Turks had ammunition enough, which I had reason to doubt, they would presently have no guns and no men to use it.

I recalled Napoleon's saying, "*Un canon sur terre vaut dix sur mer.*" Was Napoleon right? This day would show whether he was or not.

Presently we were reminded that the Allies might

yet shell the battery in front of us. A projectile screeched past us so low that we felt the wind currents it caused. A hundred feet behind us it exploded.

Our first impulse was to find another point of observation. But there was no place along the strait that might not be taken under fire. We decided, therefore, to stick it out where we were.

The Allied observers, aerial and others, must have learned shortly that much of their fire was going to waste. It was not so much a question of inaccuracy of aim as it was one of pointing errors multiplying with distance. To overcome that the line ships presently came in closer.

By 1.45 P.M. they had materially lessened the distance between themselves and the Turkish batteries. I was much interested in finding out what effect this would have on the emplacements.

The effect was very good for the Allies and very bad for the Turks.

Fort Anadolu Hamidieh, every gun of which I could plainly see, was being raked in a terrible manner. The Allied shells were exploding now on the parapet and traverses. The yard of the emplacement was being turned upside down. One earth-geyser rose beside the other. The barracks were completely down.

As the Allied ships drew nearer, the guns of Dardanos, Erenkoi, and the howitzer emplacements above the Shavan Dereh, got their range. For the next ten minutes both sides were pumping shells as fast as the pieces could be served.

I was watching events on the right flank of the

Allied fleet, Fuad those on the left. Swing had the center.

"She's been hit! She's been hit!" shouted Swing, suddenly.

"*Which one?*" I asked, eagerly.

"The one with the heavy superstructure!" cried my friend. "Look a little to the right of the acacia-tree."

I did as directed

One of the French ships was showing a heavy list. She was still going ahead, as the water at her bow indicated. As I watched her the stern went down until it seemed to be awash.

Four flashes from Fort Anadolu Hamidieh announced just then that the large battery in that emplacement was at work. The secondary batteries also joined in. Hamidieh was going to sink that vessel, if it could be done.

It was then two minutes of two o'clock.

The fate of that ship interested me. She lay in an iridescent patch of water. It seemed now that her stern was up again. I looked for the foam at her bow, but saw only ripples. Presently even these disappeared. The shells from Fort Hamidieh were raising water columns all about the vessel.

Suddenly a red sheaf of flame appeared above the ship. She had been struck by a shell.

An instant later her deck opened. An intense flame shot up—far above the mastheads.

The flash cooled into red and then changed into a dense cloud of smoke and steam.

When my sense of perception registered again the ship had turned over. In another instant she was

142

no more than a flat, black thing in the water. That, too, vanished—swiftly.

It was two o'clock exactly.

Some nine hundred lives had been snuffed out.

The Allied ships had ceased firing now. The Turkish guns also were mute. Everywhere in the Turkish emplacements men jumped to the parapets and traverses. And then rang out a great cheer. The Turks had drawn first blood and seemed to enjoy it.

When the *Bouvet* was first hit some smaller craft had rushed forward to be of assistance to her crew. From them boats were now being lowered. The wet oars flashed in the bright sun like things of burnished steel.

Where the ship had gone down some dark objects were floating. Whether they were wreckage or men I could not determine. At any rate, the boats were not out long. I understand that about a dozen men of the *Bouvet's* complement of 900 were saved.

The loss of the *Bouvet* seemed to have angered the Allies.

When next they took up the fire it had in it all the intensity and impotency of rage. The shells came thick and fast, but fell wide of the mark. Some of them fell into the middle of the strait between Tchanak Kaleh and Kilid-il-Bahr. Many more crashed into the Greek and Armenian quarter of the former place.

By three o'clock the bombardment was back in its old rut.

The Allied commander kept his ships close to

the Turkish batteries now. Half a day had been lost in bombarding from too great a range.

But to stay in close had its shortcomings. The Turks were getting many full hits. At 3.40 P.M. four of the Allied ships had been badly hammered. They showed lists, and two of them were blowing off steam. One of the others had lost much of her superstructure and one of her masts was down

I noticed that there was no longer much ginger in the efforts of the Allies. The firing was poorer now than I had ever seen it.

Most of the shells intended for Fort Anadolu Hamidieh were from 1,200 to 3,500 yards too "high" —that is to say, the shells went that much too far. In that manner much of the Greek and Armenian quarter of Tehanak Kaleh had been brought down The quarter was now burning. Kilid-il-Bahr, too, was again afire.

When about four o'clock the fire of the Allies became entirely a waste of ammunition, Swing, Fuad, and I decided to have tea. It was out of the question now that the Allies could do any more to-day than retire when the light became poor.

After tea the three of us intended to return to Fort Tehemenhk and mount to the tower platform for a final survey before writing our despatches. But the yard was so full of debris that we decided to go to the old sea-wall and do our observing from there.

Before long I was to see an odd spectacle there.

Some of the Allied cruisers were towing away disabled line ships. Three of them were just passing out of the entrance, beyond which I could still see the retiring battle-ships that were under their own steam.

In the Bay of Erenkoi were still two line ships, however. They were riding on an even keel, one of them in front of the Menderch mouth and the other near Cape Eski-Hissarlik. A number of small craft were standing by the latter. The other seemed able to take care of herself.

I asked a Turkish observation officer on the traverse of Tchemenlik what the ship to the left was doing. She had been abandoned, he said, volunteering also the information that the other ship was in tow, but hard to manage.

Meanwhile, the ship on the left appeared to move. From her funnel came the merest suspicion of smoke. There was no foam at her bow. She seemed to drift. She was coming toward the Turkish batteries on the back of the counter-current that sweeps north along the Anatolian shore.

The sun was now setting behind the high hills of Gallipoli. It left the hillsides of the peninsula in a deep-purple gloom, but lit up the Anatolian slopes and the helpless line ship in fine manner.

Suddenly the battery of Rumeli Medjidieh came to life. I saw the long streamer of flame of the propelling charge and then directed my glass upon the ship. A strange thing happened. The shell hit the ship full amidship. The sheaf of sparks announced that eloquently.

Again the gun in the shadow fired. This time its shell fell short. The third shell crashed into the superstructure of the ship.

It seemed for a while after that as if the ship were returning the fire. Flashes came from her.

But in that conclusion we were wrong, as the Turkish officer on the traverse informed us. Fort Dardanos had taken the ship under fire and was sheing her to pieces now. Of twenty-five shells sixteen took full effect. Then the *Irresistible* turned turtle and went down.

Later we learned that the *Ocean*, the ship on our right, had sunk in deep water in Morto Bay.

Swing and I went to the Hotel Stamboul to write our despatches. It took several copious draughts of *sharrap* to tide us over the fearful headache we now discovered we were suffering. We had been living in a hell all day long and now we had to sit down and describe it.

War correspondence is not the easiest way of making a living.

There was no time to think of eating. Swing and I wrote away like mad, and then started in, by the light of burning Tchanak Kaleh and Kilid-il-Bahr, to find the censors. But they had left town in the morning. They also had taken with them the telegraph-office.

Here was a fine state of affairs. In the end we decided to look up Merten Pasha at his headquarters in the Calvert villa, town house of an Anglo-American family owning a great deal of property along the Dardanelles.

But Merten Pasha had already retired.

Well, Major Schneider was nice about it this time. He offered to see the pasha for us. When he came down-stairs again he said that the "old" man was none too pleased with having been disturbed. I told Swing it would be best if I went up alone. I would get his despatch visaed.

Merten Pasha found it a little hard to be as congenial as he usually is. No doubt he was tired. He blinked at the papers in his hand, but found it hard to read. The strain of the day had been great and the light of the lamp was poor.

"Tell me what you have written there!" he said, presently. I told him. Then he signed his name to the despatches and returned them.

"I will have to walk three miles to-night to get these things on the wire," I said, with the intention of starting a conversation.

I succeeded.

"Well, if you can still walk three miles to-night, I should be able to read these things over," he said, with a smile. "But it is all right. Let them go!"

"What is the outlook for to-morrow, Pasha?" I asked.

The artillery expert thought it over.

"Not so very good—to be frank with you," he replied.

"Not so very good?"

"No!"

"What is the matter?"

"That I can't tell you, of course," replied Merten Pasha. "At any rate, it 'll go bad with us if the Allies return to-morrow. They have lost heavily to-day, to be sure. But I think I know the British well enough to feel that they will be back here bright and early. If you have anything around here you wish to save, take my advice and pack it to-night. Be ready to get out of here early in the morning."

Swing and I trotted off to the telegraph-station. Shortly after midnight we were back in town.

By that time we were ready to eat anything. But it was too late to go to a cookshop. So I roused the poor *kamorote* and had him start a *mangal*. As luck would have it, we had a piece of meat handy, having recently done a little cooking ourselves.

By one o'clock we had put away a good meal, and then we turned in for some sleep.

The *kamorote* called us at six this morning. To get our eyes open was quite a task. But the *tchai* and *yamourtalar*—tea and boiled eggs—had a strong appeal.

After breakfast I surveyed the entrance of the strait from a jetty in front of the hotel. No ships were in sight. At eight we were in Fort Tchem-enlik. But the danger flag, a white field with three red disks in it, was not up.

Nine o'clock came and still no Allies. At ten no smoke even could be seen behind Tenedos. The same state of affairs prevailed at eleven. Noon came and the coast was still clear. The afternoon passed and all was well. But they may come to-morrow.

March 21st.

Still no Allies!

Swing and I have been making the rounds of the Turkish emplacements the last three days. The damage done by the bombardment of four days ago is hardly what I had expected.

Fort Dardanos has had a miraculous escape.

148

WHEN THE ALLIED FLEET FOOZLED

There is a small dent in Turret No. 1. Turret No. 3 was struck by a shell fragment near the gunport. As a result of that the gun could no longer be elevated or lowered. But a little work with a steel saw fixed that. No. 5 turret is slightly damaged near the base.

In Fort Rumeli Medjidieh two guns are temporarily out of action. In Rumeli Hamidieh a gun is dismounted. Fort Tchemenlik mourns the temporary loss of a gun. One of the casemates there was demolished. In Anadolu Hamidieh a 35.5-cm. has been torn from its anchorage and its carriage has also been badly mauled. Here, too, a casemate caved in.

The most remarkable thing is the Turkish list of casualties—twenty-three Turks and Germans dead, and seventy-eight wounded. Many of these are civilians.

Considering that the Allies employed in the bombardment 276 guns larger than six inches this is not much of a showing. According to the Turks and Germans, the Allies used over 8,500 shells larger than six inches. It seems that a six-inch shell does not count any more nowadays.

But the Allies are still expected back. Every parapet and traverse along the strait has been, or is being, overlaid with an additional ten feet of sand. That will make them entirely impenetrable. Even the old covering was perforated in only two instances on March 18th, and in each case, as I was able to establish myself, the shells had gone through near the mouth of the emplacement, where the covering is none too thick.

New guns are arriving every day. They are being carted in the direction of Erenkoi and to the Shavan Dereh. The guns come from Adrianople, I learned. The Turks must be very sure of the Bulgars to do that.

More ammunition is also arriving. But it is not the right sort of ammunition. It can be used against the deck of the ships by high-angle guns. As the *Queen Elizabeth* has discovered, that is not so harmless a pastime. Five hits from the howitzers put her out of action.

The shells must have gone down her funnels, since her deck is said to be well protected by armor.

March 30th.

The Allies seem to have lost all interest in the Dardanelles. Their ships have gone to parts unknown. A few of the older tubs have stayed, however, and day before yesterday they came to the entrance and peppered something on the heights behind Kum Kaleh. It may have been one of the camps of the Ottoman Eleventh Division. At best the thing was no more than a demonstration. Swing and I watched it from the platform of the old tower.

Life in a bombarded town is not altogether pleasant. Everything still smells of dead fire.

Of inhabitants only the dogs and cats are left. Poor things! Nobody feeds them and soon they will have to either migrate or eat one another, as they did on a certain barren island in the Sea of Marmora, when the Turks decided to clean up Constantinople.

WHEN THE ALLIED FLEET FOOZLED

The café in the rue Saat Hissarlik is again doing business. Swing, Fuad, and I spend our days under the elm-tree, which is now finely furnished with foliage.

The big bombardment is still the stuff of conversation. So are certain developments on Gallipoli.

The men in Stamboul think that the Allies will try a landing there next. In fact, there are rumors that troops for that purpose are even now being concentrated. Egypt is said to be crowded with Australian troops. On Cyprus they have more of them. In Malta they are also being concentrated, and even the Island of Imbros is said to have a camp.

The Turks have not wholly disregarded that.

Liman von Sanders Pasha, head of the German military mission to Turkey, has been placed in command of the troops on Gallipoli. He arrived at the town of Gallipoli on the 26th, and is now busy putting his troops and headquarters in shape.

But for the time being there is no reason why Friend Swing and I should stay longer at the Dardanelles. We will take a look at Pera and make interviews. For one of them, an audience with the Sultan, we have laid the rails already. To-morrow we will start our farewell visits. How good a decent room with "bawth," as Swing pronounces it, will look to us!

By the way, Swing has ruined his fine fur coat. But he says the story was worth it.

V

AN AUDIENCE WITH THE SULTAN

THE Ottoman government had not been unmindful of the dangers that threatened the capital. On March 18th, the records and treasure were packed and special trains were held ready to convey them to Eski-Shehir in Anatolia, the capital of the Osmanli before they settled in Europe.

On the following day, when the situation was better understood, some of the records were taken to a freight-shed in Haidar Pasha, the terminal of the Anatolian railroad, and on the same day the household of the Sultan was mobilized. It was feared that the Allied fleet would renew the attack on the Dardanelles coast batteries at least on the 20th of March, or shortly thereafter. We, at the straits, had been under the same impression, as I have already related.

But with the uneventful lapse of days reassurance returned to the men in Stamboul. At first loath to believe that the Allied fleet would not follow up its advantages, the Ottoman government little by little began to see why it would be considered imprudent just now in London and Paris to sacrifice more ships at the Dardanelles.

The Ottoman military and naval leaders were under the impression that the lack of ammunition in the Dardanelles batteries was known to the Allied fleet commanders. That belief was reasonable enough. The administration of the Ottoman coast-defense system had been in the hands of the British Naval Commission to Turkey, and the British artillery experts in the commission could not help knowing how much ammunition there was along the strait. The commission, in fact, had bought most of it.

What shells the Turks had used during the bombardment was known to the Allied fleet commander, or should have been known. All he had to do was to detail an officer or two to keep tally. Whether or not this was done I have no means of knowing. One thing alone is certain: Had the Allied commander realized what conditions in the Turkish emplacements were he would have returned and finished his task.

I have good reasons to believe that the Entente governments had permitted themselves to be fooled by their own "intelligence" men in the Balkans. These agents were over-zealous in many respects, especially in matters affecting alleged shipments of ammunition into Turkey.

That some contraband slipped through Rumania and Bulgaria is possible. At any rate, this claim was being made with great persistence and, at times, unseemly impetuousness. But that Germany succeeded in getting to the Dardanelles

153

"blue-head" shells, or large shells of any class, is not true. The Bratianu government in Rumania had been too eager to join the Entente in the winter of 1914–15 to have permitted a sort of traffic that could not but improve the position of Turkey. While it might have been possible, as, indeed, it was at times, to bribe officials of the Rumanian state railroads and the Rumanian customs and frontier-security services, it would have been very difficult to get around the Rumanian political police and government secret service.

I was in Bucharest at the time and had occasion to occupy myself with one of the Entente's complaints that ammunition intended for Turkey was going through Rumania. I was assured in government circles, by the first secretary of Premier Bratianu, among others, that such an assertion was preposterous and a poor reward for the interest in the Entente's cause which the government was showing. Mr. Take Jonescu informed me that the protests of the Entente governments were based on nothing better than unfounded reports made by over-zealous intelligence agents eager to make a showing with their superiors. Since Mr. Jonescu was then in charge of the British propaganda in Rumania, I had every reason to believe him.

But holding, perhaps, an exaggerated opinion of corruption in Rumania, the governments in London and Paris may have deemed it the better part of valor not to press the naval operations against the Dardanelles. If the Germans had really succeeded in getting thousands of shells to the strait, there was no telling how many ships would yet have to be sacrificed before the Dardanelles were forced and Constantinople taken. The war was still too young to risk many of the line ships of the Allied fleet.

The case must have hinged upon Rumania, because there was no other way of getting shells into Turkey. The Serbs still held the Danube and the Sava lines. In the Strait of Otranto lay a large Allied fleet, keeping the Adriatic Sea closed, so that no Austrian ship could get to any part of the Ottoman Empire. The German fleet could not reach the Mediterranean. Russia had barricaded all other avenues of access to Turkey.

I may state in this connection, for the purpose of showing how desperate the need of ammunition of the Turks was, that during the early part of the siege an attempt was made by the Germans to take ammunition from Trieste to Smyrna by means of a submarine freighter. The vessel was especially built for the purpose, being merely a sort of tank capable of floating at a convenient depth. It had no motive power of its own and could neither rise nor sink by itself. It was a makeshift and a failure.

I will now return to my journal.

PERA, *April 4th.*

We are back in Constantinople—F. Swing and I.

One of the last things we did was to excavate a bit on the site of the ancient Abydos, the only Jew settlement on the Dardanelles, when the strait was known as Hellespont. So they say.

We are the first to have done that. Many

regular archeologists have in the past made application to the Turkish government for permission to delve into the secrets of the hill. They were refused, for the reason that at the base of the hill lie some very important forts and batteries. Those archeologists might gather military information as a side line, and, since every emplacement is visible from the site of Abydos, there is no telling what might happen.

It is different with us. Enver Pasha has given us *carte blanche* in return for our complaisance in subscribing to Ottoman military law, and that has greatly impressed everybody.

The commander of Fort Nagara said that under the circumstances we could dig anywhere. He also gave us eight soldiers for the purpose. Then I made a survey of the site and imagined that I had discovered the *locale* of the city walls of Abydos.

But my "spades" soon hit a pavement. That was too much for them. So I tried another spot and found a vase.

The vase is an unseemly thing. Crudeness is written all over it. The thing was fashioned by hand and burned in an open fire. The decorations on it are decidedly Trojan—black and red in a conventional pattern.

F. Swing found several little pans about the size of the saucer of a *demi-tasse*. He says that the ladies of Abydos used to keep ointments and pomades in them. My friend deduces from that that the ladies of Abydos were pretty. Later, as he found more of them, he said that the ladies of Abydos were beautiful.

156

Swing's judgment in the matter is influenced by a certain Greek lady of Maidos possessing Titian charms. Ye gods! what hair that damosel has! What eyes! And Troy is not far away—only some fifteen miles. No wonder Agamemnon stirred up a row!

The vase being all I wanted, and archeology and the like being not my domain, anyway, I suggested that we go home and leave that sort of thing to regular and scientific excavators. Not so F. Swing. We had a large row on the site of Abydos, and we then went home, anyway, a generous shower of rain supporting my viewpoint.

We returned to Constantinople on a six-knot tub. It took us almost three days to reach dear old Byzantium. When we saw the city by the Golden Horn again we felt as all good *Pérotes* do, for full-fledged *Pérotes* we are by this time.

At the hotel we had a "bawth," and then we rushed to the Petit Club, where we allowed one and all to admire us. Our fame is no small matter. Our fame is so great that we expect an audience in a day or two with His Majesty, Sultan Mohammed Réchad Khan V.

April 7th.

His Majesty did receive us in audience.

The event came to pass this afternoon. It lasted from 2.07 to 2.29 P.M.—twenty-two minutes in all, which is seven minutes more than any ambassador ever gets, no matter how much gold braid he may have on his uniform. But F. Swing and I are privileged characters hereabouts.

157

Speaking of dress reminds me that F. Swing and I had a fine time of it yesterday, trying to get the needed habiliments for the audience. The court rules prescribe what the Sultan's visitors have to wear. We did not have such raiment, and in Constantinople just now it is not so easily procured.

It was a merry chase all over the city before we found what was needed—frock-coat, dark striped trousers, patent-leather shoes, dark cravat, high collar, white gloves, and silk hat—*haute forme*.

It is a long time since I have been so busy. We scoured all Pera for a second time, and then succeeded. At that the things would not fit. F. Swing is a little too slim for store clothes, and I —well, two men of ordinary size could be made out of me.

But we took the things and then rushed off to an English tailor on the Gran' Rue. He made a fine job of it overnight. When F. Swing, who had never seen me in anything but a war correspondent's raiment, caught sight of me, he opined that I was ready to become a Senator of Texas, the Lone Star State being my place of official residence.

Of course one cannot call on the Sultan afoot. Nor were we big enough to have the court equipage sent for us, though F. Swing prayed that this would happen. We went around to the American embassy and stated our wants.

The ambassador was somewhat surprised when he heard that we had engineered an audience with the Sultan without his ken. Usually, the ambassador attends to such matters. But we were given the automobile and a gloriously attired *cavass*, for all that.

With the *cavass* looking his best in his official costume—much embroidered with gold and glorified with a sash of vivid scarlet, in the folds of which two murderous-looking pistols reposed—we made off for the audience.

Even the chauffeur did his best to make things interesting and official. He honked the horn persistently and often, as if to call everybody to the windows to see the show. *Cavass* and silk hats left no doubt in the minds of Pera, Galata, and Fyndykly that His Majesty was about to have callers.

At the gate of the Dolma Bagtche Palace they knew that we were people of some importance, even if we did not come in a court equipage.

The chauffeur was directed to drive through the large, gilded gate which is opened only on state occasions. But perhaps the small gate was out of commission just then. Next the guard was called out and drawn up. We greeted the officer of the day and then rolled on through the splendid Italian gardens of the palace. *En route* the *cavass* informed me that a high wall to the left of us incloses the imperial *hareem*.

That wall was uninteresting enough, I will say. To the disappointment of some of my readers, I will state that there are not many ladies in the *hareem;* just the four wives of the Sultan and his daughters.

We went to the *sclamlik,* as the men's part of any Turkish home is called.

FROM BERLIN TO BAGDAD

The *selamlik* of Dolma Bagtche is an imposing and pleasing structure of white marble and stucco. The building has only two stories, but each story is high enough to provide the height needed to discount the great length of the structure.

Toward the garden the *selamlik* has a fine portico. Under this lies the main ramp and stairway. As the automobile stopped, several court officials in frock-coats were ready to receive us. In stepping out of the machine I dented the crown of my silk hat. I bent the thing into shape again, looking meanwhile into the sympathetic face of a nice old Turk who was expressing his regrets. I told him that since His Majesty was not likely to see the silk hat no damage was done.

At the foot of the stairs we were received by the master of ceremonies. He was very stout and very good-natured. From his hands we passed into those of Brigadier-General Salih Pasha, first aide-de-camp to the Sultan.

Salih Pasha was standing at the head of the stairs, and looked very martial. So we cracked our heels and bowed, as becomes such hybrid beings as war correspondents—half civilian, half military.

There and then we discovered that Salih Pasha was a most congenial sort of person. He bid us welcome to the palace in a very happy manner, and then led the way to one of the reception-rooms of the palace—one of the great halls for which Dolma Bagtche is truly famous. The room lies to the left of the main foyer. It is a magnificent apartment, decorated sumptuously in the style of Italian Renaissance.

AN AUDIENCE WITH THE SULTAN

"His Majesty has expressed keen appreciation of his meeting with you gentlemen," said Salih Pasha, as he dragged some chairs before the large, open fireplace in which a fine log blaze was going on. "He is occupied with some reports at this moment. You will kindly excuse him if the audience should not take place at two o'clock exactly. Let us have some coffee and a smoke."

In Turkey they have coffee and a smoke on all and every occasion. We assured Salih Pasha that we would not be put out about it if His Majesty did receive us a few minutes late. To see him at all was the main thing. Then we seated ourselves around the fireplace and warmed our hands. Overnight the wind had shifted. It was now coming from frigid Russia, with heavy clouds and showers on its back.

Salih Pasha was greatly interested in what we had seen at the Dardanelles. I gave him some of the military aspects of the situation at the strait, and he returned opinions on German military efficiency. Salih Pasha disclosed himself as a great admirer of the Germans. That is natural enough, seeing that much of his military training dates back to the days when he was a dashing cavalry officer in Coblentz on the Rhine.

The coffee came. It was served in the thinnest porcelain cups I have ever seen. So thin were these shells that touching them with your fingers might crush them, explained Salih Pasha. That was the reason why they had been placed in holders of gold filigree. I wondered how they washed the things, and took a sip of the brew—real Mocha from Arabia, said the general.

Salih Pasha handed each of us a cigarette—thick things about ten inches long, of which length four inches were paper tube. It was a very mild smoke—denicotinized.

"His Majesty is greatly interested in what happened on the eighteenth of March," said the general, after a while. "He may ask some questions concerning that event. In case he should do so, make your replies brief and to the point. I am to act as your interpreter."

At four minutes past two o'clock the high double doors of the *salon* were swung open. Then the master of ceremonies appeared on the threshold. Before he entered the room he bowed to us, and after advancing a few paces he repeated the salutation. After that he said something in Turkish of which I could not catch a single word, though out at the front I am able already to make myself understood to the soldiers.

Salih Pasha explained that the many words meant merely that His Majesty was waiting for us.

F. Swing shook his frock-coat into place, squared up, and made generally ready for the procession. The master of ceremonies faced about. Salih Pasha suggested that, as senior, I should take my place behind that functionary. Then came my friend. The general brought up the rear.

As we filed out of the reception-room a score of court employees and officers salaamed and saluted and some of them attached themselves to us.

The procession, keeping studiously to the runners protecting the costly carpets and rugs on the floor, made its way through a great *atrium*, toward the grand stair-house. There is a flight of stairs to the left and one to the right, both of them landing on a sort of balcony on a level with the upper story of the building.

We took the flight on the right, and, going up, I had a fine opportunity to study the details of the splendid cut-crystal balustrades of the stairs and balcony. The man who conceived the proportions and decorations of that stair-house thought only in the sublime. The effect of the whitest of marble, the crystal, and the gold is marvelous.

At the head of the stairs we turned to the right, then entered a corridor at the left, turned once more to the right, and finally entered a small reception-room—antechamber to the private quarters of the ruler of the Ottoman Empire.

That seemed to end the duties of the master of ceremonies. He and the other functionaries withdrew. For a minute or two we looked around the plain room, and then a man in a plain frock-coat entered. He informed us that His Majesty was waiting, and motioned to me that I was to enter a narrow and wholly unlighted corridor from which he had stepped into the room.

This I did. After a few paces I noticed to the left of me an open door, the only thing I could see. I concluded that this might be the end of the maze through which we had been led.

I stepped to the door with my wits in good order, looked in, and saw an aged and rather corpulent man of medium height rise from a divan.

Agreeable to the instructions given us by Salih Pasha, I stopped on the threshold, looked Mohammed Réchad Khan V full in the face, and bowed three times

The Sultan was smiling quite heartily. He came toward me and extended his hand, saying something in Turkish the while. This time I was luckier. I caught the word, "*Salaam.*"

We shook hands, and then I stepped aside to let F. Swing go through the same maneuver.

These formalities over, the Sultan pointed to the chairs that had been placed before his divan. We stepped toward them, and seated ourselves as soon as the Sultan had done so. But Salih Pasha, more a stickler for form than his master, had to introduce us formally, and so we rose again as he announced our names, connections, and the purpose of our stay in Turkey. As Swing and I caught our names we bowed, and the Sultan smiled in recognition.

It struck me that the monarch was eager to dispense with much of the rigmarole that was going on. Before Salih Pasha was through with the introduction of Swing the Sultan motioned to us to be seated.

For the space of a minute Mohammed Réchad spoke to Salih Pasha, dwelling lovingly on the letter "l." All Turks have that habit, however. More time was lost when Salih Pasha thought it necessary to interpret every word his august master had uttered.

"His Majesty desires to extend to you a most hearty welcome," he began. "He also wishes that we do not stand on ceremony too much. This is an informal meeting—the first His Majesty has had with American journalists—with journalists of any kind."

He said some other pleasant things, but they need not be recorded.

I was meanwhile surveying the ruler of the Ottoman Empire and spiritual head of the Moslem world.

The sultan-caliph was very simply attired. He wore a frock-coat of blue broadcloth, trousers of the same fabric, black shoes with soft uppers, a turned-down collar, blue scarf, and the conventional maroon fez of the Ottoman. There was no jewelry of any sort about his person—not even a stickpin.

I found that the sallow and rather fleshy face was not as immobile as one might gather from the pictures of the man. On the contrary, there were moments when it was full of expression, especially when there was an occasion for a smile.

The Sultan appeared to me a gentle old man whose lot in life had left him resigned instead of bitter. For many years Mohammed Réchad was the prisoner of his brother Abdul Hamid. Youth had flown when the revolution freed him and made him ruler of an empire.

The facial traits of the Sultan are distinctly Turkish, more so even than those of his famous brother. But the face is devoid of the cruelty commonly credited to the family. The large brown eyes have a good-natured twinkle in them, though they could also search, as I noticed.

The Sultan was very much interested in the events at the Dardanelles. Before long I was under the impression that he was checking up things he had heard, but which he had taken *cum grano salis*. He was especially interested in what the losses of the coast batteries had been. When I told him how slight they were he expressed surprise, and then said something to his aide-de-camp which the latter did not translate.

Other remarks showed me that the Sultan had not hoped for so lucky a turn. He had been agreeably surprised, it seemed. He was not yet sure that there was good reason for entertaining so pleasant a sensation.

A lively conversation was soon in progress. Questions of a military character were addressed to me, while Swing had to give an account of things concerning the civil population along the strait. The Sultan was greatly interested in the fate of the people of Tchanak Kaleh.

"Yes, indeed," said the Sultan, after I had remarked that his officers and men had done splendidly during the bombardment. "They have done well. For that I am thankful to Allah and thankful to them. Not all of the spirit of the Osmanli has departed, though my people is no longer what it once was. It has gone through too many wars. It has bled too much. But the days of a long peace will come, and then the Ottoman nation will again forge ahead."

With that the Sultan turned to my friend with the question as to how he had stood the terror of the bombardments.

F. Swing is an honest man. He explained to the Sultan that most of the time he had been scared out of his wits. On March 18th he was so scared, he said, that an old Turk at Tchanak Kaleh had placed a hand on his shoulder in a fatherly way, remarking:

"*Yok, effendim! Yok—kismet!*" That is nothing, sir. It is fate!

The Sultan smiled.

"I am glad that a Turk offered you such comfort," he said. "But you do not look like a man who would fear much.

"And the old Turk did not use the right word, my young friend. He should have said, *kadar*. *Kismet* applies to the lesser trials of life, while *kadar* embraces all of our great misfortunes. *Kadar* means that our fate is in the hands of the Almighty, of Allah."

The Sultan bowed as he pronounced the word Allah. Then he continued:

"What is to be will be. This attitude of the mind is known to you of the Occident as fatalism. But that word does not wholly embrace our conception of *kadar*.

"But we must not consign everything in life to *kadar*. Some of us have a false conception of how far we must trust in fate. We have, as a race, relied too much upon *kadar* in the past, and so we have grown negligent and indolent. *Kadar* alone will not cause us to do well in life We must work, work, work!"

Mohammed Réchad wanted to hear more of the sinking of the *Bouvet*, *Irresistible*, and *Ocean*.

"It is a pity that so many young lives should have been lost," he said, when I had gone over the ground again. "What is the use of all this blood-shed, this making of widows and orphans, this destruction of what man's hands have fashioned so laboriously?

"I did not want this war. Allah be my witness! I am sure that my people did not want it. But what can we do under the circumstances but fight valiantly? That my army is doing, and will continue to do.

"Russia would take this city from us. I fail to see the justification for that. This city has never been Russian. We took it from the Greeks by conquest. We will not surrender it except we are vanquished.

"Tell your government and your people that my government and my people find great satisfaction in being at peace with them and that our relations are so cordial."

With this the Sultan rose—signal that the audience was over.

As we took leave of him, Mohammed Réchad patted Swing on the shoulder.

"You are a brave boy," he said, with a kind smile. "But remember that it is *kadar* and not *kismet!*"

F. Swing promised to do that and assured the Sultan that he would also remember always the man who had given him this lesson in Turkish. The Sultan seemed to be pleased with the compliment. We were to call on him again—every time we had something of interest to tell him. That, too, was promised.

Then we shook hands so heartily that our cuff-

links rattled. At the door we again bowed thrice
to the ruler of the Ottoman Empire and the caliph
of the Moslems, and then rushed home to write
what seemed to us a pretty good story.

April 9th.

Attended the *selamlik* to-day. The Sultan went
to worship in the *Walideh Dchami*. Though the
war has put a damper on this splendid ceremony,
it is still magnificent enough to give one a taste of
what it must have been when Abdul Hamid was
the central figure of it.

The mosque in question lies to the south of the
Dolma Bagtche Palace; its yard adjoins the imperial stables, in fact.

About this yard had been drawn up a few
mounted police and the men from nearby fire
stations. Formerly, regiment upon regiment from
the local garrison took part in the ceremony. But
these are now at the front—in the Caucasus, in
the desert east of the Suez Canal, and on Gallipoli.

What gave glamour to to-day's *selamlik* was the
assembly of officers of the Ottoman military and
naval general staffs, and officials of the government.
Most of the ministers were also present.

In the "good old days" of Abdul Hamid these
ministers had to run alongside the carriage of the
Sultan. But the revolution has changed all that.
Nowadays, the ministers meet the Sultan at the
entrance to the mosque. Instead of falling to the
ground, as formerly, they merely *salaam* in their
best fashion and then proceed to help their ruler
out of the carriage. Enver Pasha seemed to be es-

169

pecially eager to be of service to the stout old man. He is related to him by marriage and Sultan Mohammed Réchad V is extremely fond of the dashing Enver.

And that reminds me of Enver's wife. She is a princess of the imperial house, very young, decidedly handsome in a strong way, vivacious, intelligent, and energetic. At the head of a *harcem* she would be one of those able intriguers of whom the Ottoman court has had so many, and who have caused so much bloodshed and misery in days gone by; as it is she is the only wife, in the European manner, of one of the strong men in Turkey. That being the case, she finds a more natural outlet for her energy. In addition to helping Enver with his work—she has taken to military affairs like a duck to water—she runs most of the war work of the Turkish women. She manages several charitable organizations, presides over the Turkish Red Crescent, equivalent of the Red Cross elsewhere, and finds keen delight in managing bazaars and other charitable enterprises. In her moments of leisure she attends lectures at the University of Constantinople. She is a busy woman and, as I learn on good authority, a happy one.

April 16th.

Well, I am alone F Swing has gone to the Balkans to "snoop" around a bit. I am resting up from my labors by taking a good look at Stamboul—dear Stamboul.

To-day I viewed the *Atik Ali Pacha* quarter of Stamboul. Here the wealthy classes of Turkish

society live. On the way there I passed many a
fine mosque. But I do not find the large ones half
as charming as the smaller ones and the *turbeh*
(chapels). Most of these are surrounded by a high
wall, pierced here and there by large openings
barred with wrought-iron grilles of very beautiful
designs.

Behind the walls and the grilles lies a little cemetery, as a rule—shady lawns on which the Turkish
gravestones lean in all directions. The trees are
old and venerable, and through their dense foliage
come bits of white marble walls and dashes of azure
sky. There is something about these old cemeteries that causes one to understand the meaning
of the term, "Acre of Peace."

The *tashys* stand about in sweet abandon to whatever slant they have elected to take. They were set
perpendicularly, no doubt, but they have shifted as
the grave sagged. The *tashy* of the man is sur-
mounted by a large bulbous thing accepted to be
the turban, while that of the woman is plain.
Generally a man and his wife rest side by side.
In some cases the two stones incline toward each
other, in others they lean away. I saw some
cases where both *tashys* tended in the same direction; now it was the woman that leaned toward the
man, and again the opposite was true. I wonder
whether or not those gravestones picture anything
of the true relations of the two in life.

I saw many fine homes and gardens in *Atik Ali
Pacha*—I think that is the name. Of the homes
I saw only the upper stories; of the gardens no
more than the treetops. But there was peace

everywhere. It was rather different at the Dardanelles.

In and out of the sunlight-and-shadow drawings on the pink garden walls passed Turkish women in their *feredchehs*, high-heeled shoes, *yashmaks*, and *bürundchuks*. Some of them had their children with them. A Kurd hurried along with a heavy load of new furniture on his bent back. The perspiration was running over the leather strap across his forehead which helps to keep the load in place. I wonder whether the yoke is heavier to the ox than that strap seemed to be to the man. A donkey passed with a traveling meat-shop on his back—two large boxes covered with a wire netting to keep the flies off the meat that was exhibited.

"*Kassab! kassab!*" the man was shouting.

At last I discovered how Constantinople amuses itself—how it finds recreation.

The capital has a population of about 1,135,000, and not a single regular theater. Before the war a light opera troupe put in appearance now and then.

There are four cabarets, all of them more or less, generally more, shady. The *artistes*, nearly all awkward dancers and worse singers, earn, despite their use of all sorts of terpsichorean tricks and any language under the sun, the munificent sum of fifteen francs—three medjidieh—a night. They are well dressed, of course, and live in the second-rate hotels. They also ride about in the *arabas*. Fifteen francs a night will not pay for all that. But the ladies get a commission of five francs on each bottle of champagne they induce the guests to drink. Three bottles a night would be

fifteen francs more. That will take care of board
and lodging and the carriages, but not of the toilettes.
Then, too, the younger and better-looking of the
artistes have maids. They also have jewelry and
little dogs, and when they have arrived at this
degree of magnificence they begin to put on airs.

The cabarets are crowded, naturally. Officers
in the Ottoman service, government officials, diplomatic secretaries, and rich *Pérotes* and Stamboulites
about town form the elegant audience of these
amusement places. Just now a young aviation
officer is the "prince" of the *Jardin de Paris.* I
was introduced to this fine spendthrift last night.
There is no doubt that he is a high-flier in more
ways than one.

We were intimate within ten minutes.

He called me his *cher.* French is the only European language he knows. And that is enough,
anyway, seeing that his mother tongue is Turkish.

"*Mon cher,*" he said, easily and with the grace
of a potentate, "one does not know when one flies
for the last time. I have had several narrow escapes.
One of these days a hole in the air will get me. It
will be a case of down, down, down—and . . ."

He lifted the glass to his lips. I nodded. He
drank.

"You understand, *mon cher ami!*" said the aviator, bowing slightly.

"I understand perfectly. There will be a sudden
meeting of two bodies, a crash, wreckage, a fire
maybe, as the gas ignites, and . . ."

"For me death—*pour moi la froide morte. Ça
m'est égal!*"

173

Well, I suppose it is that way with aviators.

The conservative element, the capital's bourgeoisie, does not go to the cabarets. These Greek, Armenian, and Levantine families hold to the narrow path of virtue. Of course, no Turk would dream of taking his "household" to a cabaret.

That limits one to the moving-picture houses, known hereabouts as *cinémas* or *kinos*. There being a general prejudice against attending places of amusement at night, the family sees the latest Italian, French, or German film in the afternoon. The favorite subjects are historical or melodramatic. The former must be pompous and long, the latter highly emotional and tragic. At least the heroine must die in the last "take" of the film. If it can be managed, the hero also must go by the board. The Levantine has what I would call the "opera" temperament—that is to say, the lovely person who has kept us enthralled by her beauty, grace, suffering, and nobility of mind must in the end die so that we may have the subconscious satisfaction of feeling that now she is all our own.

Pera has several concert gardens. The best attended of these is the establishment of *Les Petits Champs des Morts* (the Little Cemetery).

To us of the West the thought of having a sort of large open-air restaurant in a cemetery seems a little odd. In the East they do not mind such things. The place is really beautiful. Great, somber cypresses overshadow the young acacias that have been planted to afford shade for those sitting at the table. On the graves have been

171

heaped several feet of soil and gravel. That prevents the dead from being disturbed.

The Greek orchestra does well enough. Its repertoire includes the masterpieces of Europe, a little ragtime, even a few plantation songs, and the things they call music in the East. While the leader sways his company as best he may—that orchestra lacks dash, by the way—the youngsters run among the trees and tables and chairs and scream for joy. *Maman* sips her cup of *tchai* (tea) and *monsieur père* has his *bock*. Elena munches a wafer and moistens it with a grenadine lemonade, while Theano scoops up the red-and-white ice-cream in a pensive mood. Constantin has just been called to order by *monsieur père* for blowing into the straw and making the lemonade bubble, and *maman* promises him a going-to-bed-without-supper.

Tout comme chez nous!

The conversation in the garden is mostly carried on in French. For that language remains the *lingua franca* of the Levant. The Greek does not understand Armenian, and when he understands it he does not use it on general principles, because the Armenian will not speak Greek if he can help it. Neither Greek nor Armenian speaks Turkish well or willingly, and the Turk is in a like position when it comes to the languages of his compatriots —if compatriots they regard themselves at all. Even the German officers in the Ottoman naval and military services speak French. Turkish, Greek, and Armenian are languages which even the polyglot German does not acquire. So far but few

12

here have learned enough German to speak at all well, though everybody is busy conjugating German verbs and memorizing the German vocabulary.

Around the copse of acacias runs a gravel path —the *corso*. Those who are tired sitting, and those who want to see who is there, keep making the rounds on the path. Friends meet, shake hands or *salaam*, exchange a few words, and move on. There is considerable flirting. The Levantine ladies seem to be rather fond of the officers. The lure of the brass button is potent everywhere. Present are also some *chanteuses* and *danseuses*. Most of their friends are in the several diplomatic services represented in the Ottoman capital.

At five o'clock the concert ends. The garden clears rapidly. The *Pérotes* go home to dine. Many of them stay for their dinner. There is a large terrace to one side of the garden, with majestic cypresses as a huge Spanish screen, and one has glimpses of the Golden Horn, Stamboul's sky-line of minarets and cupolas, and a splendid sunset for diversion.

It is a little early to dine when the concert ends, so one takes an *apéritif*, as one does on the Boulevard des Italiens in the real Paris, and chats meanwhile about many things—the war alone excluded. To talk of the war is a little dangerous—often very dangerous. It depends how one feels about it. Public opinion in Constantinople about the war is far from being unanimous. The Armenians at least are anti-Turk and anti-German. To say that one is either is to say that one is both. The Greeks are indifferent, and the other Levantines don't care.

At six-thirty the dishes begin to rattle, the silver tinkles, glasses clink, corks pop, and the orchestra is again at work. Never has a congregation of the dead enjoyed so much company, nor one so joyous. By eight o'clock it is a merry scene in the garden. Everybody laughs and makes merry. The *artistes* are on the boards, and when at twelve one goes home one feels that even in war not all is sadness.

On fine days *monsieur père* hires an *araba* and drives his family to the park known as the Sweet Waters of Europe. Under its old trees one may roll in the grass. At the kiosks all sorts of non-alcoholic drinks may be had cheaply, and the ambitious may rent a *caique* and exercise their muscles, rowing. The more enterprising may even go to the park of the Sweet Waters of Asia, where a sort of perennial country fair is held, while those with more means take a trip to the island of Principo or as far as Ismid, to which good suburban trains take one in very little time.

But all that does not fill life entirely. The Levantine has a very active mind, and there is little to occupy it. The supply of good reading is extremely limited. The few daily newspapers in Turkish, Greek, French, Armenian, and German bring all the same reports. The censorship is rigorous and a pest.

Good books are hard to get since the outbreak of the war. Most of them came from France, and just now France is too busy to make and export books. Greek literature offers little. Its novels are mostly of the back-stairs sort. They are written for the poor and show it. The wealthy classes can afford to buy French novels, and the needs of their poorer race brothers concern them not. One result of this has been that the newspapers carried excellent *feuilletons* (feature stories), "Continued" novels, and poems. But the war has laid low now that source of mental food. There is a great scarcity of paper.

But the mind must be kept busy. For this reason Pera, whose gossip has been proverbial for centuries, talks more than ever. Formerly this talk concerned itself largely with family scandals and the like. Nowadays it turns to war rumors. The wildest reports spring up and spread over the city in the space of hours. Tatavla being a quarter of the city in which only better-class Greeks live, some spiteful wit opined that these rumors came from the *Agence Tatavla*—equivalent for the American "grape-vine news."

The gossiping *Pérotes* occupy themselves much with the love-affairs of strangers in the diplomatic and military services. Having no love-stories to read, they take it out in talking about lovers. Whether Mademoiselle So-and-so is now the friend of this or that secretary or attaché is of great moment to everybody, it seems. On the strength of this news some dealer in jewelry, rugs, and such may call on the gentleman to do a little business. Some *modiste* or *couturière* will do the same thing on Mademoiselle. When this happens *monsieur* will know that Pera is talking about him. As a rule, he does not have to wait long for these calls.

AN AUDIENCE WITH THE SULTAN

April 21st.

Having demonstrated to the satisfaction of the American embassy that I can paddle my own canoe, the embassy is now willing to have me help them paddle theirs a bit. The American ambassador has given me a commission. I am to get Captain Morton, commander of the American *stationnaire Scorpion*, and Captain Williams, of the U. S. Coast Artillery, now attached to the American embassy for relief work, to the Dardanelles front.

I told the ambassador I could not manage that, having my hands full looking out for myself. He was sure I could manage it. So I tried. For the time being the chances are not very good. Later they may improve. That is the word I got from Enver Pasha.

There is a tea at the American embassy every Wednesday. I mention that because to-day's affair was unusually successful.

The American embassy teas are about all that remains of the social diplomatic high-life formerly enjoyed at Pera in the winter, and at Therapia in the summer. There was a time when the American embassy was not so much in demand by the socially inclined. But that time is not just now.

The Morgenthaus are charming people. Madame Morgenthau has a knack of making you feel at home. Her entertainments are simple but of high quality—rather refreshing change from other American diplomatic functions where they tell you how many dollars the tea costs per pound and how much they have to pay for this or that singer.

And at the Morgenthaus' you can meet everybody worth knowing in Pera. To-day's affair was really splendid. The company was the best. The Marquis and Madame Pallavicini, the Austro-Hungarian ambassadorial couple, and all the Scandinavian ministers and their wives were present. Several German and Austro-Hungarian diplomatic secretaries concluded the list of people from that sphere of life.

Fully a dozen pashas were there. Beys by the score. Ex-ministers and senators crowded one another. Officers in the nattiest of Ottoman uniforms and the most gorgeous gold-domed calpacs cracked heels and bent over fair ladies' hands with a grace that comes only after an inoculation with the *virus Constantinopolus*. Some of those Ottoman uniforms were worn by men who have Prussia as their place of birth, but the wearers are tanned enough to pass for Turks.

There were rich *Pérotes*—Greek merchants in olive-oil and wine, Armenian traders in wool and cotton and other produce, Persian dealers in carpets, rugs, and precious stones, and Bulgar captains of industry of various sorts.

They all had their ladies with them. I saw toilettes that would make the *rue de la Paix* green with envy. Jewelry had lost its worth and charms in that assembly of matrons and *demoiselles*. I saw a pearl necklace, thrown carelessly around the shapely throat of the American wife of a Greek merchant prince, who is an Italian subject, that would keep me in small change for many a day.

Madame Morgenthau introduced me far as she

could, and then I took matters into my own hands.

You walk up to the person on whom you wish to press your acquaintance, crack your heels, lean forward with your hands hanging idly by your side, and say your name—just your name and no more. At least that is the practice in Pera now. I am told that formerly you excused yourself for the intrusion you had so intentionally managed. To that extent, at any rate, Pera is honest and sincere. But only to that extent—no further.

The concert arrangements were good. I can't say, though, that I have a keen longing to hear any of the artistes again, though one of them, a *contralto* with a very quivery *tremolo,* commanded attention enough to let her appearance be the signal for the cessation of the lively babbling that was going on. The boy virtuoso on the fiddle I did not hear at all, being just then engaged in conversation with Halideh Edib Hannym Effendi.

April 22d.

I am ready for a trip that promises to be a wild-goose chase. I am to go to Arabia, or some other place, to meet the remnants of the crew of the German cruiser *Emden.* When heard from the remnant was near Hodeida on the Red Sea, heading north in search of the Fatherland. Word has now been received that Lieutenant von Muecke and his trusty band are still alive and somewhere in the interior of Arabia.

Tears come into my eyes when I think that for some weeks I may not see Stamboul and Pera, and fears creep over my mind when I think what may happen in that time to Constantinople—and to the service, which I am leaving in the care of a professor of history and literature, the last person in the world qualified to be a "journalist."

Copyright, by Underwood & Underwood

TURKISH BATTERY CAPTURED BY ARMENIAN COMITADJES AT VAN

VI

ARMENIA'S RED CARAVAN OF SORROW

THERE had been much talk in Constantinople, throughout April, of trouble between the Turks and the Armenians. I had ascertained that something was wrong, but had failed to get at particulars. In the Ottoman Ministries they would not discuss the question. It was admitted, however, that there had been "slight local troubles." But I knew just a little better, though unable to give my sources of information. Several despatches I wrote on the subject were suppressed by the Ottoman censors and I was finally told that the affair was over.

Since not a word of the Armenian uprisings was permitted to be published in Constantinople, and since there was a most rigorous censorship of all telegrams and letters, the city was entirely out of touch with the state of affairs in the provinces. That there had been trouble was generally known, but even the best evidence obtainable just then favored the conclusion that nothing serious had happened.

Such, indeed, was the general impression. The first Armenian troubles started in the Ottoman

armies in the Caucasus. Many of the Armenian
soldiers had gone over to the Russians. The result
of this was the disarming of all Armenian troops
and their employment in the rear at road-building
and the like. As yet the insurrection had not
spread into the Armenian districts. The Armenian
civil population was still quiet, and with the Armenian troops in the Ottoman army disarmed the
belief prevailed that the trouble was ended. Such
was not the case, however, as the entries in my
journal show.

ESKI-SHEHIR, ANATOLIA, *April 23d.*
The Anatolian railroad does not run at night.
Why that should be so I do not understand. The
track is good and the rolling stock is in excellent
condition. But the road goes to sleep every evening.
That is why I am in Eski-Shehir.

Seen on the map, Anatolia does not give one
the impression of being much of a country. Yet I
have never traveled through a more interesting
one.

From Haidar Pasha to Ismid the road passes
through an endless variety of suburbs, villas,
tchiftliks, gardens, orchards, olive groves, fields,
and hillsides upon which young and old shepherds
mind large flocks of sheep and goats in true Attikan
style—they play the flute while their charges graze;
it is a sort of a pastoral *table d'hôte avec orchestre.*

I can well understand why the old Byzantians
were sore when the Turks took over all there was
along the Gulf of Ismid. For scenery the country
on both sides of the gulf is hard to excel. On the

184

north shore the hills rise gently. Fertile acres lie on their slopes and their bases are wrapped in the most luxurious foliage of fruit-trees one can imagine. This is the home of the cherry—so it is said—and to see how this tree flourishes here makes one need no further proof of the assertion.

Flowers grow in profusion. Just now it seems to be the turn of the poppy to do its best. It does not shirk its task. The red, red faces in the high grass nod in the gentle breeze and make one feel that nature is indeed generous.

Little *tchiftliks* stud the country. The red tile roofs peep from the parklike gardens most coyly. In the field a span of black water-buffaloes strains faithfully under the yoke. You notice that the plow is the one which Adam patented, and one wonders how such crops can be produced by so primitive a method of cultivation. The plow is nothing more than a piece of wood with an iron point, fastened to a straight shaft. How can such a primitive implement raise the taxes the *tchiftlikdschi*—plain Turkish for farmer—has to pay and then keep himself and family in a fair measure of comfort? But it does it. The soil is rich and the climate good.

On the gulf stand out lateen sails. The water is clear, so that one can see even the patches on the sail in the boat's image. Beyond the sail lie red-roofed villages, hamlets, and *tchiftliks*. Then the ground grows steep. Beyond the olive groves and vineyards on the foothills lie pleasant beech and oak forests. The higher elevations are preferred by the pines and birches, and finally the eye rests on the half-naked slopes of Mount Olympus

—one of the many mountains of that name, this one having with the Turks the name Sultan Dagh. But there are as many Sultan Daghs as there are Mount Olympuses, so the Turkish name does not help you any.

The Ismid country is indeed a sort of paradise.

Reached Lake Sabandcha about noon and had another feast in scenery. Its beauty excels that of many a Swiss lake. Near Arifleh the railroad runs through a rich agricultural district. The heights here are covered with tall conifers of all sorts.

All day long I dashed through mulberry plantations. Anatolia produces a great deal of the world's silk. They would plant mulberry-trees on their roofs here, if it could be done. The business pays well according to Oriental standards of living.

Passed through a gorge somewhere that was wildly romantic. Then we came to a place I once read of in history—Biledchik, the Belokoma of the Byzantians. In the old castle above the town lived the beautiful Nilfur whom Sultan Orchan married after keeping her a prisoner for a time. The story is very interesting, but too long. At any rate, I am sure she had the sort of hair F. Swing likes so much on a woman. Nilfur infused the first Byzantian blood into the *padishah* family.

As the train pulled out of Biledchik some Greek urchins ran alongside, crying for *gazettas* (newspapers). Having a goodly supply on hand, I earned their gratitude—maybe! At any rate, I saw the same boys again half an hour afterward, when we were well above the highest of the town's roofs, having needed that long to worm our way up the steep escarpment which must be scaled here by the railroad. About sundown we reached the crest, over many a viaduct, through many a tunnel, and over many a steep grade, one of the latter, I noticed, being one in forty.

The crest forms the divide between the Anatolian hill country and the high plateau. To the north lies a country as rich as can be found, to the south a geological roof as bare as they make them—so said the man with whom I share my compartment, an inspector of the Anatolian railroad, an expatri- ated Pole. I was to look out for the "paved" mountains that we would see to-morrow.

We reached here shortly after dark. Took a spin about town in an *araba*, and saw several fine mosques from without. The place is interesting for the reason that it is the cradle of Ottoman power, and that quite recently the Ottoman government in- tended to again make it its capital—almost like com- ing home to die.

Konia, Anatolia, *April 24th*.
The Polish Anatolian railroad inspector is a god- send. He knows this country like a book. Outside of Eski-Shehir he showed me some of the farms of the Ottoman crown—crown lands. Can't say that these farms are very up-to-date. After that we ran through a fine batch of "paved" mountains —massive rocks from which denudation, brought on by the lips of the goat, has carried the last bit of soil. The *daghs* (mountains) have fitting names, I noticed. The names when translated mean dry,

187

black, gray, slate, lime, thirsty, hungry, and similar unlovely things.

A sign at the station of Duewer said we were 1,125 meters—about 3,375 feet—above sea-level. The country looked it. The mountains, bare of all vegetation and soil, the valleys buried under gravel and other denudation deposits, and the water-courses, stained white with alkali, made no pleasant picture.

About noon we reached the district in which the Phrygians were supreme once upon a time. To the left and right of the railroad stand to-day the cave cities they cut into the soft limerock. One of the "buildings" I could have touched with my hands from the car window.

It was built in this way: A large boulder was selected as both the site and the building material. This done, the good Phrygian set to work with his chisels and cut out what rooms he wanted to have "built." This detail attended to, he carved the external architectural details into the "building" and moved in.

By noon we came to Afiun-Karahissar—the Black Opium Castle. The name comes from the fact that the poppy flourishes here as it will nowhere else. For miles and miles the fields stood in poppy crop—a splendid picture of greens and all shades of pink, the real opium poppy being that color.

I found the steep castle rocks about the place very interesting. The inspector says that one of the ruins is the remainder of a castle built by the Crusaders. I am evidently not the first person to come this way.

Early in the afternoon the inspector showed much interest in apples and that sort of thing. We had come to Ak-Shehir, the ancient Philomelion of Old Pisidia, otherwise known as Pomphilia, I think. Back of the town lies the original Sultan Dagh, home of the apple, peach, and grape. Sultan Dagh was still covered with snow, and innumerable streams were gushing down its massive expanse. The inspector pointed out to me some of the larger wild-apple forests, peach forests, and the like. I suggested that in such a climate any fruit might grow in forests and that this was not necessarily proof that the plant had originated there. In the end I agreed that the apple might be autochthonous of the district—just to have peace in the compartment.

But the Sultan Dagh is something really worth while in mountains. It is the major landmark in all that country. The streams and river coming from its vast snowfields make that part of Anatolia a veritable granary. All day long I passed through villages whose little freight stations were glutted with wheat ready for shipment. Much of the wheat had been exposed to rain and had sprouted. The inspector said that his road had not been able to cope with the traffic, owing to the heavy military transports. I suggested that they should run some of their trains at night.

I understand that Frederick Barbarossa, the Great Crusader, passed this way. That may be, but I do not believe the heroic yarn which claims that his enemies were so thick that he had to go clean across the Sultan Dagh. The plains about the mountain fastness are wide, and a much better reason for not believing this tale of an ancient court press agent is that the Sultan Dagh is not negotiable by an army.

BOSANTI, ANATOLIA, *April 25th.*

This is a sorry Sunday night. The rain beats down upon the shack which I share with an Ottoman officer, an engineer, who has the task of keeping the pass road to Tarsus, through the Cilician Gates, in good repair. I have eaten another meal from the tin can, and strewn more insect powder upon the couch where I am supposed to pass the night —if the bugs will let me.

Coming out of Konia this morning I made the acquaintance of a very interesting chap—Moustaphe Nadir Effendi, irrigation engineer and imperial irrigation commissioner for the Konia plain irrigation enterprise. His card gives this full information.

Thousands and thousands of acres will be made productive when the great irrigation system in the making here has been completed. Nadir Effendi was enthusiastic over it. He rattled off figures in terms of cotton-bales and hundredweights of grain that took my breath away. Two lakes are being tapped by means of tunnels. Most of the work has been done. The plain south of Konia is already intersected by irrigation ditches in a most liberal manner.

After running through another Kuru and Bos Dagh the train took me into the fertile and hot plains of Eregli, the *Herakleia* of the ancients.

Eregli in days to come will be a big city again.

The plain around the town, and the neighboring valleys, boast of a rich soil, and the adjacent Cilician Taurus has what is rare in the East—primeval forests of vast extent. It is asserted that coal is to be found not far from the city. Certain it is that the Tchakyt River,' which thunders a few paces from the shack I am in, would supply enough hydro-electric energy to make Eregli a manufacturing center of no mean sort.

Since leaving Konia I have been traveling on the international bone of contention, known as the Bagdad Railroad. The Germans and English had many an interesting fight in *notes verbales* and *mémoires* about this line, and much of the animosity between the two nations is due to it.

It is a good line, so far as it is in operation. The roadbed was laid down to last, the stations are pretentious, and the rolling stock could show itself anywhere.

Beyond Eregli, the building of the line required much engineering skill. After leaving the plain it ascends the pass in the northernmost ridge of the Cilician Taurus, doing this in a series of ramps or steep grades. At Bulgurlu the road is 1,056 meters above sea-level; twenty-nine kilometers further on it reaches an elevation of 1,467 meters, the highest point in the line between Haidar Pasha and Bagdad.

From there on the line descends toward the Cilician plain, running through as wild a bit of mountain country as one can find. Mount Aidost is about 10,700 feet high, and most of the peaks around it, past which the railroad runs, are not much lower. Many places in the gorge in which the

Bagdad Railroad and the Tchakyt River crowd each other never see the sun for longer than three hours every day. To leave room for the wagon road the rail line has to run on high stone embankments, get into tunnels, and straddle the river in many places.

After the ride across the flat lands of Anatolia, the trip through the pass was a treat. I have never seen anything quite so picturesque, nor so majestic. Above you the peaks of lime lose their snow-covered heads in the clouds. Further down stand old forests in which the ax has never been heard. Then come alpine meadows, fields pasted against steep slopes, vineyards and orchards, and then more fields.

The wagon road meanders along, entering a cut here and crossing the river on a camel-back bridge there. I noticed places where the road had been shifted four times. The river had either washed it away in part or some landslide had buried it. Dozens of good stone bridges, some of them built by the Romans, had in this manner become useless. The road had to be led some other way, and the bridge could no longer be utilized.

The great fall of the river is made use of by many small water-mills. Little donkeys were taking grain to these mills, and others were taking home the flour.

Many of the villages and *tchiftliks* are far above the gorge—idyllic spots where the war will never be a reality. The father or son may never come back, but the war itself cannot trouble these people. Yet there were times when this was not so. There

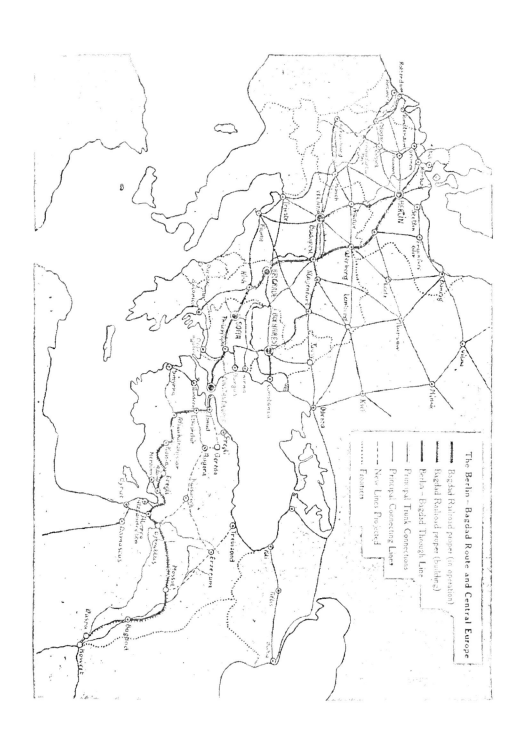

The Berlin–Bagdad Route and Central Europe

Bagdad Railroad proper (in operation)
Bagdad Railroad proper (building)
Berlin–Bagdad Through Line
Principal Trunk Connections
Principal Connecting Lines
New Lines Projected
Frontiers

was a time when through this gorge tramped the great armies of antiquity.

Passenger service on the Bagdad Railroad goes as far as Bosanti. That's why I am here. There are no hotels, no restaurants, no stores, no town at all. Bosanti is the camp of some railroad construction gangs, and some Turkish troops who keep in repair and guard the great pass road to Tarsus. Some day Bosanti will be something, maybe. To-night it is but a name.

KAWAK HAN, FOOTHILLS OF TAURUS, *April 26th.* A memorable day!

As if to convince me that there is no rest for the wicked, a mighty babble outside of the shack in Bosanti woke me this morning. I looked at my watch. Five o'clock! Not so far from starting-time, anyway. But what was the cause of the noise outside? It seemed to me that hundreds of women and children were weeping, crying, sobbing, talking, remonstrating, scolding—all at the same time.

It was still dark and the insect powder had been very efficacious, so I turned over in my mind the thought of sleeping another two hours, as I had planned. The Ottoman pioneer officer was slumbering sweetly, if his snoring was any indication.

But the noise outside would not cease. I poured some water in the rubber wash-basin, fished some soap out of my baggage, and completed a hasty toilet.

Then I stole out of the shack.

Near the railroad track a lamp swung from a pole in the chilly morning air. It was raining. The lamplight showed me a sea of wet faces and wet clothing—those of women and children, mostly.

What was this? Were these people passengers for the morning train? They were, as I soon found. These wretches were Armenians from Tertiul and Zeitoun. But what were they doing here? Didn't I know? The Armenians at Tertiul and Zeitoun had massacred a Turkish garrison and had been banished to the Anatolian high plateau to atone for the crime. All of which was hot news to me.

That was the version of a Turkish soldier—the official interpreter at Bosanti.

I mixed with the crowd. None of them spoke English, French, German, or anything else I knew.

All they could say was:

"*Effendem, ekmek! Karnym adchdyr, effendem, ekmek!*" ("Sir, give me bread. I am hungry. Sir, give me bread").

Some of the voices were feeble from hunger and hardship. I could tell that without seeing the face of the speaker.

I circulated among the crowd, still hoping to find somebody able to speak one of the languages I know.

In the end I found a woman who spoke English brokenly. Unlike her sisters in misery, she was not dressed in red calico trousers and red waist. She had on a much-bedraggled black skirt, and across her narrow chest and shoulders hung a large woolen shawl. She was soaked with the rain like all the others.

What had happened? I asked her. Where was she from? Where was she going to?

Her story was very incoherent. I made out that she was from Zeitoun and bound for Konia in banishment. The young Armenians of Zeitoun, said the woman, had been told that the English and French had taken Constantinople and that the Turkish government was a thing of the past. Thereupon they had decided to do away with the Turkish garrison of Zeitoun. The barracks of the Ottoman battalion stationed in the town was attacked, and in the fighting a good many Turks had been killed.

For two days the Turks had held their own, however. Then reinforcements had come up, obliging the Armenian *comitadjis* to seek refuge in an Armenian monastery on the outskirts of the town. This had been shelled by the Turks. But the Armenians had fought their way out of the trap they were in and had gotten safely into the mountains. Then the Turks had rounded up all the inhabitants of Zeitoun, and had sent the able-bodied men in one direction, and the old men, women, and children in another—toward Konia.

I fetched some biscuits for the woman, and while she ate them I cross-examined her. There was little else to tell, it seemed. The poor soul's mind had been under such a stress that she could remember very few details.

In some cases the Turkish officials had permitted the Armenians to carry with them a few of their household goods and some food. The Armenians from the rural district about Zeitoun had also been allowed to take part of their live stock with them. The artisans who had proven that they were not implicated in the revolt had been permitted to take with them their tools.

Daylight crept over the high peaks and ridges. It continued to rain. The exiles went on lamenting and calling for bread. Children whined piteously. Old men groaned. Whatever fortitude there was was shown by the older women. Stoically they sat about on the wet ground, their lean, brown hands folded over their shins.

Well, there was nothing I could do for these miserable beings. About seven I drank a cup of black coffee, and then climbed into the *yailah* that was waiting to take me to Tarsus.

I had asked the pioneer officer what would happen to the exiles. He didn't know. During the day cattle-cars would come from Eregli to take them away. He had no food to give them. They would get something to eat in Eregli.

Along the road I noticed more of the exiles. Most of them were men advanced in years. They had taken possession of the little *hans* (road inns), and they were drinking coffee and eating bread which they had bought there.

At about nine o'clock my *yailah*, a sort of covered, four-wheeled carriage, reached the little plateau of Tekir, made famous by the elaborate fortifications which Ibrahim Pasha, the Egyptian, caused to be erected there in 1836, during his campaign against the Turks.

Such weather! A driving cold rain was coming down in torrents. There was much snow in it. The road was muddy to a depth of a foot.

There was something wrong with the harness,

so the *arabadshi* pulled up to mend it. That was a chance for me to see the country, since the low roof of the *yailah* had hampered my vision. I leaned out of the carriage. Splendid scenery, despite the bad weather! Above me frowned a huge parapet of limestone, 9,000 feet high. To the right yawned an abyss, fully 600 feet deep, without a break in its walls. In front of me lay a narrow slit, a mere cleft in the mountain masses—the Cilician Gates—the ancient *Pylæ Ciliciæ.*

I was indeed on historic ground. This way had come and gone, in victory and defeat, most of the armies of the ancients. The great generals of antiquity had passed along this very road—names who in my youth had roused all the fire of heroship within me—Xerxes, Darius, Cyrus, Alexander the Macedonian, scores of others.

Through the pass had disgorged upon peaceful peoples the wild hordes of history's twilight zone, followed by the armies of Chaldea, Assyria, Babylonia, Persia, Media, Egypt, Judea, Phœnicia, Syria, Parthia, Phrygia, Greece, Rome, Arabia, and the Crusaders.

Those walls about me had heard the chant of victory and the wail of defeat; had resounded with the tramp of rugged foot and horse; had heard the death-rattle of the captives unable to drag themselves to a less forbidding place of death.

What stories those rocks could tell if their tongues could be loosed, I thought. Stories of national and racial aspirations and personal ambition realized, and stories of all hope abandoned. How many captives had passed them with "the light

199

of their eyes put out" and the "sound of their tongues forever taken from them," as says an Assyrian *stélé*. How many captive women had here of nights mourned their loves and wept over their fate, and how many had here made up their mind to be some other's "paramour in a far and distant land"?

Fixing harness is no easy matter, if you don't know how. I concluded that my *arabadshi* knew how, but that he had a rather difficult job on his hands. So I busied myself with my binoculars, viewed the fields against some lower slope, wandered up and down the narrow alleys of a mountain village, counted the cattle and sheep in an alpine meadow, and measured some of the tall pines near by. They were venerable old giants. That they had not been cut was not the fault of man, but a virtue of the inaccessible places they stood in. Everywhere I saw patches of deciduous trees— just taking on their summer dress—but conifers predominated. High up there was some stunted growth, and then beyond that boulder fields that looked as if Cyclops had tired of his job in Mount Vesuvius and had come here. Around the snowline of the mighty range drifted thin clouds, promise that the weather would improve during the afternoon, according to my driver.

But what was that? Coming around the bend of the old pass road was a caravan, afoot and clothed in red—a dirty, wet red.

More Armenians! I could not see the pass road near or beyond the actual gates, but some two miles farther on a short stretch of it was visible.

Either the train of sorrow extended that far or this was a new one.

The *arabadshi* had finally gotten under way again. He was inclined to go off at a smart pace, but I cautioned him with several *yawash! yawash!* (slow' slow!). I wanted to have a good look at the Armenian exiles. I might be able to file a story from Tarsus.

Old men in rags; women in red calico pantaloons, red waists, red shawls, and some of them in red veils; children of all ages, dressed like their elders; the halt, the blind, the sick made up this miserable column.

Stoically they drudged on. Some of the men glanced at me furtively. The older women begged for bread, the younger ones pulled either their veils or their shawls over their faces. They seemed to fear that I might hurt them.

The crowd stepped readily out of the way of the carriage, and I had trouble keeping the driver from going off at a trot. I could see that the road ahead was very narrow, especially in the gate, and I was not minded to have an accident on my hands.

It was well that I had taken this precaution. Beyond the bridge across the Tarsus Tchai the crowd was dense. A few high-wheeled ox-carts hove in sight. They were packed with light baggage and children. I saw some cows in the train. Children rode on them. On other cows and steers packs were carried.

The spectacle was pitiful. The rain was still coming down in a cold drizzle. It was cold up in that elevation—a sort of March weather. Few of the exiles had shoes; all of them were soaked to the skin, the clothing hanging to the weary bodies limp and wet. All faces showed suffering—hunger, exposure to the cold and wet, together with mental anguish about their kin and the future.

An old woman led a blind man by the hand. The woman was bent with age and sorrow. The man walked beside her erect. A great white beard was flowing over his broad and naked chest. His face had something noble in it—maybe nothing more than the resignation to do without sight forever. The empty eye-sockets were directed upward in search of the blessing that never came.

In the wet grass by the roadside lay an old woman. I halted the *yailah* to see if anything could be done for her. She was still alive, I found. I poured some brandy between her teeth. She opened her eyes and with them motioned me away. I suppose she wanted to die in peace.

Near a bridge a cart had fallen into the ravine in which the river runs. The dead oxen were still in the yoke. From under the wreckage protruded parts of four human bodies. On the other side I passed the body of a dead man. He was young. It seemed to me that tuberculosis had been the cause of his death.

Five miles I had gone, and still there was no break in the column. Since the exiles walked in groups and preserved no uniform marching order, I could not estimate their number. All I can say is that the exiles numbered no less than 4,000.

Then I came to the stragglers. The picture grew yet more harassing. It was composed of men and women trying to help some sick relative or friend along. Some of them sat by the wayside, tired and disconsolate, while the object of their care lay in the wet grass, resting or asleep. Two men were digging a grave. I passed a woman who was groaning under the weight of a large boy she carried on her back. To judge by the size of the child's head, I should say that he was a cretin and not in control of his withered limbs. Another woman was leading a blind man. More carts with sick and children aboard came, their screeching wheels filling the ravine with dismal sounds.

It was afternoon before I got beyond the red train of misery. The sun had come out. The horses had been fed and rested at a *han*, and we were going along at a fast clip to make good the time we had lost.

A new picture!

As we made a bend in the road in the foot-hills, I heard the sound of a *kawal*, a fife, and a drum. I thought at first that some soldiers might be coming up the road, and cautioned the driver. But that was not the case. Several hundred Armenian soldiers were sitting by the roadside, breaking rock. The Turkish officer in charge of the party explained that there was less intention in the music to entertain than design to get the work done. The "band" was employed to make the working-party keep time with the hammers, more rock being crushed in that manner. He had hit upon the plan himself, said the officer.

The Armenians, I learned, were part of a regiment which had just been disbanded and disarmed. "We cannot trust them any longer," explained

203

the officer. "So we took their arms away from them and put them to work improving the roads."

He had ten Turkish infantrymen to control the party of nearly 500 Armenians. I wondered how he managed to hold them in check.

"Oh, they are easily managed," he remarked, lightly. "The first one who makes a false move dies." The officer patted his revolver. "You know the Turkish proverb, 'God made the hare, the snake, and the Armenian'?"

And still what could the Armenians do? They might have butchered the few Turks who stood sentry over them, and could then have taken to the mountains, to be hunted down one by one or starve to death.

TARSUS, *April 27th.*

Arrived here late last night. Am installed with a Greek family—all *hans* and hotels being full because to-day is the anniversary of the ascension to the throne of Mohammed Réchad Khan V, Sultan of the Ottoman Empire, Caliph of all the Faithful, etc., etc., etc.

I viewed the patriotic exercises in the Konak (government building) this morning. Afterward I called upon the *kaimmakam* to get information concerning the Armenian trouble.

The pasha did not say much. He regretted it all. The affair had given him no end of trouble. Yesterday he had commandeered every wheeled vehicle in Tarsus and vicinity to get the Armenians to Bosanti. It had not helped much. Most of them had been obliged to go afoot.

I knew all that. How had the trouble started? He didn't know exactly as yet. The matter was being investigated by officials of the vilayets affected by the revolt. It was a sad affair!

I agreed with him on that point and asked for his assistance in getting a despatch to my "base" man in Constantinople.

"I would like to help you," said the pasha, "but to be frank with you and not have you waste your effort, I do not think it can be done. Wait until you get to Adana. The *vali* there has the authority to act in the matter. I have not."

The pasha was frank and polite, and with Adana but forty kilometers away I thought it best not to press the point.

IN THE CILICIAN PLAIN, *April 29th.*

I am the guest of a Bedouin sheik to-night. Left Tarsus in a hack, bound for Adana, got caught between two rivers running over from the heavy rains, and finally gained this hill. There is a flood all around. The elevation in question must be one of the signal-hills of the Romans. At any rate, it rises out of the plain without good geological reasons. My driver, when he spied the black, goat-hair tents on the hill, refused to go on to Adana, saying something about a river further on that would surely drown us.

Anyway, I am sitting on a dry rug, and the goat-hair fabric around me and above me is both water- and air-proof. The sheik is busy with something outside—maybe the evening meal. He has made several passes of his hand to the mouth. That is always a good sign.

After the meal.

Had plenty of pilaff and *shish-kebab*. A servant of the sheik's brought in the stuff on a large wooden platter. Then the two of us squatted down and ate. There being no spoon, I followed the example of the sheik by making a sort of shovel of the pancake-like bread of which the servant brought in a stack. Not a bad meal! After the pilaff, etc., we had a sort of sweetmeat, flavored *ad nauseam* with very rancid mutton fat—the sort they render from the caudal ornament of the fat-tailed sheep.

But the sheik's coffee drove away that awful taste, though it was long in the making. First the sheik had the servant bring into the tent a small *mangal* with live coals in it. From a sort of carpet bag he took a small metal pan fastened to a handle—a roaster. Then he brought a sheep's bladder from a pocket of his brown burnoose.

I got the idea by that time, but still had that taste in my mouth. From the bladder bag the sheik took some green coffee beans and put them into the roaster. They were roasted quickly enough, but there was no coffee yet.

Another search of the carpet bag produced a cylindrical coffee-grinder. Away he ground and ground and ground, while the servant was bringing the mixture of water and sugar to the boiling-point.

Four times the aromatic beverage in the dirty little pot had to rise in protest before the sheik filled two small cups and handed one to me.

ARMENIA'S RED CARAVAN OF SORROW

ADANA, SYRIA, *April 30th.*

That sheik proved to be one of nature's gentlemen. He made me comfortable in his tent, with all the carpets and rugs he could find. He even took some away from his women folk in another tent.

Since I could not make myself entirely clear to either my driver or the sheik, I had a hard time making my host understand that in other parts of the world it is considered very good taste to pay for one's keep. When I offered the sheik a little hard cash he held up his hands in horror. Then he smiled obligingly.

So I thanked the son of the desert in Turkish, which he could not understand, his own regular language being Arabic. At any rate, we parted the best of friends.

I must vote this place the least attractive I have seen. The houses have a neglected look about them and the poorly paved streets are anything but clean.

But that is not all. Adana's recent history is repulsive, loathsome. In 1909 the Armenian population, three-quarters of a total population of about 50,000, was decimated by massacre. How many Armenians perished I did not learn, but estimates given me by residents placed the number at about 11,000. Race hatred has no such monument anywhere.

A good half of the town is still in ruins. The quarter in which the Armenians formerly lived is a vast field of roofless and windowless walls. Though the heavy rains which fall in the Cilician Plain have washed off much of the smoke-stain and

soot, one can still form a good picture of the conflagration that raged here while the Kurd butchers
of the Turks put the population to the sword, knife,
and bayonet.

No quarter was shown by these fiends. The
young and aged, strong and weak, man, woman,
and child, perished that awful afternoon and night.
And it was not even death in a quick form that
overtook them. The Kurds set out on that day
to establish for their despicable race of beasts of
burden a new record in brutality. To disembowel
their victims and then let them linger on in agony
was their favorite procedure on that terrible day.
Nothing more shocking has ever been heard of.

The tortures to which many of the men were
subjected are quite indescribable. Let the statement suffice that mutilation was only a part of
them. But the women fared worse yet. The
German consul at Adana is my authority for this
statement. He saw some of the Kurds open the
abdomen of *enceinte* women with their knives and
tear from the living body the pregnant womb.

Be it said to the credit of the official that he
single-handedly charged a group of these Kurd
butchers, but was overpowered and knocked sense-
less by them. He would have been killed himself
had not a Turkish officer recognized him in good
time.

I need not dwell on a full list of the deviltries
that were perpetrated that day. What befell the
younger women and girls may be imagined. In
the end even they were butchered in the most
revolting manner.

Meanwhile, the Armenian quarter was in flames —a white-hot furnace. Many of the Armenians had barricaded themselves in their houses. The fact that but a few had firearms made defense difficult, and so it came that many of the houses that were not fired by the Kurds were set ablaze by those within. It was far better to die in the flames than to fall into the hands of the fiends outside.

The Adana massacre is one of the things that must cause us to consider whether or not the Turk has a right to rule others. I suppose that question is easily answered. A government that tolerates mob violence, or which even encourages it, is so low and contemptible a thing that nothing whatever can be said in its favor.

The Ottoman authorities at the time excused themselves, and, strange to say, had this excuse accepted by the polite governments of the entire world. The statement sufficed that the horde of Kurd and Turkish soldiers who perpetrated this most vicious crime of our age had become unmanageable. That means that soldiers in this instance became a mob and acted like one, quite the last thing that should be condoned in a government.

That the men in Stamboul did not issue an order for the massacre may be believed, but that does not absolve them. A government that cannot even control its own army is no government at all, and, being that, it has no *raison d'être*. There is another aspect of the case. A government may not always be able to protect every person within its domain, but it must be able to afterward punish the crime committed—and punish that crime in such a manner that the punishment will be a deterrent to others. For mob violence there can be nothing but reprisal.

Even in this the Ottoman government failed. Instead of hanging the entire garrison of Adana, one half for taking part in the massacre and the other half for not coming to the assistance of the Armenians, the troops were transferred and a few of the leaders of the riot were shot. But this leniency toward these vile brutes may have been due to the disinclination of the government to let the Armenians have justice—to put it mildly.

I spent a day among the ruins. It was a sad sight. The rectangular spaces formed by the bleak walls were filled with the debris of the upper floor and roof. Broken furniture, rusty bedsteads, decayed mattresses, and the remains of other household furnishings could still be seen. I was told that hundreds of bodies were still under the debris. On the window-sills flourished grass, and vines from the neglected gardens had crept over the walls. Here and there the branches of trees had spread across the ruins. It was a beautiful day and one could not help thinking of the line:

Where only man is vile.

OSMANIEH, SYRIA, *May 2d.*

On the road again—this time trying to get over the Amanus range.

I am spending the first night in my young life in a regular Turkish *han*. The place looks most uninviting. But there is some European company —two very taciturn Germans, whom I met on the train from Adana and who confess to be going to Aleppo—I mean, who aver that.

It is their baggage that excites my curiosity. Each of them has a small trunk, and the two of them together have about a dozen of sheet-iron boxes about the size of a large suit-case. The things are very heavy, as I discovered when, innocent-like, I tried to help them get the things on the wagon. We'll see!

There are all kinds of epidemic disease in this town—everything "blessed" Syria has in that line, cholera and typhus not overlooked. I propose to pass the night on the gallery. I arrived at that conclusion after I had surveyed the little cubicle of a room assigned me. The building must be at least a century old and it has never been renovated. The room may have been cleaned occasionally. It certainly has not been swept in a week.

There is a peculiar sort of bed in the room—a board with a narrow and thin cotton mattress on it. On the mattress lies a sheet which once was white, but which is now of an asphalt color. The pillow-case is not much better off, and the one blanket is black, heavy, and stiff with dirt. A small home-made table of pine and a rickety chair complete the furnishing. The floor is bare and dusty, and the walls are black with smoke. There is no fireplace, of course, and since the winter in the Cilician Plain is often severe, a *mangal* is put in the room. When the charcoal is not well burnt through an uncomfortable amount of smoke is generated by the *mangal* fire.

But the *han* is an interesting place. The building, like most others of its type, is in the form of a "U," a quadrangle open at one side. A wooden gallery around the yard gives access to the rooms. In places this gallery has sagged, so that one gets the sensation of walking on a roof.

Most of the guests turned in early. With a long overland journey behind them, and another before them, they were a tired lot. There being no eating-place attached to the *han*, the guests ate anywhere and anything they had brought with them. ·I did the same With the filthy yard reeking with every smell imaginable, that was not easy, and the unlovely habits of the camels thrown in, or out (those who have traveled in the East will understand), eating was not an enjoyable task.

The crowd in the *han* is an interesting lot. Its most inviting members are the Turkish officers.

Many of them are on leave of absence from the Caucasus and Suez Canal region. They have traveled far, but do not show it. The uniforms of most of them are spick and span. Faces are shaven and clean, and show a good spirit.

The other guests seem to come from all parts of the empire. Those in store clothing are Greeks and Armenians, and Syrians of the city. Business of one sort or another causes them to move about in these parlous times.

The men in the cloaks—burnooses—and fezes and turbans would make a fine side-show in any circus. They are a most picturesque assembly. Headgear divides them, for me, at least, into Syrians, Bed-ouins, Arabs, Persians, Kurds, and Turkomans. I suppose some expert could split them up better.

What the business of these travelers may be is not so easily determined. The camel-trains in the yard belong to them. The many bales of merchandise the animals brought in seem to contain mostly wool, finished textiles, and carpets and rugs. One of the befezzed ones seems to be a merchant in silks. One of his bales needed repacking. While he and a servant were busy with that I took stock of his wares. Seeing me interested, the Arab—such he seems to be—motioned to me to step closer and inspect his stock.

I could do a little business with those silks on Fifth Avenue. Simply gorgeous are those fabrics! The man explained to me, in the poorest of French, that his silks are dyed with vegetable colors. They look it! He had a piece of yellow silk of so fine a texture and hue that one would take it for a sheet of beaten gold. The Arab was proud of this. As he looked at the silk he smacked his lips. Whether it was the beauty of the fabric or the prospective profit that caused his satisfaction I do not know. At any rate, he will sell the silks at Damascus.

I made some inquiry concerning the pass road across the Giaur Dagh. An Ottoman officer, whom I approached on the subject, was of the opinion that it was a most difficult one. He suggested that I would do best not to ride in the *yailah* going down toward Islahiah. Something might happen to the brake and then I might fall several hundred feet without striking once, and then for the last time.

VII

IN THE LAND OF RUINS AND ROMANCE

SOUTH of the Amanus mountain chain lies a very interesting part of Asia Minor. It is a part of the earth for the possession of which many nations and kings have fought. The battle-fields of old and our own era crowd one another. Whoever held the *Pylæ Syriæ* was master, for a time, of Syria and the adjacent countries. But nobody ever held that gate for long.

Of course there was something to fight for. Once upon a time, before the great forests of the district disappeared, the site was well watered. The soil is rich, and the climate one of the best for the husbandman. Through the Syrian Gates also moved much of the world's trade anciently, and to the ports of the Levantine Sea came the best merchandise carried on the Mediterranean.

Large cities came into existence. They are no more. Even the sites of most of them are not known; Tigranocerta, capital of the Armenian king of kings, Tigranes, is such a case. Quite recently accident led to the discovery near Sendchirli of the site of what is said to be the capital of the Hittites. It is not so very long ago that Baalbec was exca-

241

vated. The most interesting part of Damascus should lie some fifty feet under its present surface. In Deerat we have one of the many towns in the Syrian desert that are being overwhelmed by their own cemetery. The burial-grounds are ten times greater in extent than the area covered by the hovels of the living.

To Deerat and other places of that sort the war could make no great difference. So far as I could ascertain, the war mattered nothing at all to the people of Deerat. What difference could it make to an Arab in a desert settlement who ruled in Constantinople or who collected taxes of him?

So, while there was fighting at the Dardanelles and on Gallipoli, while it was once more "open season" for the Armenians, the actual background of the Ottoman Empire knew hardly that there was war. For the desert men will not fight and in a desert the others cannot fight. And the background of Turkey is desert—desert in more respects than one.

But Syria is pre-eminently a land of romance. For centuries it was the scene of martial clash, the incubator of lust for empire, and now and then the monument of human achievement. If the Syrian cities could rise from their ashes we would have a real fairy-land. One metropolis would crowd the other in a setting of fertile fields, splendid vineyards and orchards, mighty forests, and snow-capped mountain ranges.

But the soldier and time have destroyed the magnificent capitals, and the man with the axe and the fat-tailed sheep and the goats have ruined the countryside.

The Turk could have prevented the latter. He would have done it had he ever taken an intelligent interest in the domain that fell so easily into his hands.

With that I am not concerned here, however. This is a simple account of Turkey in war.

ISLAHIAH, SYRIA, *May 3d.*

A *yailah* is about the most uncomfortable thing one can travel in. It resembles a barrel on wheels. Usually it is drawn by two horses or mules.

The *yailah* is built to suit the habits of the Orient, where people still prefer to squat on their haunches instead of sitting on a chair. It is this fact that makes the conveyance a thing of torture to the Occidental. The floor of the carriage is flat. There is no seat. You can sit baby fashion, or *alla Turca*. You can lie down full length, even—to discover how bad the roads are. Each jolt upsets your internal arrangement. You are constantly in pain. So what you do is to sit again baby fashion, or *alla Turca*, hoping that the trip will be over soon.

In a *yailah* my trip from Osmanich was continued, across the Amanus range and into the plains south of it.

As far as Mamoreh we had a fairly good road. Then the ascent of the Giaur Dagh began over interminable serpentines, through deep gorges, and along precipices affording a would-be suicide a clear drop of many hundred feet.

Everywhere the Turks are building new roads or improving the old ones. I was struck by their endeavors in that line, though rather disgusted at the same time, because my *yailah* had to go over many miles of roads freshly covered with crushed rock. It was the worst form of traveling, and progress was not rapid. The road improvement is in charge of Swiss, German, Austro-Hungarian, and Ottoman engineers. Most of the work is done by the hand labor of Armenians. I passed two rock-crushing plants and about a dozen steam-rollers, whose coughing must have sounded odd to the old mountains.

New grades were being laid to replace the old. While the road has occupied its present site for centuries, it had not been used to any extent for wheel traffic. The camel caravans prefer short cuts. But the war has changed that. For artillery-parks and supply-trains easy grades are needed. The Turks are now about to provide them.

The Amanus range, while not as high as the Taurus, is nevertheless a magnificent mountain chain. Little denudation has been going on here, so that even the highest peaks are covered with vegetation. Splendid forests of deciduous trees and conifers abound. Here and there one sees groups of venerable cedars—brothers of the trees that have made the Lebanon famous.

There is much pasture in the range and horned cattle is plentiful. The soil of the valleys is rich and well watered. Elevation and soil and climatic conditions produce a great variety of crops, among them the following staples: Indian corn, wheat, barley, oats, rice, tobacco, sugar-cane, cotton, opium, and mulberry for silk culture.

With the completion of the Bagdad Railroad

217

the district is bound to become one of the most prosperous in the Orient. Together with the Cilician Plain and the Aleppo country it will become a veritable granary.

Of course, it rained some more in the morning. The air was sultry, so that, when we had to get out and walk in order to spare the animals, we perspired freely. After many uncomplimentary remarks concerning Turkish roads and Turkish things in general, the *yailah* included, we got to the head of the pass, thinking that from now on it would be easy sailing. All of which was a mistake.

The road from the head of the pass to Sendchirli, where the long tunnel of this part of the Bagdad line has one of its openings, is about the most dangerous bit of mountain road I have negotiated in a four-wheeler. The high ridge over which the road runs drops into the valley of Islahiah here without any sort of warning, as it were. There is a spot where an overturned carriage would roll and fall some 4,500 feet—from the crest of a high escarpment to the level of the Mediterranean. When I looked into this frightful chasm and thought of the poor brake the *yailah* had, and of the advice given me by the Turkish officer, I decided to walk. My two companions had seen worse in Persia, they said.

In Persia?

But I noticed that they, too, left their *yailah*, when on a steep grade the harness was almost stripped off the horses, because the brake refused to hold. That not every one of these *arabadchis* has been hurled into eternity off this road shows how kind Providence can be to imbeciles and fools.

So I drudged valleyward in the hot noon sun. But the discomfort of this exercise was forgotten in contemplating the spectacle offered by wagon wrecks and animal skeletons hanging in the tree-tops below the "trail" road.

At Sendchirli we reached the foot of the Giaur Dagh, glad that ascent and descent of it were behind us. I had a peep at the entrance to the big tunnel of the Bagdad Railroad, which is 5,100 yards long, then got into the *yailah*, to go at a fair clip through a very pretty woodland country in the foothills.

Beyond that lay fields upon which the crops were ripening. The valley of Islahiah, in reality part of the Armenian plain, has a rich soil and a warm climate, as I deduced from the dust.

At sunset we bumped into Islahiah and put up at another *han*. Had a supper of *yaourt*, cucumbers, and bread, and then, dead tired, turned in, defying fleas, bugs, and every disease known to humanity.

RODJO, SYRIA, *May 4th*.

Climbed across another range of steep hills, the Kurd Dagh, this morning, and then followed the Hamus Tchai almost to the Mediterranean. At first the road was fairly good, but about ten o'clock we had to get on the right-of-way of the Bagdad Railroad. Noticed that everything was ready for the line—roadbed and stations, but there were neither ties nor rails in evidence. These were to come from Germany to Alexandrette, the nearest port, by ship, but the Allies' fleet has spoiled that part of the program.

Saw a very odd and interesting natural phenomenon this morning. From a lone hill in the valley spurted the finest of spring water in all directions. I counted sixteen brooks having their sources in the hill. Evidently a geological fault. Most of the water in the Hamus Tchai comes from this valley.

About noon we reached the foothills of the Kurd Dagh. Another laborious ascent had to be made over innumerable serpentines. From the valley near Karababa we could see that the pass road was very animated. My glasses showed that a great deal of artillery, also some infantry, was coming toward us.

While the long column passed us our *yailahs* had to stop. The dust almost suffocated us. The troops were part of the force which the Turks have kept near the Suez Canal. They were being raced back, because, as we dimly learned, something has happened on the Gallipoli peninsula—the Allies have landed there. I prayed that my "base" man would have enough initiative to take care of the situation.

My two companions are not quite so mysterious now. Little by little I have gathered enough data about them to know what errand they are on. They are going to Persia on a mission of some sort. The freight of the sheet-iron chests is gold—minted gold. One of the two—I can't give their names—has been a physician in Shiraz, and the other has in the past been connected with the German legation in Teheran.

Copyright, by Underwood & Underwood

It would pay some desperate *arabadchi* to drive their *yailah* over a precipice, he jumping at the right moment of course. They insist that their "baggage"-wagon always travel in front of them, and that it never get too far ahead. What has surprised me is that they do not unload the gold at the *hans* and have it brought to their room. They are not so foolish, however, as to direct attention to the "medicine"-boxes in that manner. They stand guard over the treasure at night, watching the wagon from the window, when they cannot find a good excuse to sleep on it.

Well, it's none of my business, anyway.

Here at Rodjo ends the French-Syrian railroad. The French never were great railroaders and this line shows it. The station here is a puny affair. There will be a train some time in the afternoon, says the Armenian station agent. The Turkish officer in command of the *étape* is quite the funniest thing I have seen in a long time. His grade is that of major. But that does not keep him from running around with his tunic open, showing a dirty undershirt. At the end of a short pair of legs, incased in riding-breeches, swing a pair of red carpet slippers. His calpac sits in the nape of the neck.

ALEPPO, SYRIA, *May 5th.*

Nobody here knows when the next train leaves for Damascus. I wouldn't mind that so much if I hadn't just learned that two German journalists passed through here two weeks ago, bound for Arabia to pick up Lieutenant von Muecke and his

Emden crew somewhere. Even that I wouldn't mind, were it not that von Muecke is reported as having reached Djedda, near the head of the Red Sea.

Well, one can't do more than one's best. They want too much for a special train to Ryak, so I will have to wait. I do hope that the news I got at the local "base and line of communication," that no newspaper report may be telegraphed from south of Damascus, is correct. That is a point in my favor.

Aleppo is not a bad place. It is fairly modern, except for the old castle in the center of the city. It has several parks, electric light, and other modern improvements.

SOMEWHERE OFF THE LEBANON, *May 7th.*

As luck would have it—and when has luck ever deserted me?—I got this train last night, and now I am bumping along over the "Homs & Hama Extension R. R.," through a country that has more history than is good for it.

To the right of me lie the eastern reaches of the Lebanon—worst scenic disappointment I had in my life. The only thing that looks at all worth while is the snow-cap on a central peak; the remainder of the view is just flinty barrenness—rock walls, boulder fields, stony expanses without trees, without scrub, without grass. Where are the charms of the Lebanon? I see none of them.

It is a little better in the valley I am going through. Ahead of me lies what seems to be a park. From over its treetops rises in majestic

222

proportions a portico—six columns supporting an architrave—Baalbec the Splendid.

The trains come to a halt in the station at Baalbec Through the fruit-trees I see a complex of massive walls, of more columns, of towers, of ramparts. I can make out the outline of what seems to be a temple. But all that when I come back. Right now I am busy running down a story.

DAMASCUS, *May 8th.*

At eight to-night my train leaves for Arabia over the Hedjas Railroad. So far all is well. Lieutenant von Muecke and his men left El Ullah this afternoon, bound for the north. I am to meet them somewhere along the line on the special train which Meister Pasha, chief engineer of the Hedjas Railroad, has ordered for himself.

So far my favored colleagues have not been able to file any part of their story. They may not "scoop" me, after all. They won't if I can still prevent it. But the chances look slim. The German newspaper-men have too much of a start over me. Maybe hard work will do it.

The trip on the narrow-gauge line from Ryak to Damascus was most interesting. First we crawled through a hilly country exceedingly well cultivated, and then we descended into the cañon of the Barada River—the parent of Damascus.

I am not surprised that the engineers who planned the line decided that they would have their hands full with a narrow-gauge, let alone a standard, line. It seems to have been a question how to get from the heights of Mount Hermon to the lower desert floor upon which lies the city. And then, I suppose, it was also somewhat of a problem how to get up again.

As if afraid to start downhill, the line hesitates in many zigzags near the head of the gorge. It bends this way, squirms through a maze of dolomite crags, and finally makes up its mind that the southern wall of the cañon is the most likely for its purpose. The tunnels are not long, but they are many. Much of the road lies on high stone revets. The curves allow one to shake hands with the engineer. The smell of hot brake-shoes is constantly in one's nostrils.

The rickety old cars squeak and tumble along over a roadbed where every fishplate needs attention. There is one consolation—should anything happen, the car will not fall far. The tall poplars which fill the valley, as cornstalks do a field, would break the descent without fail.

These poplars, by the way, are one of the singular features of the Barada Cañon. They are planted closely together, have no foliage except for the crown, and, having to fight for every ray of daylight, they are unusually tall and slender of trunk, even for trees of that family.

Under the trees runs the Barada in the deepest shade. What little light the high cliffs and walls permit to enter is absorbed, as it were, by the poplars. The Barada races along in semi-darkness. Its bed is a succession of falls and cataracts and rapids. There is enough water-power here to supply all of Syria and Palestine with electric current. So far this energy is utilized only in part.

The cliffs and walls of the gorge show many caves. All of them were inhabited in prehistoric times, when man was either too stupid or too lazy to build himself a house. In historic times they have often been the place of refuge of the inhabitants of the district when the invader came.

At last we seem to have struck bottom somewhere, as the Ottoman engineer officer in my compartment put it. He is going to El Arish to bring the water-supply of the Suez Desert into good shape. He is not very optimistic, however.

Where is Damascus? I ask.

We are now below the garden-levels. The water of the Barada tumbles about us from a thousand irrigation sluices. It breaks from the foot of garden walls, issues from culverts of the road, runs along on little stone ducts, disappears in tunnels, and rises in siphons.

The officer explains that Damascus would not exist were it not for the Barada.

"I would place a statue to the river in the city," he says. "Whatever Damascus has and is has its origin in this body of water."

The train runs through gardens. Such gardens! In them stand the stateliest of nut-trees and chestnuts. Fruit-trees of every variety crowd one another for space and sunlight—for the ground is costly and must be well used. The corn is ten feet high and has from two to four cobs on it. Vegetables stand thick. I saw *salade romaine* two feet high. And flowers—only Mexico City has such flowers, on the floating islands in the lake.

Near the station the Barada is no longer the

impetuous youngster of the gorge. They have forced it into a broad and deep masonry channel here So it meanders along, under bridges and past public buildings, toward the Bahrets Sherkiyeh and El Kibliyeh, out of the desert, still dispensing largess *en route* to the tillers of the soil who care to lift its water upon their parched lands.

And still some people wonder why river worship was at one time so fashionable.

I had to make things move when I heard that the *Emden* party was on its way up. There was no regular train, of course. So I went to the management of the Hedjas Railroad to hire a special. That was out of the question. They didn't have a locomotive to spare for the work. Was there no gasolene hand-car? Never had such a thing on the Hedjas! I suppose not. What they don't do here to-day they do to-morrow, or not at all.

But luck is a faithful servant of mine. I was informed that Meister Pasha, chief engineer of the road, was going south to meet the party. Maybe he would take me along. He has promised to do so.

DEERAT, IN THE GREAT SYRIAN DESERT, *May 9th.*

The special pulled up here early this morning to wait for the "Emden Special" from El Ullah, which was due about 11 A.M.

That being the case, I decided to have a good look at the "city" of Deerat. I saw the place from the station platform—a line of low buildings on a ridge in the desert. It did not seem worth while until Meister Pasha explained that the high walls to the south were the remains of a Roman settlement of some note.

It was then seven o'clock. But the heat was stifling even at that hour. I was told that the smoke and steam of the "Emden Special" would be seen across the desert an hour before it reached Deerat, and that I could not miss it. With so much time on hand I decided to look over the "city." I might never get that chance again.

The first Deeratians I met were some Arab maidens at the well. But Jacob was not looking for a Rebecca, though several Rebeccas were present. They were drawing water from the well in a manner followed throughout the East. A jar is fastened to a rope, lowered and manipulated until it is full and then pulled up.

Though Mohammedans, these Arab women here do not wear the veil. I suspect that they are too homely to make that necessary. And then it is frightfully hot here. Most of the women wore but a single garment, the *goemlek*, from which we Occidentals have made the word "chemise"—the wearing of shirts having originally been a strictly Arab fashion.

I thought I would have a drink of water. The fluid the women were pulling from the well seemed palatable and cool. It was both.

There was no difficulty in making the Arab girl understand what I wanted. She smiled and handed me the jar. I noticed that an olive branch had been tattooed into her chin. That did not improve her looks greatly. The design was done in a dirty green tint. Apart from this disfiguration the girl was not bad-looking.

To my question, did she speak Turkish, the young woman replied, "*Heir, effendim!*" ("No, sir!"). That much she understood, anyway. Then she salaamed deeply and gravely, loaded the jug on her shoulder, and walked away.

I was going in the same direction, but did not want to press my company upon her, so I gave her quite a start. But she heard me coming, stopped, and waited until I had caught up. She made a remark and laughed roguishly. I said something in Turkish.

"*Tuerkdche as bilirim*," she said, with a smile. "*Arabdche bilirmissinis?*" ("I do not speak Turkish. Do you speak Arabic?").

It was my turn to say, "*Heir, effendim.*"

We walked on. She kept up her prattle. Evidently she could not fully comprehend why I did not understand Arabic. Looking full into my eyes, she would repeat and repeat the same words, and shake her head when I shrugged my shoulders.

I thought the incident ended when we reached the first of the adobe hovels of Deerat. The girl thought otherwise. I had salaamed her in parting. This she would not accept. With a smile she motioned that I should follow her. I was puzzled. But there was no good reason why I should not accept her invitation. So I followed.

It seems that my companion lives under the ceiling of an ancient Roman temple. I say under the ceiling because the interior of the temple was filled with debris to within twenty feet of the ceiling.

228

IN THE LAND OF RUINS AND ROMANCE

An adobe wall has been placed between the columns and capitals of the dilapidated portico. There is a door opening with a mat as portière, which had been drawn back.

The interior of this odd home was well enough arranged. On the ancient walls hung several prayer-rugs. The floor was being swept by an elderly woman as the girl entered.

The young woman set the jar on the ground and began to tell the other something, pointing to the door where I stood. The older woman seemed annoyed or frightened. But that did not seem to worry the girl in the least. She poured some water into a smaller jug and handed it to me. It struck me that I was very much *persona gratissima*.

While I drank she prattled again. I caught the word coffee after she had repeated it a dozen times. Of course I would wait for coffee. I might never again have the chance of being entertained in a Roman temple at Deerat in the desert.

I was glad, moreover, to get out of the broiling sun; so I sat down on a mat, rested my back against a column carved by a Roman, and surveyed my environment with much interest.

The girl had brought a little *mangal* from a recess. Into this she heaped some dry cow manure, struck sparks from a steel and flint, and then fanned energetically with her breath the spot where the fire had started. No doubt I was to have coffee.

I had coffee. I have drunk better, but I have never sipped any under equally interesting circumstances.

But I had a train to look out for—a train which

229

I had come many miles to meet. I wanted to leave, but my little hostess would have none of that.

"*Yawash, yawash*," she would say.

I was in a pretty pickle now. I could not make her understand, and to my insistent repetitions of the words, *Demip jolu* (railroad) she would merely say, "*Yawash, yawash*," meaning that there was no hurry.

By means of the sign language I finally got the girl to understand that I wanted to have a look at the town. She seemed agreeable to that.

So I was to have company for the next hour or so. The girl left the temple with me, and, bright thing that she was, led me to the remains of the Roman settlement of which her home seemed to be a disjointed part. We walked through a long alley flanked with adobe walls in whose doors stood wondering inhabitants, and then came to what had been a Roman *aquarium*—one of the places in which those people gave their aquatic spectacles.

Deerat in those days must have had more water than it has to-day. The *aquarium* could not be filled in a week by all the water now available. Near the big tank lie the remains of a temple or villa; nothing of any importance, however. Without knowing the history of Deerat, I should say that it was never more than a garrison of the Romans.

Later we came to the cemetery of Deerat. One could not miss it.

Deerat's prominent feature is its cemetery. Around the town and stretching far into the country lies this *mesarlyk*. The town may cover one-half of a square mile; the cemetery extends over at least five square miles.

And what a cemetery! Not a single tree in it. Nothing but thousands of gravestones, most of them down. Between the gravestones stands thin bunch-grass, upon which a multitude of goats was feeding.

After a long and purposeless stroll among the gravestones we returned to town, where I met Meister Pasha and some other officials of the Hedjas line, who had come to meet the train.

When the girl saw them she salaamed and walked off. She seemed to be a little angry. I could not help wondering what was passing in the mind of this simple child of nature.

I have come across some old things here and there, but I had never seen a church turned upside down until I came to Deerat.

The town has two mosques. The larger of them, whose minaret can be seen for scores of miles in the desert, was a Byzantine church at the time the Arabs took Deerat. The Greeks had followed the Romans in the possession of the town. A church was built by them. It cannot have been much of a structure. When the Moslems came they converted it into a *dchami*.

For some reason it must have become necessary to rebuild the structure. And then, by some method of reasoning all their own, the architects decided to set the many columns of the church on their capitals. But that is not the worst of it. It was found that more columns were needed. There being no more carved ones at hand, the builders took huge slate splinters from a nearby quarry and set them between the columns to support the roof and ceiling of the mosque. The effect is most bizarre.

In all that country there is no wood—no trees. There is enough adobe for walls, but the substance does not lend itself to the construction of an arch or vault. Still, the houses of Deerat had to be roofed. In the end this was accomplished—as it had been done in the desert ever since some of its inhabitants tired of living in tents.

The material in the slate quarries was used. The huge blocks of stone are split with wedges until beams of the desired size are secured. These beams are then used to support the ceiling and roof. On them is placed the material of which the roof is made.

Much ingenuity is displayed in some of these "stone"-beam ceilings. After all, it is not easy to secure many good stone beams. One or two of them, as a rule, is all the average Deeratian can afford. But this quota would not hold up his roof. That is done, however, by trestling up on the main beam the smaller splinters in such a manner that a primitive arch results. Woe to the tenants of the house if ever one of the splinters breaks.

Meister Pasha has taken a great interest in this sort of construction. He proved an efficient cicerone, therefore. He told me that throughout the desert this system is in use. He has been in places where even the little furniture needed by the "urban" Arab is made of stone deals and timbers.

232

We took another turn through a part of the cemetery, walked again through the ruins of the Roman city, and then, having seen a tiny puff of steam on the hot horizon, we hurried to the station.

DAMASCUS, *May 9th.*

Everybody reads newspapers. Few people ever give the collection of news a thought. There is no profession that lives more by its wits than the newspaper-man. In fact, the man who is not endowed with a liberal quota of wits—resourcefulness—does not last long in our business. Competition is keen. Only the alert survive.

As I have already stated, two German newspaper-men—and I may say that they are prominent in the Central States—had rushed into Arabia to get a "beat" on everybody. Somebody had tipped them off two weeks before I learned that the men of the *Emden* were nearing the head of the Red Sea. They had gone to El Ullah, and even if they had not been able to get their stories on the wire, they at least had had ample time to write them. I was in Deerat, with not a single word of the really extraordinary account in my possession.

When the train pulled into Deerat I jumped aboard and began to interview Lieutenant von Muecke and his officers and men. It was hard work getting the story pieced together from the somewhat fragmentary accounts I drew from the weary men. But by the time Damascus was reached I had a clear picture of what had happened to a part of the *Emden's* crew out in the Indian Ocean, and later in the interior of Arabia, a country in which but few Europeans had ever been.

My first despatches consisted together of some 4,400 words. The total of the story ultimately ran into 15,000 words or 15 newspaper columns. Meanwhile my German competitors were ready to file their stories; mine had still to be written.

Here was a fine dilemma! I began to write as I had never written before. Only speed could save the situation for me, and then, knowing how things are handled in Turkey, I decided to have my story censored by the *vali* himself. I would also ask that almighty official to issue orders to the telegraph service that my despatch was to have precedence over all others. That was the only chance I had of getting my account through first.

It was almost seven o'clock when my copy was in shipshape. I got into an *araba* and instructed the driver to take me to the *vali's* palace. My many *chabuk! chabuk!* (quick! quick!) could not induce the *arabadchi* to take a friendly interest in my affairs. But a *medjidieh* (five francs) had an electric effect upon both the driver and the horses. Of a sudden life came into the man and animals. We speeded toward the palace at a clip that caused the street to be cleared five hundred yards ahead of us.

Luck was not having both eyes on me at that moment. As we came to the gate of the palace some outriders emerged, followed by the state coach of the *vali* and more men on horseback.

My driver could not understand what I said, but he was a good guesser. Thus it came that back of the *vali's* cavalcade trundled my *araba*.

I wondered where the *vali* was headed for, and had visions of having that manuscript still in my pocket next morning—a most unpleasant thought.

After much driving the *vali's* procession stopped in front of a *cinéma*, as they call a moving-picture house in Damascus—moving pictures in Damascus! I remembered then that the sailors of the *Emden* were to be given a moving-picture entertainment that night. The *vali* was to attend.

I hate being too forward. But this was a case of professional life and death with me. That story would have to get on the wires that night.

A sort of reception committee in frock-coat and silk hat rushed from the door of the movie to meet His Excellency. I got out of my *araba*, permitted the storm of enthusiasm to pass, and then joined the tail end of the *vali's* entourage.

A Turkish policeman held me up on the stairs. He wanted to get some *vesika* or other paper. I showed him the passport Enver Pasha had given me. The man couldn't read, anyway, so it made no difference to him. He remained obdurate until I said the magic word, "*Aleman!*" ("German!")

That helped instantly. No doubt the faithful *asker* thought I was an officer or something of that sort, an impression which my attire might easily create.

The house was dark when I got in. I could see the flicker of the moving picture on the ceiling.

235

No doubt the *vali* was in a box—in the center box of the house, if things were run regularly.

That box I found. I peeped into it. The box was dark. After a while I discerned the outlines of two men against the screen on which sailors were marching and counter-marching. Then I noticed that four men were seated on chairs. Back of them stood three policemen. I had found the *vali*.

I strolled leisurely into the box, sat down, and waited. They were showing some war picture—and a long one it was, as it well might seem to a man who had intruded thus into the presence of the great.

When the film had been run off the lights were flashed on, and the crowd applauded energetically. The *vali*, being a man willing to please, also clapped his hands. I didn't.

I was busy wondering how an introduction might be gracefully effected, when the *vali* looked around. He saw me and didn't seem to understand the situation. I could not blame him. I introduced myself. The *vali's* eyes grew bigger. So did those of the two men with him.

"I am here on very important business, Your Excellency," I said, in French. "I wish to have a newspaper despatch censored by you—the story of the *Emden* party."

One of the men with the *vali* grew indignant. I ignored him.

"But that is out of the question," said the *vali*, coldly. "In the first place, I am not the proper official for that—that lies within the domain of

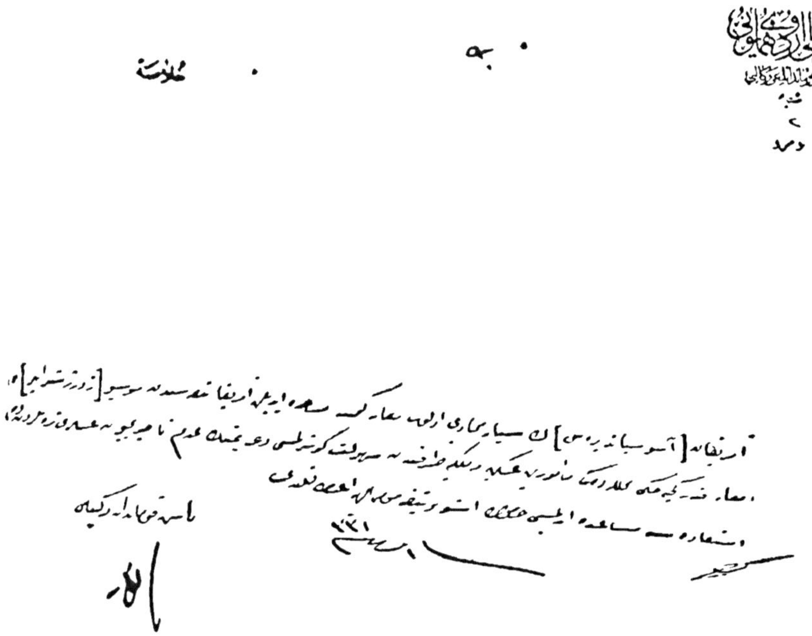

REDUCED FACSIMILE OF MILITARY PASS GIVEN THE AUTHOR BY ENVER PASHA

It entitles the holder to call for assistance upon all Ottoman civil and military authorities as far as Maan, the southernmost station on the Hedjas R R , to which Unbelievers may travel The heavy "pot-hooks" on the lower left constitute Enver Pasha's signature An Ottoman official seeing that signature could generally not do enough in his efforts to please the military authorities. And, secondly, I am here at an entertainment and can't be bothered with such matters. How, by the way, did you get into my box?"

I replied to that question in my politest French.

When I was through explaining, the *vali* had not yet made up his mind as to what he should do. The three policemen were ready to carry out any orders, and since the *vali* has rather far-reaching power over life and death, I speculated what those orders might have been a few years ago. That night they could be nothing worse than that I should be thrown out of the box without ceremony. But that was exactly what I did not want to happen.

But the *vali*, like so many Turks in high position, turned out to be a very reasonable human being. When I told him again that the story had to get off that night, and that there was nobody but he who could prevent my trying trip from being an utter fiasco, his heart softened.

"Have you got the story with you?" he asked.

Did I have that story with me!

"But it is in English," I said, regretting that I had not written the story in French, as I had at one time planned.

Dame Fortune had both eyes on me in that moment.

"My dear sir," said the *vali*, in fluent English, "I speak English almost as well as you do. Speak it better than French, and certainly write it better."

I could have kissed that *vali*.

He read the first three pages of the despatch. There were fourteen pages, however.

"It is very long," said the *vali*. "Tell me briefly what the despatch contains."

They switched on another film just then. While it was filling the dark, hot hall with its trembling lights I told the *vali* what my story contained.

"That's all right," he said. "I will assume the responsibility for it—seeing that this is a special occasion. When the light returns I will sign it."

But that film drama was long! I was glad when the lady committed suicide by plunging into her heart a dagger concealed in a bouquet of roses—paper roses, no doubt.

The light was flashed on. The *vali* signed with a red pencil.

"Now, Your Excellency, there is another matter," I began as he returned the copy. "The telegraph wires are usually overloaded, with the result that long despatches are put off until the rush has eased up. I cannot afford to have that happen to me in this case. Will you kindly instruct the telegraph office, by some words to that effect on the back of the copy, that this message must have the right of way over all others?"

The *vali* could see the point and forthwith exercised this kingly prerogative of his. Then we parted with several *salaams*, the movie show proceeded, and I raced to the telegraph office.

The first thing I showed the man at the *guichet* was the notice of the *vali*. Its effect was astonishing. The superintendent happened to be near. The receiving clerk called him.

"Certainly, certainly, monsieur! Your despatch will get on the wire this instant. As the clerk counts the words on a page he will hand it to the operator."

The clerk counted and counted. I paid my bill, and then asked the clerk what the *vali* had said in his instructions.

"He says that this office must see to it that the message must have the right of way over all others," read the clerk.

There is a great deal in mental suggestion. I had started by asking the *vali* that my despatch should be sent in its turn. I had finished by asking that it have precedence over all others. The *vali* had written that order.

With that great load off my mind, I spilled a little largess. One Turkish pound to the receiving clerk, and two for the two operators who were handling my story out of Damascus on two wires.

May 10th.

I have scooped my competitors so far as Constantinople. Don't know what the fate of the story beyond that point will be. I am not going to worry about that.

Reception last night at the *konak*. My friend, the *vali*, presided. Everybody worth while in Damascus was there to do honor to the *Emden* crew.

There was enough honor in the speeches for everybody. Tons of flowers of the most fragrant sort filled the large hall. The table groaned under the load of good things to eat. Champagne was served by the case—for, mark you, while the Moslem is not allowed to drink wine, he is allowed to drink champagne, for the all-sufficient reason that

240

the *Qua'raan* does not expressly forbid it. The great prophet had no means of knowing that ultimately there would be such a thing as champagne, so he did not include it in the list of beverages proscribed. The Moslem knows that, and naturally assumes that Mohammed has no objection to a glass of fizz. I am sure he hasn't.

The affair was really high class. There had been a movement on foot to have the non-commissioned men and privates of the *Emden* crew eat in another hall. But the *vali* squashed that promptly. He was a democrat, he said, and men who had shown such qualities were fit to eat with the Sultan. He had his way—and my company at table. I sat across from him. He was still amused over my resourcefulness.

There are many people from his vilayet in the United States, he explained, which he also gave as the reason for his being so well informed on American affairs. He maintained that the United States was no greater a democracy than the Ottoman Empire.

"We Ottomans are all equal. We have a Minister of the Interior who started in life as a telegraph operator. That ought to appeal to you especially," he said. There was a funny look in his eyes. I am willing to bet good money that, on second thought, he had arrived at the conclusion that I had taken advantage of him.

The speeches were short, and the dinner soon over, therefore. The *vali*, showing again what a sensible individual he is, made the following remark in his address to the *Emden* crew:

"And I will not say any more. I want you to have a good look at Damascus before you leave here. It is a city worth seeing. This hall, moreover, is hot. I did not prepare a speech, and I am sure the other gentlemen whom we shall have the honor of hearing to-night will not detain you long."

The hint was accepted. Those who had come to the banquet to air their oratorial talents decided to do that some other time—for which I was duly thankful. I had had a very busy day.

In the morning I had visited the bazaar and had imbibed much Oriental atmosphere; most of it is rugs. I was shown enough Bokharas, Persians, Syrians, and what not to supply a city of a million inhabitants. There were many dissertations on the fine qualities of vegetable dyes and their advantages over chemical dyes of the aniline variety. One of the things that interested me most was the heaps of arms from all Eastern lands, some of them dating from the days of the Crusaders.

A restful place is that bazaar. To believe what some Oriental travelers palm off, one would think that a bazaar is bedlam. Well, that of Damascus is not. The merchants sit on their piles of rugs and keep the *narghileh* bubbling and gurgling, sipping meanwhile fine coffee with a nonchalance that made me think twice before asking them to show me a thing. The venders of arms are no less aristocratic, and when it comes to the jewelry- and antique-dealers—Persians in black *kaftan* and black fez—why, I would not think of addressing one of Their Highnesses without salaaming my deepest.

Through the glass roof of the bazaar comes bright sunlight. Here and there the multicolored carpet awnings have been spread, so that the long, broad corridor, formed by the bazaar stalls, shows all the colors light and shadow can produce on the gorgeously tinted rugs and silks exposed for sale. Parts of the bazaar lie in dark arcades of masonry. The sunlight hits their interiors on the slant, showing in broad, yellow ribbons of light that would be the delight of any painter.

Camel-trains arrive and depart. The animals enjoy the coolness of the bazaar and kneel down with many a grunt of satisfaction that the end of the journey across the hot desert has been reached. The merchant counts his bales or boxes and makes out a receipt with a paint-brush which he dips into an inkstand the size of a young barrel. The *dewedchi* (camel-driver) gets a *bakhshish* (tip) and all goes well. Odd to say, the word *camel* is not heard in the Orient, *dewe* being used.

There are many women in the bazaar—Arabs mostly. Contrary to their sisters in the rural districts, they go veiled, the fashions in *yashmak*, *burundchuk*, and *feredcheh* being the same as in Constantinople.

Most of the women are slim, like the men. The Arab is not given to obesity; nor is the Turk, for that matter. Our notions in that respect seem to come mostly from people who know only the habitués of the Pera restaurants.

The dress of the men here is interesting. Many of them are clothed *à la mode*—store clothes. Then come the various garbs of the Turk—baggy trous-

243

ers, and others not so baggy, but all set off by a flaring sash belt. Some wear cotton pantaloons of white, with even a broader and louder *kushak*. Outing shirts and short jackets, both of them usually embroidered, complete the costume. There is the omnipresent red fez, and footwear of all descriptions.

But the Arabs from the desert who come in here to sell rugs and wool are the most picturesque in the crowd. Most of them can be singled out by the white turban which encircles the Ottoman fez of red. The turban hangs over the neck and covers much of the face. The body is draped in a brown burnoose of generous folds. The feet are in sandals.

Those faces are interesting. Brown from exposure and natural tint, clean-cut like a cameo, lean, and withal in repose, they convey an impression that is not easily shaken off. There is much dignity in the face of even the humblest son of the desert—a dignity stamped there, I take it, by the subconscious realization of the mind that it has passed the ordeal of elimination and proved its claim to fitness. Those who survive on the desert are one hundred per cent. fit. Life there shows no favors—the weakling perishes without exception. Hence these strong and handsome faces; hence also the lithe body, revealing strength and grace in every movement.

There are also brutalized Kurd *hamals*, and cowed Armenians—poor devils!—for whom it is once more "open season." Proud Persians strut about. Syrians waddle up and down as if they had learned to walk on a Paris boulevard.

IN THE LAND OF RUINS AND ROMANCE

It is an ever-changing picture—and one that is not fully appreciated except you happen to be in the right mood.

A few steps from the bazaar and all is different. A clanging street-car shoots past; you see that in the streets electric arc-lamps swing from pretentious cast-iron posts. The shops show "marked-down" tickets. You cannot read them, but you know what is meant by drawing a heavy black line through a higher amount in piasters and paras, and putting a lower one under it in red ink.

They don't do that in the bazaar. The Turk and Arab have one price. You pay that or no transaction takes place. The Greek may ask twice as much as he will take in the end, and the Armenian will even go to three times the sale price; but at any rate they do not expect you to believe that they could not write anything they pleased on a piece of cardboard, delete it, and then write something else under it in red ink.

Damascus is a strange mixture of the old and the new. It is a sort of little whirlpool in this part of the world where the Orient and Occident swing around in eddies, with the Orient still getting the better of it. The tallow candle has made much room for the incandescent lamp that gets its "juice" from the Barada River. The street-car, getting its current from the same source, has driven the *araba* into the background. And yet Damascus remains a delightfully Oriental city. Its architecture is still what it was in the palmiest days of Ottoman power, and its gardens are still the abode of the bulbul and the rose.

FROM BERLIN TO BAGDAD

BAALBEC, SYRIA, *May 13th.*

Baalbec the Magnificent lies beyond my windows. Still farther on is the bare, denuded Lebanon. I wonder whether those gentle slopes were as barren in the days of Cæsar Augustus, who caused Baalbec to be—shall I say built or created?

I have sat under the portico of the Temple of the Sun and marveled at the proportion of column and architrave. What master's mind conceived those relations of beauty to strength? I have wandered under the colonnade of the Temple to Bacchus and tried in vain to picture the mind that harmonized, with so striking a success, the forceful with the delicate, the intricate with the simple. It is difficult to associate those giant columns with the delicate design on the far ceiling, and still they belong together.

To-day Baalbec is a splendid ruin. Its courts are filled with masses of prostrate columns, shattered stone beams and masonry. The excavators ceased to work when the pavement had been reached. It was not their business to reconstruct. They had merely set out to discover, and they did discover, what is undoubtedly the acme of Roman architectural glory—if there be such a thing, for most of Baalbec is as Greek in its lines as the Parthenon on the Acropolis.

But here is a case in which the lines,

> The glory that was Greece
> And the splendor that was Rome,

blend well indeed.

Much of this splendor is left. Baalbec the Fortress was of great military importance to the Romans. Baalbec the Temples proclaimed to the Syrians that their masters in that far-off city on the Tiber ruled not by arms alone.

Time has not effaced this splendor. Though the Temple of the Sun be all down, with exception of the great portico; though the Temple of Bacchus be no more to-day than three great walls, and that of Venus but little more; though all the lesser temples have fallen completely, their very location upon this fortress platform of hewn rock and earth shows that worship was conducted here on a scale so magnificent that we of to-day find it hard to appreciate it.

But it is not of material splendor alone, nor of religious splendor alone, that Baalbec speaks. The empire under Augustus was liberal, and so the temple which in Rome would have been dedicated to Jupiter Zeus was here dedicated frankly to the sun—Baal. Rome had come to understand that you cannot force all men to believe the same thing, any more than all of them will call the same woman beautiful.

The mighty ramparts are still well preserved. The parapet is in place, the towers have not yet wholly yielded to the elements. All of these, like the temple structures, were of such strength that neither time nor the hand of the vandal could damage them much.

I found parts of the subterranean vaults occupied by the horses of an Ottoman cavalry regiment. Anciently these tunnels served the same purpose. Apt allegory! As the temples of Baalbec stood above the war-horses, so rested the Roman Empire on its military strength and prowess. And maybe the Ottoman cavalry horses support no more than a ruin. *Quien sabe?*

KARABABA, SYRIA, *May 17th.*

I am sitting in front of the shack inhabited normally by the engineer who is building a tunnel that runs under the shack, and which some day will allow Haidar Pasha-Bagdad passengers to get under, instead of having to go over, the Kurd Dagh, as I did again to-day.

To-night the engineer has company—the *Emden* officers and myself.

At Rodjo I found the major again, still dressed as before, despite the military crowd he had to receive. As a hard-boiled egg soldier he has no equal within my ken. But the important part of our meeting with Rodjo was that we had brought our wheel transportation along from Aleppo. The good *arabadshis* of Mamoreh and Osmanieh had heard we were coming, and fearing that they would be pressed into service—with little assurance that the government would ever pay them—they failed to look for business going southward. The *vali* of Aleppo, reminded of this peculiarity of the drivers in question, had signed an order for the requisition of the needed vehicles in Aleppo. The Aleppo drivers protested, but their plaints fell on deaf ears.

There is nothing like a good military training to make you careful. Proof of this, if proof were needed, is in the fact that we reached Karababa to-night instead of next week.

IN THE LAND OF RUINS AND ROMANCE

ISLAHIAH, SYRIA, *May 18th.*

Reception by the *kaimmakam* this noon. The official insisted that the column stay there for the night, but common sense and the prevalence of typhus in the place said him nay.

The reception was nothing to brag of in dimensions, but the spirit was there and the one thing that was good. Never tasted such awful tea in my life.

There was an entertainment, of course—a novel one at that. Other forms of visual pleasure being hard to obtain, the *kaimmakam*, bless his heart, ordered a number of bear-trainers to put in appearance. They did, and brought with them some real Taurus bears, also a monkey.

To the stopless notes of the *kawal* the bears danced until their tongues hung from their snouts by the foot. Being a humane sort of person, I suggested finally that the player of the *kawal* be given a chance to breathe, seeing that he had taken his last breath fifteen minutes ago, as far as I could judge by the breaks in his music.

Well, I learned something there and then. It seems that the *kawal*-player breathes *sotto voce,* or *sub rosa,* as you might say. The flute-player, for instance, has to breathe after so many notes. Not the *kawaldshi.* By some trick of his pneumatic system he manages to take in air even while he is expelling it. This enables him to run all of his notes together into that plaintive yelp in which he usually delights.

We were not the only spectators of the bear dance. To one side of the *konak* stands the prison, a small, one-story building of but a single room. Into this room had been crowded about forty prisoners of all conditions, many of them soldiers. I approached the place, but was driven off by the smell. To judge by the laughter of the prisoners, when the bears did something that seemed funny to them, they cannot have been in much anguish. Things in the Orient are generally different.

VIII

SOME CURIOUS PEOPLE AND ODD EVENTS

WITH the expeditionary forces of Great Britain and France fairly well rooted on Gallipoli by this time, I might now undertake a description of the landing operations and the position warfare that ensued.

But I am dealing principally with the events behind the scene. One of these was the activity of the British submarines in the Sea of Marmora. The commanders of these sea-hornets had finally learned how to get past the Turkish mines in the Dardanelles, and were giving the Turks no end of trouble. The more essential safe traffic on the Sea of Marmora became to the Ottoman forces on the peninsula the more hazardous it grew. For a while the Turks lost no more than one or two ships a week. It was not long before they lost from four to six.

With the supply of shipping very limited at the outbreak of the war and with no means of building new ships the problem soon became serious.

When I returned to Constantinople from my trip east and south I found that my friend, Raymond E. Swing, had returned also. He had looked over the Balkan countries and was now ready to view the operations on Gallipoli. After a great deal of trouble and delay he had been given permission to do that. But the British navy also had to be consulted.

Those who have read Rudyard Kipling's *Sea Tales* will remember the story of an American journalist who, under tragic circumstances, interviewed in the Sea of Marmora the commander of a British submarine. That Yankee reporter is my friend Swing.

I listened to his tale of woe with much interest and ill-concealed amusement.

"Say," said Swing, savagely, "tell me if you find that funny. I don't. I was almost drowned, and now I have a bad cold from exposure. I know I'll never get out of Turkey alive."

"Have some cherries," I said. "They were presented to me by a Turkish lady at Herékeh, who must have thought me one of the *Emden* men. The bunch of red roses tied with the red ribbon was also thrust upon me by the fair damsel."

"Of course you must always get your share of everything," commented F. Swing, eating my cherries, but still resenting that I had not taken a tragic interest in his sad experience. "I suppose she was very good-looking. What did she have over her face? *Yashmak* or *burundchük?*"

"*Burundchük*," I said.

Swing was now interested. He loves women under thin veils.

"Thought so! Homely women might hand you a sandwich. They haven't the go in them to fool around with flowers and cherries. Takes the good-looking ones to do that and do it right. Eh, what?"

The story F. Swing had told was good. I got him to go all over it again. I must immortalize it.

"Well," he started, "I wanted to have a look at things on Gallipoli. You had beaten me on this *Emden* thing, so I wanted to beat you on the other."

I nodded—to show my friend that his generous intentions were appreciated.

"I got the passports in the end. Then I took the first boat going to Akbash. Well, she wasn't a bad tub, but mighty slow.

"So when we got off the southern point of Marmora Island a periscope comes bobbing out of the water to port. I happened to be bending over the rail and saw the plagued thing first.

"By the time I had made the skipper understand what was what, the conning-tower of the submarine was above water and so were several feet of the forward deck of the little tub.

"The skipper understood that better than he did my Turkish.

"From out of the manhole of the conning-tower crawled a man—a British officer. Up to that moment I still hoped that the submarine would prove to be a German. Now I knew it was all up.

"The Turkish skipper had lost his tongue, it seemed. So I took up the conversation. The officer asked:

"'Who are you?'

"'I am Mr. Swing, war correspondent of the Chicago *Daily News*,' I shouted.

"'I don't want to know who you are. What

253

I want to know is what ship that is,' said the officer.

"'Then why didn't you say so?' I remarked.

"'Never been spoken to at sea, I suppose,' returned the officer, sort of fresh.

"'Not in that manner,' says I.

"'Well, what bloomin' ship is it you are on?' he asked.

"'Don't know,' I replied. 'Her name's on her bow in red letters. But I can't read it. Maybe you can.'

"The officer had squinted in the direction of the bow several times, but the Arabic pot-hooks were too much for him. They were for me.

"'What sort of cargo does the ship carry?' asked the officer, next.

"'Don't know,' I said. I knew that she had several guns and a bunch of ammunition aboard. But that wasn't my business. Was it?"

I agreed with my friend that it wasn't.

"'Are those sailors from the Turkish navy or are they merchantmen?' was the next question.

"'Merchantmen,' I replied, without knowing whether this was so or not. I didn't want to go to the bottom of the Marmora without making a bid for getting ashore somewhere.

"'What are they wearing those red hats for?' asked the officer.

"'All Turks wear red hats,' I answered. 'Those things are fezzes.'

"'I see,' remarked the officer. 'Tell the captain that he and his men will have ten minutes in which to get off the boat. I am going to sink her.'

"The Turks had already swung out two of the boats, and were getting the third clear of the davits. But there was great excitement, nevertheless. The skipper was one of the first to bring his precious hide into safety—never mind the passenger. The crew ran about in all directions, and in the end the submarine artist lost his patience. I was keeping my eyes on him, for fear that he might make a false move and fire a torpedo while I wasn't looking.

"'Tell those Turks that if they aren't off in two minutes, I sink the tub with them on,' shouted the officer.

"Two minutes seemed a short time to me. So I didn't bother about my baggage. I jumped to the nearest davit, seized a rope, and slid down into the boat. Then we rowed off.

"Well, the tub went down in two minutes. That fellow believes in being as good as his word. My baggage went down, of course—camera and all, such a good camera at that. All of my field equipment is gone, also my canned stuff."

Poor F. Swing!

"And after that?" I inquired.

"Well, we rowed out of the way of the explosion. The *E 14* dived out of sight and we started on that long paddle to Rodosto. They wouldn't let me land there at first, seeing that my passport read for Akbash. My landing at Rodosto was not entirely regular, therefore. The commandant of the place realized in the end that it wasn't my fault. There is something to that effect on my passport, which he wrote in red ink to have it

17

separate from the other authorizations. Then I got an *araba* to Muradlu, took the train there, and here I am—almost busted."

Such is the tale of shipwreck of Raymond E. Swing Effendi.

May 31st.

There is one thing which but few Occidentals do in Constantinople or anywhere in Turkey— see the inside of a Turkish home. F. Swing and I have done that on some other occasion. This afternoon we attended a tea.

It was Fuad Réchad Bey Effendi, the student officer from the Dardanelles, who suggested this. Since he became a full-fledged lieutenant he is hard to keep in check, anyway.

"I would like you to meet my sister," he said. "Let's go to the house this afternoon and have tea."

If he thought that reconcilable with the notions of a Turkish household, then far was it from me to say him nay.

F. Swing was delighted.

We hired a *caique* or *caik* or *kaik*—the thing is spelled in all possible ways—and had the boatman pull us across the blue Bosphorus. Never saw a body of plain salt water look so attractive.

Dear Bosphorus! The water, as said, was blue, in its best blue. Right above it perched the terraces of Pera and Galata, on the left; while to the right lay, dormant in the hot sun, that oddest of cities, Stamboul. I caught a glimpse of the Serai Park and the long façades of the Sublime Porte, of the hundreds of minarets, extending like frosted icicles into the burning sky; of the little pink houses in the treetops, and the old Byzantian wall on the water's edge, and felt that while a man might hate to leave paradise, he could do so willingly if the Bosphorus shores were to be his future abode.

The Leander Tower beckoned to me not to mind the ugly Gothic traits in the Haidar Pasha railroad terminal, and from Iscutar smiled other pink, yellow, and brown houses from the opulent foliage.

The Greek *caiquedshi* perspired freely. He was pulling against the current. That gave me time to enjoy the Bosphorus all the longer. There was the Galata Tower, rearing its proud form above the houses at its base. Further down were several marble mosques and their white minarets. Then came the Dolma Bagtche Palace, with the Yildiz Palace right above. The frowning, massive front of the German embassy in front of *Les Grands Champs des Morts* seemed to say that it had a right there — things diplomatic do have a way of intruding.

To the right was Kuskundchuk, with its villas and gardens. The Judas-tree was in bloom, and the wistaria had run riot. The oleander and murwer trees were blooming as they had never done before, I swear. Greens of the most opulent and softest shades greeted the eye everywhere, and out of them stood, in majestic gloom—as a reminder that after summer comes the winter, and after life, death—the tall and somber cypress.

We were pulling along the Asiatic shore now, to get out of the current. The houses bathe their feet in the cool floods of the Bosphorus. The cellar walls are pierced by arches, and under the arch stands the family's *caique*. Little jetties and piers run into the water at the end of the streets that climb up the steep hills—on stairs, if there is no other way. And still from everywhere dashes of Judas-tree, wistaria, oleander, and murwer. What a world to waste your life in! For wasting life on the Bosphorus is not what wasting it elsewhere would be. It is not a sin—it is a virtue.

The *caiquedshi* said he would wait for us at so much per hour. The price he demanded suggested that he thought he was dealing with patrons bent on a gallant adventure. We disabused his mind quickly.

So we walked under the trees, peeping curiously over the garden walls, climbed a stair uphill running in a wistaria bower, and came to the house of Fuad Réchad Bey Effendi, son of a former *juge de cassation* at an Ottoman court in Stamboul.

Fuad had telephoned, so we were expected. The Greek servant said as much when Fuad told her to notify his sister that we had arrived.

The house is large and comfortable, furnished in quasi Occidental fashion—at least the reception-hall and *salon* were. A sort of study and living-room combined was similarly furnished.

Carpets, of course, were splendid. One does not find poor carpets and rugs in a Turkish home. The cheap stuff is sold to the stranger. The furniture, what little there was, was good.

In the spacious *salon* there was but a single table, a Louis Quatorze thing with a heavy onyx top.

Six Louis Quatorze chairs, and a similar ottoman, completed the garniture. Fine lace curtains were floating in the breeze entering through the five open windows.

Beyond the windows facing the Bosphorus lay a wooden veranda. Underneath the veranda was a well-kept flower-garden, to one side a vegetable-plot, and in front nothing, the house standing on a steep slope. Over the garden wall I could see the roofs of the buildings in the street far below.

I returned to the *salon*. The maid had announced that the lady was about ready to come down.

F. Swing and I are very fond of Fuad. I am sure we could not love a brother more or better.

Again the maid entered. This time she stood aside to let a young woman pass.

We rose.

"My sister, gentlemen—Lahika Hannym! Allow me to introduce our guests," said Fuad, in polished French.

As Fuad mentioned our names we cracked our heels and bowed.

Lahika Hannym salaamed—greeted us as only the Turkish woman can greet. The grace of her slight bow, the short swing of her hand, the inclination of the head, the words she said, formed a perfect picture of what a greeting should be. Then she gathered the folds of her silk gown in her small hand and walked to the other end of the room, where she sat down.

The full longitudinal extent of the large room was now between hostess and visitors

As tea was being served Lahika Hannym grew

more sociable. She sat near us and began to ask questions—questions concerning the Western world, the world she wanted to see, to know, to understand. She knew nothing of the Occident, she said. All her knowledge of the other world, as she put it, came from French novels, and recently she had become convinced that the French novelists did not understand the part of the Occident which was not strictly theirs.

"Oh, I am not so lonesome!" she smiled. "There is my mother. You know she wouldn't come down. I asked her to come, seeing that you are such good friends of my brother's. But *maman* is still of the Old Turkey. I am a little more modern—just a little, not so much.

"And do you know that I had asked a friend of mine to meet you? Well, she, too, was afraid. She thought that her parents and friends might not like it if it became known that she had been seen by Christians.

"I told her she could wear a *burundchuk* or even a *yashmak*, if she wanted to. At first she was half inclined to do that. But in the end her courage failed her.

"Have you seen our garden? What do you think of it? It is not as large as we would like to have it. But father wasn't a rich man, and my brother here says the place is good enough for us. Isn't this war terrible—*très terrible?*"

Lahika Hannym had demonstrated that she could be communicative. Fuad smiled at some of the droll things she said. He began to tease her.

"Well, I can't know as much as you do," she

said. "You have been in Paris. I—well, I have spent all my life here. When I go to Pera it is quite an event. To go to the *magasin* becomes a veritable trip. Father used to take me along when he had business in the country. Since he died I haven't been anywhere.

"Fuad, you see"—she turned to her visitors— "never takes me out. And, anyway, since he has been in the army he hasn't had the time. Do you think we will win this war?"

We spent two most enjoyable hours at the house. Then we had to leave for Pera. Lahika Hannym waved a handkerchief as her brother and we went down the hill. A charming young woman indeed!

June 6th.

Well, we newspaper-men must work when there is work. We could never belong to a union regulating the days and hours of work.

F. Swing and I interviewed Captain-Lieutenant Otto Hersing to-day. The captain, commander of the German submarine *U 51*, had just been notified that his august master, Emperor William of Germany, had conferred upon him the order "Pour le Mérite" for having sunk on May 25th, at 12.30 P.M., off Ariburnu, the British line ship *Triumph*, and on May 27th, at 6 30 A.M., near the same spot, the British line ship *Majestic*. The captain has some other exploits to his credit. On May 27th, about 9 A.M. he sent a torpedo into the side of a British line ship of the *Agamemnon* type, and three days later he sank a troop-transport near Lemnos.

Before that, September 15, 1914, he had sunk the British cruiser *Pathfinder*, two French transports, and had shot up the port of Brest. Coming out of that port, he had disposed of five British merchantmen.

He is the first German submarine commander who has made the trip from Wilhelmshaven to the Dardanelles by way of Gibraltar. He needed just a month for this exploit, leaving the German port on April 25th and getting into the Sid-il-Bahr offing on May 25th, an hour before he fired his first torpedo.

This modern corsair proved a most interesting man. He is about thirty years old, tall and slim, blond, blue-eyed, hook-nosed, steel-jawed, tanned, and ninety-five per cent. good humor.

The fact that he had sent to the bottom of the deep some three thousand men in his time meant nothing to him, he said. That was his duty. When he was on duty he could not be monkeyed with; when he was off duty—well, would we have another bottle of champagne?

Like most German naval officers, Captain Hersing speaks English with a fluency that is surprising. Captain Hersing used slang phrases of American origin. Oh, he had been in the States. He knew them well. Had made many good friends in Buffalo, in Boston, in New Orleans. Did he know the States!

"Well, that fellow I got on the twenty-fifth didn't know what struck him," he said. "I can understand that. It's not to be expected that a thing that has never happened before in that spot should just happen to you. I fired the torpedo and got from under. There was no exchange of cards.

"But that I got the *Majestic* so easily surprised me. Of course she was duly surrounded by cruisers and torpedo-boats. But I got my line on a cruiser, let her go over me, lived in a sort of big drum as the propellers churned over my cockleshell, and then—bingo!

"Have another?

"You see this submarine life is good so long as it lasts. Every time we go under the water we may have closed our own coffin-lid.

"But you get used to that. . . . My! this stuff is good! You know I am a great admirer of the French. Their champagne is certainly what Homer meant by nectar. Was it Homer? I am not sure now. Well, it doesn't matter, anyway!

"And then life on a submarine is all hard work. Six-hour shifts, you know. Six wet hours, when you are out of the water, and twenty-four hours of bad air when you are under. You can't stretch in the blooming thing. When you poke your foot under the table you have upset the equilibrium of the shuttle, and when you eat a meal you have to rearrange the other cargo.

"Here is to a merry life, even if it be a short one!"

June 12th.

The building of the Ottoman Ministry of War in Stamboul is noted for its large rooms. Right above the main entrance are located two of the largest of them all—the antechamber to the offices of

Enver Pasha, located on the second floor, and the waiting-room on the floor above, where the visitors of Colonel von Bronsart cool their heels.

I was sitting in the *teneffuss odassy* of Enver Pasha this afternoon. It was about the time of the *muezzin's* afternoon call for prayer. His Excellency, the Minister of War and Vice-Generalissimo of the Ottoman Army, just then also charged with the duties of the Minister of Marine and a few other things, was very busy, I had learned, but would receive me as soon as he could.

I began to study the vast hall. I judged it to be sixty feet long, fifty feet wide, and twenty-five feet high. Noble proportions. On the floor was a rich carpet done in blues, slates, and white The walls were of neutral buff tint, the ceiling being very plainly decorated. There are mantels at both ends of the room. Over one hangs a picture of the first Turkish aviator—dead now.

Between the large windows, looking upon the great square, is a high mirror with a white frame. On the console in front of the glass stand two clocks, one showing the hour *alla Franca*, the other *alla Turca*.

The furniture in the apartment is richly upholstered in red tending strongly toward maroon —the red of the Ottoman fez. Four ottomans stand along the walls, there is a heavy carved table in the middle of the floor, and around it a dozen *fauteuils*. From the high ceiling hang candelabra of cut glass, relieved by disks in blue-and-white enamel

A very, very modern room. Nothing so far to

suggest that we are not in some Western Ministry of War.

But the wall facing the windows is very Oriental, very Turkish. In huge glass cases, divided in their middle by a door draped with a maroon portière, stand and hang specimens of all the arms ever used by the Ottoman army, and some of the victorious Ottoman standards—flags of red and green, all of them faded, all of them torn, all of them embroidered with the name of the organization that carried them into battle; also the star and crescent, and the peculiar snarled lines representing the name of the *padishah*.

There are arms here of every description. Firearms range from the most ancient flintlock to the prototype of the old Snyder. There are rifles and pistols—rifles that must have been served by two men, and pistols which only the brawny fist of an Anatolian could handle.

In swords and scimitars, daggers and stilettos, the collection is richer yet. Most of the blades have that vicious look which bending and flaming gives them. Some of the scabbards are handsome pieces of the gold- and silver-smiths' art. Many of the blades are damascened so finely that any little piece of them would make a handsome brooch or some such bauble. The same may be said of the many different forms of stirrups and other trappings in the cases. Every item in the collection is worth its weight in gold to the collector.

I was wondering from how many battle-fields these arms came, how much they contributed to the rise of the empire, and how much they had left undone to prevent its downward career when the *muezzin* in the open court began his summons to the faithful to come to *Allah* for prayer. I tried to picture to me an Ottoman staff-officer leaving his work at four o'clock in the afternoon to spread out his prayer-rug and pray for ten minutes. I tried to imagine what Enver Pasha would say to that, Enver Pasha, the indefatigable, the ever-ready and almost omnipotent genius of the war.

The *muezzin* continued. At first his voice was natural enough; then it reached a sort of falsetto, shrill and penetrating, rising and falling; now plaintive full notes, then quavers of uneven and disagreeable duration. Again the chant fell to the *muezzin's* natural tenor, and again it rose—rose to a pinnacle of shrillness that grated on the nerves like the screams of a saw under the file of the sharpener. Then it fell again—to die in several *Allah, Allah, Allah's.*

Boom! crash! Down in the courtyard bass drum and cymbals had taken up the lead in a modern military march. The light brasses and flutes were racing off in inspiring runs, while some oboes were leading the melody. The heavy horns brought up the rear with much dignity.

The Ottoman army's best band was giving its regular afternoon concert in the building. It followed the call of the *muezzin* like thunder follows lightning.

And yet the two did not fit together, it seemed. As objects of contrast they could not have been better selected. There was something astounding in the change from one to the other. The summons that had been heard a billion times from thousands of graceful minarets in the dormant cities and peaceful villages, and out on the still desert, did seem to be too good a companion for the crashing, blaring march the band was playing.

I turned to see what effect the thing had on the waiting visitors in the room. Most of the faces were wrapped in resignation to wait until their turn should come. They all wanted to see Enver Pasha, and many of them had been on the list yesterday, would be on the list to-morrow. Some of them would be on the list next week, next month.

It was not an uninteresting assembly. Several were in uniform. Ottoman officers, and German officers in the Ottoman service and uniform. They were dressed in olive-drab, booted and spurred, sabers hanging from tan belts, head being covered with the fur calpac, despite the heat.

A rather fit lot, I thought. Two of the officers had either come from, or were going into, the field, to judge by their *enveriahs*—a field headgear made of stiff cloth in the form of a helmet.

A goodly number of civilians were in the room. Turks in the regulation Ottoman frock-coat—cut like any other, but having a plain collar closing high around the neck; Arabs in turban and burnoose; an African sheik similarly dressed but black of face; two Persians in *kaftan* and black lamb calpacs; a dervish in a brown burnoose and high felt calpac, gray of color; two *hodjas* in gray frocks and green turbans; and a Greek contractor whom I happened to know. The Swedish military attaché came in, nattily attired in a dark-blue uniform, cavalry cut, faced with a lighter blue. A student-interpreter of the American embassy appeared.

The band in the courtyard took up a Wagner overture and played it well. I fell once more to studying the collection of arms.

I saw Enver Pasha. We discussed the latest phase of the operations on Gallipoli. But no interview resulted.

"You can use what I told you," he said. "But don't mention my name. I hate to see my name in a newspaper"

Smart child of a clever mother, I thought The wise statesman never gets into the newspapers with his consent.

June 26th.

The man and I—I can't mention his name; it would not be ethical—were having dinner in the Petit Club together. We were sitting at the "American" table, in the large general dining-room on the ground floor. My *vis-à-vis* did not know what I had in store for him, seeing that my invitation that he dine with me came quite casually.

"Joe" had served our *demi-tasses*. We had lighted our cigarettes.

"Got something to tell you," I said. To prepare him for the shock, I added: "There is nobody in the room I can tell you here."

My guest's eyes widened. I saw that he paled a little. I wanted to hear him speak, so that I might the better judge to what extent my words had touched him. But he wouldn't. Instead he looked at me in a mixture of amazement and dread.

"Might just as well tell you the worst. I'm sure you can stand it. They've got your number," I said, somewhat indignant, now that the man had dragged my profession into the mud.

"Got my number? What do you mean? Who's got my number?" asked my *vis-à-vis*.

"The Turks and the Germans—also the American embassy. Your passport wasn't renewed," I said, lightly, not wishing to add to the troubles of the young man.

"How do you know my passport wasn't renewed?" he asked, hoping to prove me wrong in what I knew to be a fact.

"I know it and you know it. You were told two days ago," I explained. "Now don't get fussy about this. I think there is a boat for Constanza to-morrow morning. You better take that and shake the dust of this city and country off your shoes. If you are here longer than the next boat the Turks will arrest you and try you for spying. The case against you looks bad—as you ought to feel, if not know."

Instead of showing a little appreciation of my efforts, the young man began to argue with me. I had to show him where he had been and when he had been there. In the end he admitted it. The great barracks in Haidar Pasha, where the troops for the Gallipoli peninsula were assembled, had been one of his favorite hunting-grounds. He had been in or near every arsenal around Constantinople. Only yesterday he had been seen loitering near the Osmanieh wireless station—he had, in fact, not overlooked a single point of mili-

269

tary interest, down to the anchorage of the *Goeben* at Stenia.

"I think you owe your freedom at this moment to nothing but the fact that the Turks and Germans still believe that you are an American citizen, which you know you are not. The American State Department has turned down your application for a State Department passport. How you got the other one from the American embassy in London I don't know. It is none of my business. Just take my advice and sail on the next boat for Rumania. It seems that the Sublime Porte does not want to have any trouble with the United States government concerning you. All that will change when they discover that the State Department has turned down your application. It will interest you to hear that I know that you were born in Scotland, are a British subject, and have served as a lieutenant with the English army in France."

The young man had nothing to say.

"That you want to help your country is very proper—is your duty," I continued. "But I do not think you ought to do it with an American passport. That you do it as a newspaper-man I must resent. For that I could see you swing from a tripod in the morning without turning a hair. Most of us try to play this ticklish game in a fair manner, and we can't stand for every Tom, Dick, and Harry fouling our nest that way. You better take that boat. If I were you I wouldn't stick to that game. You are not built for it. Permit me to say that I do not think you are smart enough. You must leave that sort of business to a slicker person."

Photo. by Underwood & Underwood

So we parted. It was a case of love's labor lost. I don't think the young man will ever appreciate how near he came to paying the penalty of spying.

July 3d.

F. Swing and I met Lieutenant Firle, commander of the Ottoman torpedo-boat *Muhawenet Millie*, to-day. In the night of May 13th he sank the British line ship *Goliath* in as daring a manner as any one could imagine.

Firle is a slight young man. My first impression was that I had met him somewhere on a picture showing a dancing-master in the act of pirouetting as a graceful example for his little girl students to follow. He looked positively frail. His face had something superintellectual about it. I never should have picked him as a naval officer—least of all for one who could have done what he did on that night.

It seems that he had for a long time occupied himself with a certain pet idea. That idea was that he could go out of the Dardanelles and torpedo one of the Allied battle-ships off Sid-il-Bahr.

Admiral Souchon and the Ottoman naval authorities had listened to this proposal with considerable patience but little interest. How could one of the lame ducks of the *Muhawenet Millie* variety venture out to Sid-il-Bahr and return? The wheezy engine was able to make fourteen knots, and the coal available would raise enough sparks under draught to show the boat twenty miles up the straits.

But Firle persisted. He wanted to do something,

18

and was sure that the something he had picked was within reason and reach.

In the end he won.

He waited for a sultry night—hours in which there is low visibility. All day long the *Muhawenet Millie* had stood by under the cape at Kilid-il-Bahr. When night came, Firle, hugging the shore, slipped down as far as the Shavan Dereh and waited.

Luck stood by him. He had good reason to believe that part of the Allied fleet lay in Morto Bay. Taking the risk of running onto a Turkish mine, he cut a little into Erenkoi Bay, and spied the lights of some boats under Eski-Hissarlik.

There was no longer any use sticking to hide-and-seek. Quite frankly he held for Morto Bay and ran into three British patrol-boats. He was not challenged by them; evidently the scouts were under the impression that the torpedo-boat which so unconcernedly plied the bay was one of their own naval force.

The *Muhawenet Millie* kept to her course for Morto Bay, but had not gone very far when she passed a British destroyer. Firle felt a little squeamish then. A destroyer makes upon the commander of a mere torpedo-boat about the same impression that the birch makes upon the bad boy. The destroyer is the particular enemy of the torpedo-boat, just as the cat is the particular enemy of the mouse.

Firle set his teeth and went on.

Around the Eski-Hissarlik promontory came much battle-ship noise. Also, as the lieutenant noticed, a signal spelling the Morse letter "O."

That was awkward. But Firle thought quickly. He didn't know what the letter might mean, but concluded that it was a question—one he could not answer. The best thing to do was to repeat that letter "O," impressing the other side with the fact that at least something had been understood. So Firle morsed "O" with his flash.

From the dark came another "O." Firle, holding the bow of his boat for the silhouette of the nearest big ship, again replied with "O."

For the third and maybe the last time the letter was flashed—from the silhouette he was making for, as the lieutenant now saw.

The *Muhawenet Millie*, three hundred yards from the line ship, the *Goliath*, laid to port, churned ahead until she was fully amidship of the big ship— and three torpedoes left their tubes simultaneously.

Three blinding flashes flared over the night; three deafening detonations, and the *Goliath* was a thing of the past.

The wash of the troubled waters nearly capsized the *Muhawenet Millie*. In the excitement that followed she got away.

Lieutenant Firle was modest about it. He thought it could not be done again in a hurry. I agreed with him, as did others.

July 6th.
They call it *Les Petits Champs* for short. Its real name is *Les Petits Champs des Morts*. It is part of the cemetery mentioned in Claude Ferrar's "*L'Homme Qui Assassinat*" as the meeting-place of Lady Falkland and the Colonel-Marquis.

FROM BERLIN TO BAGDAD

The unfortunates solicit no longer among the Turkish gravestones, however. Bedri Bey, the energetic chief of police over in Stamboul, has made that impossible. Now and then a veiled woman still flits through the cemetery, but the Levantine *demoiselles* who sit under the acacias farther up are keen rivals; so that, after all, the virtue of the cemetery is not entirely of Bedri Bey's making.

It is *Les Petits Champs* under the acacias, not *Les Petits Champs des Morts*, which I refer to.

Part of the cemetery was converted into a small amusement-park. You pay an *entrée* in paras—*iki grush*—for the privilege of walking on the gravel paths, sitting under the trees with a *consommation*, and listening to a band that might be much better.

That band has just murdered a certain Suppé overture. I watch the crowd under the acacias and on the paths and wonder. Ottoman officers, of Turkish and German origin, well uniformed and carefully groomed, stroll about. They are from the Gallipoli and other fronts. After the trenches, and with death a constant companion, this place looks very good to them. Their demeanor shows that while life lasts one must make the best of it.

Greek, Armenian, Turkish, and Occidental civilians are plentiful. They have come to enjoy the cool air, the music, and the sights. Levantine families sit at the tables with tea or *grenadine*. All are happy. There is much laughter, and conversation in French, Greek, Armenian, and German. I hear some Italian, but no Turkish. They do not speak Turkish in Pera, when it is not strictly necessary. Though most of the people there know the language after a fashion, Turkish is a sort of linguistic *sanctum sanctorum* which few enter who do not have to.

The *demi-mondaines* and *badannas* mix with the crowd. In the Orient such little things do not matter much. Most of them wear expensive and tasteful toilettes; all of them stand in French shoes. Somehow the high heel seems more at home in Constantinople than in any other place I know.

The waiters rush about, serving the guests, and seeing to it that they are on the spot when a patron wishes to light a cigarette. On the number of matches they scratch for you depends the size of the *pourboire*. For some they carry letters to some other part of the park.

The band plays the last piece—a march suggesting that the afternoon's fun is over. Soon the crowd gathers its hats and parasols and disgorges through the two gates upon the rue Kabristan.

On the terrace of the restaurant linger a few Ottoman officers, among them General Merten Pasha. I take a walk on the gravel path myself.

The pasha intends to eat in the garden.

"It's too plagued hot everywhere except here," he says.

I sit down.

"A pretty spot indeed," continues the officer. "I am on sick leave. How did you like the March eighteenth affair? Haven't seen you since then. Where have you been?"

I explain.

Behind Stamboul sets the sun — sets in that "blond" mist for which the event is famous all over the world. Through openings in the tender filigree of the acacias break dashes of the Golden Horn —patches of purple water with shipping on it. A lateen sail floats past. A *mush* leaves a trail of white steam hanging in the gloaming on the water.

"Beautiful Stamboul," says Merten Pasha.

I agree with him.

Behind the royal blue silhouette of roofs and mosques stands the *blonde brume*, a sheet of dull gold through which the sun shows like a disk of the richest Indian yellow. The sky directly above the Golden Horn melts from the color of a hot sheet of brass into lighter yellows, delicate greens, dashes of azure blue, and farther up advance the sentinels of night—deep blues and purples.

A marvelous picture!

I try to see how many of Stamboul's details can be distinguished. There is still visible a part of Serai Point. Above that loom the long walls of the Sublime Porte, broken by the massive body of the Aja Sophia and its four minarets. I can make out the mosque of Sultan Achmed. Its six minarets point into the sky like blue icicles. From the sub-profile of the city comes the Yeni Walideh mosque. Beyond that lies a group of public buildings and the Mahmud Pasha mosque. The great block over the Suleimanieh is the Ministry of War. I recognize the minarets of the Shah Sadeh and Sultan Mehmed mosques. Hundreds of other minarets and cupolas stand above the roofs and parapets of Stamboul Tall and purple cypresses show where the cemeteries are.

The whole is a fairy-land.

Now the Golden Horn can no longer be observed. Its far shore is lost in the gloaming. The lights of the shipping become visible. The sun has dropped from view. An arc of dull red shows where the scarlet disk disappeared. Above Stamboul float thin clouds and mist streamers of rose and blue.

The banks of light far below us are the lighted ports of the Ottoman men-of-war. There is more illumination along the quays now. The dreamy twilight is gone, the electric arcs in the street and the lighted windows of the houses usher in the night.

It is still under the acacias. No dinner guests have arrived yet. One eats late in Pera in the summer, and especially in *Les Petits Champs*, so that the evening concert and entertainment may be enjoyed.

A soft breeze blows. The waiters in white aprons and big shirt-fronts lean against the balustrade of the terrace, glad that there is a moment's respite.

"Why the Turk should be such a fatalist I am beginning to understand," says Merten Pasha. "After seeing such a sunset there is little more that can please. And still I would see it again. Would see it every evening. There are times when I would prefer being a beggar in Constantinople to anything anywhere else."

"The *bacillus Constantinopolus* has made terrible inroads in your case, Excellency," I remark.

"And in yours?" he asks.

"Pretty bad, Pasha, pretty bad. It will take a powerful antidote to get it out of me, and when it is taken out I won't like it."

FROM BERLIN TO BAGDAD

The cypresses below us, in *Les Petits Champs des Morts*, stand like columns of a temple to eternity—a temple as lasting as the peace of those resting around the roots of the tree giants. From a minaret somewhere comes the evening call of the *muezzin*.

Yes, *Allah* is great indeed.

July 7th.
Nuit blanche.

I sit at the open window. In the tower of the Greek church across from me the bells are ringing—have been ringing twice before. What is the matter?

The bells are quiet. From the interior of the church comes soft singing—hymns that seem wafted across celestial space. The voices seem troubled. They come in a plaint, rise a little in supplication, and then return to the pianissimo in which the hymn is carried.

The *muezzin* calls. In the east the new day breaks. Over Taxim and Pankaldi rises a blue light. The light lifts the walls and roofs about me from the darkness of the cañon-like streets below. On the gray stone and stucco the blue morning light produces tints of remarkable softness. Some genius of a painter is putting high lights on the picture of the city with the most delicate of pastels. The panes in some windows reflect a stronger light, the source of which I cannot see.

The singing continues.

Down rue de Bairam comes a herd of sheep, bleating. The ragged figure walking ahead is leading the animals to the slaughter-house.

Behind the sheep comes a baker, crying his wares—bread twists which he carries on a stick.

"*Simitchi! Simitchi!*" comes from his hoarse throat. "*Simitchi!*"

A milkman passes along. The commodity is carted in a leather bag on the loins of a donkey.

In the church somebody is now praying. There is a single voice—heard in chant.

But from the head of the rue de Baiiram comes other singing. It is the blind beggar I have heard so often. The man is led by a boy. To the melody of an old Greek hymn that may have been heard in the Parthenon, for all I know, the man sings how God robbed him of the light of his eyes when he was still young. It is a pathetic story. I throw a piaster. The white face looks up, while the boy fishes the coin from the gutter.

There is suffering in that face—not the suffering of material want, but grief over the long night.

The sound of the blind man's voice has been lost in the labyrinth of streets and alleys. Rue de Baiiram is quiet again.

The portals of the Greek church open. The head of a procession emerges from the gloom of the interior. A pope, followed by boys with white shawls over their shoulders, appears. Back of them, carried high on the shoulders of four sturdy men in black, follows a coffin. The coffin is still open. I see the outlines of the body under the satin coverlet, then the folded hands and a venerable face adorned with a long white beard.

What an odd practice to carry the dead to the grave in the open coffin!

FROM BERLIN TO BAGDAD

The procession descends the rue de Baiiram. The face of the dead man is turned toward the fleecy morning clouds. At the corner the sad train enters the sunlight which is now floating down a street from the Taxim.

I do not like to see those that have died a natural death. I am more at home among the hundreds and thousands of dead on a battle-field. This dead man reminds me too much of the possibility of having to die in a slow and lingering fashion, with one's face to the wall and people standing about the bed. The end I would have is the sudden and swift departure, with nobody around to see how I am standing the ordeal.

IX

A LITTLE TRIP TO "HELL"IPOLI

TROOPS *en masse* were landed by the Allies near and on Gallipoli on April 25th. The French landed at Kum Kaleh, held the beach and part of the village for over a day, and then withdrew. It has been said that this was a feint. I have no means of knowing whether it was or not. Meanwhile the British had set foot ashore at many points of the south and west shore of Gallipoli—at Eski-Hissarlik, Sid-il-Bahr, Cape Helles, Kum Tepeh, Sighin Dereh, Kaba Tepeh, and Ariburnu. But it required four days before Sir Ian Hamilton could look upon the operation as a success.

Despite the effective co-operation of the Allied fleet, the landed troops had great difficulty holding the positions above and on the beach. The Turkish infantry fought with unprecedented bravery. But in the end it had to give way. It retreated to better positions and a savage position warfare followed. Much of this is described here in a non-critical manner.

Üsünköprü, *July 10th.*
To-day I discovered what I am pleased to call the southernmost boundary of the *Sauerkraut.* Üsünköprü, in fact, is a sort of demographic boundary.

F. Swing and I are bound for Gallipoli. F. Swing, having been shipwrecked in the Marmora, decided to take the land route to the peninsula. He also decided to have me come along. I am such a comfort, he admits.

To Üsunköpru by railroad. Here we are.

The station-master, an Austrian, was glad to meet us, and to prove that he was glad he invited us to come to his house and have something to drink. His wife, equally glad and hospitable, insisted that we have a bite to eat. The sauerkraut boundary was established in that manner. Incidentally we hit upon the northernmost limits of rose jam and rose lemonade.

The sauerkraut was accompanied by broiled chicken. Then we had a *Mehlspeise* with rose jam. After coffee we had the rose lemonade. Future historians, wishing to draw a line of demographic demarkation between the Occident and Orient, can take Üsunköpru as one of their basic points.

Now we are in a *han*, waiting for the morrow, when an automobile will take us to the headquarters of Field-Marshal Liman von Sanders Pasha, at Yalova.

Points of interest here: The long bridge— *usün kopru*—across a flood-level, in the center of which now runs a trickling stream of muddy water. The bridge was built by the Romans.

KASHAN, *July 11th.*

Spent the morning conjugating Turkish verbs and drinking coffee.

The automobile did not arrive. Instead came

a motor-truck, overloaded before we and our baggage got on it.

Overloading even a motor-truck is bad. The result was that the motor balked. Don't know what is wrong with it, being in that respect the equal of the driver, who appears totally innocent of mechanics of any sort.

From a neighboring village we hired two water-buffalo carts for our baggage. After that we started on a weary tramp to Kashan. The road was none too good. It was dark, and I wanted to practise economy with my electric torch.

I am much in favor of having the roads ballasted — have been a good-roads advocate all my life—but I do hate to be first to go over the crushed rock. It's painful and tedious, especially in hot weather. At times it will even cause me to swear like a trooper, which is also bad.

Our march started at 6 P.M. sharp. It was sultry and hot. At 10 P.M. we saw the *luz* of Kashan, a large gasolene flame which lights up the central square of the place.

That was promising enough. But I have never seen a light for such a distance, nor ever followed so delusive a will-o'-the-wisp. At 11.30 P.M., tired and disgusted, we got to the place.

The Bulgars may be a gentle people, as they claim with emphasis, but I cannot say that they deserved this title while they occupied Kashan. Two-thirds of the houses are in ruins. Two-thirds of the population have gone to other parts.

BULAIR, *July 12th.*

Left Kashan in a hack. Four rode in that hack. F. Swing; a young Turkish lieutenant, M. Hadi Bey, 7th Comp., 9th Reg., 2d Division, South Group, Gallipoli, to give his full address; Mehmed Murad Bekdach Bey, son of Husani, and now member of the Ottoman General Staff, so reads his card; and I.

Our baggage follows on two escort wagons of the Ottoman army. F. Swing and I travel heavy this trip: tent, field beds, portable kitchen and toilet equipment, three hundred pounds of provisions, personal belongings, paper and carbon-sheets and pencils; maps, field-glasses, medicine, bandages, flea powder, eau-de-cologne, camera, credentials, and fairly good opinions of ourselves.

These opinions are due to the fact that we have persuaded the Ottoman General Staff to break, for our benefit, the rule it made after a certain pseudo-American, mentioned afore, had emerged as a full-fledged British spy. Major Sefid Bey, chief of the second division of the General Staff establishment in Stamboul, listened to reason, but only because we were the petitioners.

The ride was hot and dusty. Things improved a little while we crossed the Kuru Dagh, an inter-teresting hill range along the Gulf of Saros, covered with wood-lots and pastures, sown with villages and *tchiftliks.*

When we reached the end of the pass road, on the very shores of the Saros, we noticed a British cruiser on patrol off Bulair. It was after sunset, or else we would have drawn a few shells. The road is impassable in daylight, I am told. The British take care that no traffic goes over it so long as visibility is good.

The horses needed watering and a rest.

There are two islands a little way out. The cruiser headed for them when its commander had satisfied himself that near Bulair there was nothing to attend to. Near the larger of the Xeros Islands was another craft—a peculiar affair. Just a large kettle on a thin dark line—a submarine. It seemed to be greatly attached to the cruiser and yet not on friendly terms with it. For, as the large ship drew near, the submarine decided to take a plunge. No doubt it was a "U."

We watched the scene for some time, expecting that there would be an explosion soon. But nothing happened. So we turned to the *kawal* player who was entertaining his Anatolian brothers-in-arms.

The concert was made more elaborate after we joined the group. One of the men began to sing the song of the "Warrior's Bride," a song in which the warrior tells his love how much and how often he thinks of her. It is a bit of Anatolian folk-song of considerable charm and delicious *naïveté*.

We had to reach Bulair that evening. After a cup of coffee we went on. How uncomfortable an overcrowded hack can be! The legs of the four passengers were interlaced, so to speak. It was impossible to even wiggle one's toes. We were overjoyed, when we landed in the ruins of Bulair, to stretch our limbs.

A shelled city is no pleasant sight even in

daylight. At night it offers a most mournful aspect.

The split and wrecked walls of Bulair were performing a *dance macabre* as we bumped over the debris-littered street. At the fountain we got out to lave our great thirst. We had seen precious little water all day—since six in the morning, and now it was eleven at night.

Quite recently Bulair has been bombarded by the Russian armored cruiser *Askold*. I must say that the Russians made a thorough job of it. Not a house is undamaged. But firing upon a defenseless town is quite different from shelling a battery.

We were told that the *Askold* had wrecked the mausoleum in the cemetery—last resting-place of Selim, commander in chief of the Osmanli troops of Sultan Orchan. The general, landing upon the shores of the peninsula, swore that he would never return alive to Asia. He did not. He and his kind were to stay in Europe. After giving the Byzantian empire the *coup de grâce*, they overran the Balkan and all of southeastern Europe and then besieged Vienna.

A shell had struck the mausoleum, pierced the two walls, and then exploded without. The two sarcophagi in the interior had not been hurt, save that flying rock had chipped the stucco burial-casks a little.

No other Giaurs had ever been permitted to enter the mausoleum. So F. Swing and I, though used to being the first in many places, inspected its interior in the appropriate frame of mind and with the aid of matches. The sarcophagi, made of

286

stucco, as mentioned, are plain and homely affairs. Just two long cases with a "roof" top, the head of the top slanting toward the feet.

The Turkish officers in our company resented this piece of "vandalism" very much. I cannot see how anything but a wanton lust of destruction or the poorest of marksmanship could have sent shells into the cemetery, seeing that it faces the sea and was in plain view of the *Askold*.

The tomb of Kiamil Bey, modern Turkey's best-beloved poet and writer, had also been hit by a shell. The kiosk had fallen, and the iron fence about the tomb had been torn from the ground.

From several shell-craters nearby the Turks had gathered the remains of the bodies and buried them in another spot. Such is war. It does not even permit the dead to sleep undisturbedly.

YALOVA, GALLIPOLI, HEADQUARTERS LIMAN VON SANDERS PASHA, *July 13th.*

Had a much-needed bath, something to eat, and am now writing to the sweet melodies of the bulbuls, singing in the pines above the tent. The nightingales of Gallipoli will perch in a pine and sing all night to heart's content.

Awoke early this morning on the pavement of Bulair, near the wrecked cemetery wall. When I am tired I can sleep anywhere. Friend Swing cannot. He is now stretched out on his comfortable field-bed—in silk pajamas—and is sleeping the sleep of the tired just.

We found this morning that our *arabadchi*, an Ottoman soldier, had gone over the hills. Neither the man nor the vehicle could be found. Our search was general and long, and when it was fruitful something happened. One of the Turkish officers, exasperated by the foolish trick of the man, first broke his riding-crop over the *asker's* head. The measure of punishment being not yet full, more was added with the fist. It was a most undignified proceeding, but I regret to say it was not altogether undeserved. Later I put balm on the wounded feelings by an application of largess.

Meanwhile I had been reproachful to F. Swing. I blamed him for many things. If he hadn't insisted on the land route I would have saved myself much trouble, I opined. If he was afraid of British submarines, I was not. Instead of a long, hot, dusty, bone-breaking, and muscle-wrenching trip across country, I could have sailed on a torpedo-boat to Akbash in comfort. But F. Swing is patient with me. Later I apologized in the most abject fashion. F. Swing forgave me and even said that he was a little to blame.

The city of Gallipoli had been shelled. The hospital had drawn several large bombs, and so had other buildings. There is no telling when the place will be under fire again. We were warned against going into it.

But I was dead opposed to more travel on dusty roads. And Swing also was tired of it by now. The Ottoman officers were of the same mind. So we hired a *mahonic* and set its lateen sail for Akbash—chief base of supplies of the Ottoman forces on Gallipoli, and our destination.

The sail down the Dardanelles was a delight.

The wind favored us, the sky was blue, the water bluer, and the sun rays were tempered by the breeze. It was always possible that an Ally submarine might poke her nose out of the water—with dire results for us. But nothing of the sort occurred.

After some delay we landed in Akbash, and after more delay, on that malodorous and hot beach, with its hundreds of camel- and buffalo-trains, its thousands of Kurd *hamals*, and thousands of tons of all sorts of military supplies, we proceeded by escort wagon to headquarters.

Major Prigge Bey, chief of staff of Field-Marshal Liman von Sanders Pasha, gave us what in his frigid manner is a warm welcome. Later the pasha interested himself in us, selecting personally the site for our tent and pledging us his unstinted assistance in everything we might wish to undertake.

July 14th.

I can't see why the French units of the Allied fleet should have decided to celebrate *le quatorze juillet* in so outrageous a manner.

This is noon. The sun beats down on our camp. The rosin runs on pine and cedar and fills the air with its fine aroma. Across the little valley waves a wheat-field whose grain is overripe. Birds twitter above me in the trees. Butterflies flit about. There is no battle noise. All is serene and beautiful —and yet all is not well.

F. Swing and I rose suddenly this morning, 6.25 being the hour. The first out of the tent and in search for a bomb-proof was F. Swing. I was a close second—a very close second.

I woke in time to see F. Swing's field bed collapse under a swiftly rising figure dressed in silk pajamas. I thought that just a second before I had heard a great noise outside—the explosion of a large shell.

I was still in inert surprise when F. Swing began to kick me in the side with one foot, while he was sticking the other into a shoe which was made for the foot that was kicking me.

"Get up! get up! the camp is being bombarded!" he shouted.

That something of the sort was going on I had surmised by that time—for, cheeeeesherorrrrrrr— tzaw—brrrrrr, another shell exploded in much the same spot. At almost the same time much daylight entered the top of our tent near the head of the pole. A piece of shell or a rock had rent the canvas generously.

F. Swing fell into his trousers, snatched up a shoe, and then raced off, down the slope, across the dell, and up the further hillside. I, similarly attired, a few seconds later raced after him, sped by a salvo of four shells.

Fine reception to get on our first day at Yalova.

Still mindful of the fact that I have a soldier's reputation to maintain, I had taken along soap and towel, and while the first parts of the shelling were reeled off I took a bath in the officers' swimming-pool in the lee of the hill, where F. Swing sat disconsolate under a cypress.

All things come to an end, and by 7.30 *le quatorze juillet* celebration was over. No casualties on our side, because the ammunition was none too good. The fire was short, moreover, falling mostly in a meadow at the foot of the hillside it was intended to reach.

Ali, the orderly who attends to our chores in the camp, made a fairly good breakfast by 8.30, so that by 9.30 our spirits were once more on an even keel. F. Swing's are inclined to show a little list now and then, and my jib doesn't seem to take the line as well as it might; we are to stay on the peninsula for at least three weeks. And what we had this morning is the regular thing around here, no square foot of the terrain being safe for a single second in the day. We have a hot program ahead of us.

July 15th.

There was no bombardment of the camp this morning. But an *escadrille* of fliers appeared thrice, for breakfast, luncheon, and dinner.

It is the habit of these aeroplanic bomb-distributors to sail to Akbash three times in the day, so that the supply machinery there may not run too smoothly for the Turks. Against that I have no particular objection.

There being from eighteen to twenty planes in the *escadrille*, some of them also "lay a few eggs" *en passant.* To-day they laid them three times near the headquarters of the man who is responsible to the Turks for the military operations on Gallipoli.

So we had aerial bombs with our coffee.

F. Swing, who has as good an ear for aeroplanes and bombardments as he has a nose for news, heard them first. I listened. Sure enough. That humming of bumblebees up in the blue sky could be nothing if not the noise of an aero motor.

Just then the anti-aircraft pieces of the Turks began to yelp. We saw now that the "birds" were right above us, coming from Ariburnu, and making for Akbash.

The shrapnel of the Turkish anti-aircrafts did not do any damage. The little flashes and fleecy clouds of powder fumes which the shrapnel gave rise to were short or long, high and low, but never close enough to give anybody but us much concern. Somewhat familiar with the operation of the law of gravity, we surmised that soon we would have a hail of shrapnel balls and fragments about our ears.

No sooner thought than it happened. Plopp, plopp, plopp, all about us. Swing stepped under the sheltering twigs of a pine, and from that moment on kept the tree trunk between himself and the direction of the spot where the bombs—fellows of the 80-pound variety—were coming to earth.

So far F. Swing had not spoken. When the *escadrille* reappeared at noon he was plainly grieved.

"Seems to me, old top, that we are going to have *some* time around here," he said, attacking the remainder of his cold food.

"Seems so," was my laconic reply.

Between teatime and supper we had the third visit. This time the aviators "laid their eggs" farther up the slope, so that we did not have to care much. But as the shrapnel again rained on us, in reality we were but little better off.

During the day we interviewed His Excellency,

Liman von Sanders Pasha. He is of the opinion that, given enough ammunition, he can hold the peninsula forever.

While stretched out on the moss and needles under the pines, F. Swing and I composed a poem to the "Wheat-fields of Gallipoli." It is a touching thing, of course. Full of maudlin sentiments about the man who guided the plow, the ox who pulled it, the woman who scattered the seed (we have no authority for the statement that a woman did the sowing, but say so, anyway, because it sounds so much more poetic), the reaper who is now absent, the sail windmills which are now idle, and so on. Later we will add poems on the neglected olive-groves and vineyards to the collection.

It is cool under the pines, and the rosin sweat is sweet to the nostrils and balmy to the lungs. We watch the supply-trains go over the hills, and when tired of this always return to our wheat-fields. The breeze goes over them all day long, causing the surface of the fields to be agitated in waves, like a sea. It is a pleasant picture, and still not without its pathetic feature. The people who plowed these fields, who sowed them, and who hoped to harvest on them are no longer on the peninsula. The war has driven them to other parts, where they may harvest, but not reap

The village of Yalova, not far from us, has been shelled. The inhabitants are gone. Many of the houses are down. The gardens are neglected. The vineyards need the care of the vintner, and the olive-groves—well, I don't know what they need, but they need something.

Even the windmills have been razed in many cases. Why so venerable a thing as a Gallipoli windmill should have been destroyed I do not understand, but it strikes me that they offered splendid guidance to indirect fire, owing to their elevation. Anyway, most of them are gone.

In the dell the bulbüls sing undisturbedly. There is moonlight, and this is the season when the nightingale sings at its best.

But the concert can be enjoyed here only in snatches. When night falls the two battle volcanoes, at Ariburnu and Sid-il-Bahr, wake from the sleep of the heat of the day. Artillery begins to boom, mines are exploded, and hand-grenades are thrown. The machine-guns begin their tu-tu-tu-tu-tu-tu-tu, and when they have spoken awhile the small arms join in volleys or scattered fire. After that, I know, men attack one another with bayonet and knife.

July 16th.

I must admire the grit of my friend Swing.

F. Swing confided to me yesterday that never before in his life had he sat on a horse.

"Then how do you propose to get to Ariburnu?" I asked. "You can't get there on foot, nor on a wagon, nor in an auto."

"I am going there on horseback," he said, coolly enough.

"You won't if I have anything to say about it," I put in. "You know that part of the road lies in the British fire-zone. When we get there we'll have to ride for all there is in the horses. You can't go there. You'll break your neck. Stay here and I'll go halves on the story with you."

To that F. Swing would not listen. Said he didn't want to show himself in my feathers. He was for clean newspaper work—he was!

Thus we started this morning. Soon I discovered that a correspondence course in equestrianism would never be a success. During the evening I had initiated my friend in some of the essentials of horsemanship—how he was to mount and dismount, how the reins had to be held, how the boot had to be kept in the stirrup, and this and that.

The Turkish officer who was to be our guide to Ariburnu made big eyes when he saw F. Swing trying to get in the saddle from the wrong side. Ibrahim Bey is one of the smartest cavalry officers in the entire Ottoman army; being wealthy, he keeps a string of good horses, and came near winning the endurance race from Vienna to Constantinople a few years ago.

I was mortified when my friend made this *faux pas*.

Ibrahim Bey frowned. I could not blame him.

"*Monsieur Sweng*," he said in his choicest French, "I fear very much for your safety. Had you not better remain in camp and go to Ariburnu some other time? Part of the way we will have to ride like the devil himself. You will fall off the horse. The British bullets will hit you. I cannot be responsible for you."

But *Monsieur Sweng* was obdurate.

So we got him into the saddle. Ibrahim Bey rode on Swing's left, I on his right,

F. Swing could keep in the saddle at step. Trotting hurt his "inners," he said. Canter he could not. As for a stretched gallop, why that was not to be thought of.

We kept up an easy pace until we got to the cemetery of Eskikoi. What little trotting and cantering we had done so far had been done in order that Ibrahim Bey and I might get our hands in, keeping the hapless man on horseback in the saddle.

"When we get to the point where the road to the right branches off we will have to ride as fast as we can," said Ibrahim Bey. "You hold *Monsieur Sweng* on that side, I on this. *Monsieur Sweng* must try to keep his feet in the stirrups. He had better hold the reins a little tight if he can. Do you think you can remember that, *Monsieur Sweng?*"

F. Swing thought he could. I doubted it, however.

At the fork of the road we broke into a full gallop, Swing between us. I had part of his upper sleeve in one hand, and Ibrahim Bey was doing as much on the other side.

We were off. I do not usually wear spurs, but on this occasion I had put them on. It was well that I had done so. We had not gone very far when a British machine-gun began to strew pellets in the road, ahead and behind us; the chew-chew-chew of the bullets as they went past us was anything but agreeable. I spurred my horse into a wild stretch. Ibrahim was doing the same. Both of us, by means of forceful kicks, kept Swing's horse going, holding on to the man for dear life meanwhile.

For half a mile we kept this up. Then we slowed down, with our burden somewhat out of breath, but still with us, alive and unhurt.

Essad Pasha welcomed us warmly. We had lunch with him and his staff—an event which was duly recorded by the menu decoration—an American and Turkish flag entwined. One of the soldier scribes at the Essad headquarters had drawn the flags with red and blue pencils.

The day was spent studying the Ariburnu terrain. One of the Turkish officers made us an excellent sketch of the British positions. An observation station near the headquarters made it possible to view every foot of the position.

It was hot. Though there had been an armistice some days ago, so that some 4,000-odd bodies might be buried, the field again was strewn with dead. Each little breeze from the Ægean Sea brought a wave of stench into headquarters. At times the odor of the decomposing bodies was overwhelming. It was the first time that F. Swing had smelled anything of the sort. He yearned for *eau de cologne*, which he had forgotten, of course.

In the afternoon we had the attention of three Allied aviators. They threw bombs of the large variety—long steel cylinders with three chambers, one above the other and intercommunicating. The crash of the explosion was unpleasant, and several of the bombs fell just a little too close to be quite comfortable.

Essad Pasha proved a most willing and delightful

297

host and cicerone. The war-tried hero of Janina explained things thoroughly and spoke of his own work with the greatest modesty. Like all good soldiers, he did not underestimate his adversary, nor speak of him in other than terms of respect.

How to get home that evening was a problem. The road we had come was altogether impossible in the afternoon, owing to more favorable light conditions for the British. We had to take a route across the hills, and that route was a most difficult one. It entailed the descent of a steep slope down which the Turks are building a road in serpentines. As luck would have it, the worst part of the slope had not yet been overcome.

F. Swing was to get a second instalment of high-school equestrianism.

When we got to the slope, Ibrahim suggested that he go first. But while he was a splendid horseman, I had gathered *en route* that he had never done much rough-riding. With much experience in that line on the South African veldt, I suggested that I make the trail. Swing rode second, Ibrahim Bey brought up the rear.

We could have dismounted and led our horses down. It would have been the natural thing to do. But there is etiquette—the etiquette of the cavalry officer—which I had to bear in mind. Ibrahim Bey would have turned such a proposal down, and I would have been disappointed had he accepted it.

Down we started. I held to what seemed in the twilight to be a goat trail. But soon I discovered that the trail was covered with round pebbles, which, lying on the baked ground and on flat rocks, made it hard for the horse to get a firm footing. So I turned off, when the ground afforded a chance, rode a bit uphill to gain a better grade, and then, holding to a ledge running high above, but parallel to, the *donga* below, landed safely enough at the bottom. My companions did the same.

The end of the ride proved very annoying. F. Swing complained of pains all over his anatomy, and we, anxious to get home, paid little attention to his woes, though our speed was greatly reduced by the necessity of having to bring our comrade into camp.

NEAR ALI BEY TCHIFTLIK, HEADQUARTERS OF WEBER PASHA, *July 17th.*

F. Swing is at Yalova, unable to do more than move his arms. That ride yesterday was too much for him. It will be days before he recovers. But company is desirable on these excursions. I have attached to my person the Gallipoli correspondent of the *Continental Times*, Mr. Bleck-Schlombach. Attached am I to one of the worst mounts I have ever straddled—an Arab stallion, built like a camel, with the strength of a locomotive, and a mouth as hard as if it had been lined with tin.

Ibrahim Bey recommended the beast to me. Said it was the best horse for speed and endurance in the camp. He is right. He should have stated also that it was the most unmanageable Waler he ever knew.

There is nobody in camp who likes the horse, it seems. The *onbashi* (corporal) who is to act as our guide said so. So the Arab stays in the bomb-proof and feeds his head off.

He was full of oats when I mounted him this morning. With main effort I got into the saddle. My foot was hardly in the off stirrup when the son of the desert made off like a cannon-shot.

Well, I let him have his way. We careened across the Gallipoli landscape like mad, got over the ridge south of Yalova, and then raced into the valley of Maidos. If he could stand it I could. We broke across fields, dashed along roads, and cleared ditches—one of them so wide that I was sure there would be a spill. But the Arab made it and could have stood another foot or two into the bargain.

Meanwhile my companion and the *onbashi* had been lost sight of. There was time to spare then, so I had a look at Maidos—Maidos so utterly and completely razed to the ground by the bombardment of the Allies.

That *onbashi* did not know the road as well as he thought. So it came that he headed what the British must have thought a little cavalry offensive. I had my doubts when he insisted that the road to headquarters ran over the ridge south of Ali Bey Tchifthk. But he said he had been there, so, despite my conviction that the mountain on the left was Atchi Baba, I followed him. He changed his mind shortly afterward when he saw trenches before him and heard the little messengers of death chirp through the air.

Weber Pasha, commander of the South group and one of the members of the German military

Copyright, by Underwood & Underwood

TURKISH TROOPS IN THE GREAT SYRIAN DESERT

The Berlin-Bagdad Railroad being not yet in operation, Ottoman troops needed in the Mesopotamian campaign were obliged to march across the desert after having detrained near Aleppo, in Syria. No small feat when heat, lack of water and distance are considered.

Photo. by Underwood & Underwood

CAMEL MILITARY TRAIN IN MAIDOS, GALLIPOLI

mission, said there were no secrets in his sectors, that I could see them all. I could start that afternoon, if I wanted to.

After a very late lunch I made off for the sector west of Krithia, a Captain Westerhagen, once a banker in New York, being my guide.

West of Ali Bey Tchiftlik we reached ground that had borne the full violence of the bombardments incident to the landing of the Allied troops at Sid-il-Bahr and Ariburnu on April 25th–6th–7th. The fields and pastures were plowed up. Crater lay beside crater and fragments of steel strewed the ground like stones in a field.

The little rest in the afternoon had once more put fine fettle into my Arab. He pirouetted, danced, pranced, and bucked to heart's content.

"Like to know what he will do if we draw a shell or two," said Captain Westerhagen in the best New York English.

I had thought of that, but, knowing my steed by this time, felt sure that I could handle him under any conditions. That I was mistaken was proven a little later.

We entered the long approach-trench, wide and deep enough for wheel traffic, and then continued in a ravine running parallel to the British left-flank trenches. A fight started as we rode along. The machine-gun and rifle bullets of the British went over our heads, and most of the shells fired by some British battery ashore hit on the grassy slope immediately above the wall of the ravine on our right.

Two places had to be taken at full gallop. They

could be "seen into" by the British. But the British had other work on hand just then and did not bother with us.

The last stretch of ground we made on foot.

They were just prying loose from a narrow niche in the backed bank of the ravine a Turkish soldier who had been hit by large pieces of a hand-grenade which had come from the British line directly above us. His intestines threatened to come through the large rent in his clothing.

"Dangerous place to have your headquarters in," I commented to the captain whose men were lying on the rim of the ravine.

"It is dangerous, but the best place I have been able to find," said the officer. "Do not stay outside. Come into my bomb-proof."

It wasn't much of a bomb-proof he had. A mere shack leaning against the wall of the ravine and protected on top by a few beams holding up several feet of earth in bags.

We had coffee and cigarettes.

"I can't recommend that you go on top now," said the officer, when I suggested doing that. "It's too dangerous. It is near sunset, and then, as a rule, the fun commences. Come back to-morrow morning. It may be better then."

That much of the day's work had been wasted.

They had covered the body of the Turkish soldier up with a bag when I bade the captain farewell. I learned, however, that he had been totally disemboweled.

Such is life!

We made our way back through the ravine.

Half of the distance had been covered when we came to where an approach-trench ran to the part of the line where the fighting was going on. Long lines of stretcher-bearers issued from the deep cut, bound with their loads of suffering and anguish to the field hospital over the hill. Three of the wounded had died. The stretcher-bearers had thought it useless to carry them farther, so they deposited their burden on the grass near the road.

Most of the wounded stood the ordeal well, but quite a few moaned and groaned. All of them had the impression that they had to salute, painful as the effort might be. Their *merhaba* was weak.

In a recess in the ravine a company was waiting to relieve a similar organization from duty in the trenches. The men had lined up along the road to see the wounded pass. I noticed that many of the *askers* shared their scant supply of water with the wounded. Encouraging words were spoken. Well, it might be their turn to-morrow.

Captain Westerhagen was on a tour of inspection, it seemed. He had to go to the Krithia sector. Did I want to come along? Certainly.

"But it is very risky," he said. "We have to pass a long ridge in full view of an enemy battery. I draw their fire every time I cross. How about it?"

I was going, I said.

From the main approach-trench, running almost due west, runs another to the south, toward Krithia. This one we took.

"You ride first. Follow the road!" said Captain Westerhagen, as we emerged from the approach-trench, which could not be continued

20   303

through the ridge, owing to the rocky ground. "Then Mr. Schlombach, I, and the orderly. Stop when you get into the next communication-trench at the end of the road."

That little spurt was what my Arab wanted. I had great trouble stopping his mad flight when I reached the communication-trench. The others arrived soon. Not a shot had fallen.

We approached the British trenches to within fifty yards. The captain ascertained what conditions were, and then, after a short inventory-taking in Krithia, we decided to return to headquarters.

We rode in the same order returning over the ridge. The captain must have had a narrow escape there. He never tired of telling us how dangerous the spot was, adding that the Allies had acquired the bad habit of using artillery even on single individuals.

I cleared the communication-trench, emerged upon the road, and had gone about a hundred yards in the open when the first shell came. It exploded in the field fifty feet to my left. The second shell crashed thirty feet ahead of me, the third about a hundred feet to the left, the fourth I merely heard close by, and numbers five, six, seven, and eight exploded on more or less the same ground as the difference in sound, due to the increase of distance between myself and the apex of the ridge, told me.

By this time my horse was frantic. I tried to guide him into the communication-trench, without the slightest success, however. I worked bit, knee, and heel as hard as I could. Nothing checked his mad plunge across the crater-torn fields. Once he fell to his knees, and the shock nearly unhorsed me, but he was up again and broke into another mad stretch.

There is nothing to do in a case like that, provided you have the necessary room, but to let the animal tire itself out. It is the best method of teaching a horse that it is foolish to waste effort in that way.

I had dismounted in the cypress grove of Ali Bey Tchiftlik when the others caught up with me. Going to camp the Arab was gentle enough —so tired, in fact, was he that I had to urge him on.

"That British battery has the range to that ridge down to a fine point," said Weber Pasha at supper that evening. "It's funny, though, that so far they have not killed or wounded anybody who has gone over the road."

He "knocked wood" as he said this.

July 18th.

Up at five this morning, after a very active day yesterday. Could have slept till noon easily.

Went back to the western sector to inspect the Turkish positions. The same old trenches. No fighting was going on. Even the artillery had shut up for once

Life in the trenches would cause nobody to leave home and mother, I thought, after I had made six kilometers in them, half of this in a stooped position The soil here is not deep, and the Turks have not yet been able to do much with the hard lime they are standing on.

It is stiflingly hot in the ditches. Not a breath of air can get into them, and the sun beats down mercilessly. Water is scarce.

Many of the *askers* were sitting on the earth bank they leave standing to reach the parapet during an action. They were playing with pebbles, like so many children. Anything to pass the time, it seems. Some were employed improving their trenches and the little holes in which they rest and sleep. Others were sewing on buttons and patches. Rifles were being cleaned and bayonets burnished.

I noticed that all the Turks carried large knives in the windings of their puttees. It seems that they prefer the knife in hand-to-hand combat. Invariably this knife is drawn across the throat of the adversary, a fact which is said to have made a bad impression on the British.

Met Lieutenant M. Hadi, of the Ninth, again. He has just been promoted to a first-lieutenancy. He was happy when I congratulated him, and insisted that I have coffee with him. I enjoyed the aroma of the coffee more than its taste. Holding the cup close under my nose, I was able for a time to shut out the awful stench floating over the field. Between the two barbed-wire entanglements lay several hundred dead British and Turkish soldiers. Each night a few of them were being buried, explained the lieutenant to me, but the difficulties to be overcome were so many that the work was slow.

"You can't stick your nose over the trench and not have it shot off," he said. "They go so far as to shoot at the shovels we use in trench-work. Many of them have holes in them."

Walking around the trenches was the hardest sort of exercise. The "seen into" stretches had to be covered on the run, with head and shoulder well out of the way. Men were constantly passing back and forth, necessitating either squeezing against the trench wall or kneeling on the earth bank until those coming in an opposite direction had passed.

I took a peep over the parapet. Directly in front of me were "Spanish riders," a sort of long saw-horse covered with barbed wire. Beyond this line came the entanglements of the Turks—a field of barbed wire running the entire length of the space between the two trench systems, and from twenty to fifty feet wide. Beyond that lay a sort of "Nobody's Land," then came the entanglements of the Allies.

The grass on the field between the lines was dead, but rather thick and high. The dead lie in it like so many mole-hills, the khaki of the British and Turks giving this color impression. I counted the number which lay in the field described by the legs of a "Spanish rider"—twenty-eight. To make an estimate of the total number of dead was difficult. I could see possibly 400 to 450. A survey of some of the nearest bodies with my glasses showed that they were in all stages of decomposition. Most of them were bloated to almost twice their normal size. In others dissolution had gone much further, the "heap" being little more than the uniform and skeleton of the body, the tissue having completely collapsed.

The Turks in the trenches did not seem to mind the sight. Some of the more venturesome characters go over the parapet at night to search the bodies and take from them what seems of value. War loses many of its terrors by constant association with them.

On Atchi Baba there was an artillery control-station which I wanted to see.

The way there was most tiresome. It led through a long communication-trench giving access during the day to the center and east of the terrain. The roads leading there can be used only at night.

We must have been seen by some British artillery observer. Long after we had passed the last of the Turkish batteries, so that there could be no question of the shells having been intended for one of them, we were taken under a most violent fire. There were only four in the party. Why the British should have thought it worth while to throw so much ammunition at them was more than I can understand.

Two volleys from a battery of four pieces came. And the fire was perturbingly accurate. I thanked my stars that the things were shells and not shrapnel. As it was, the base of a shell hit the edge of the trench so close to us that in falling it landed between Captain Westerhagen and the orderly.

When the storm had blown over we proceeded, scaled Atchi Baba in a very narrow communication-trench, into which the sun beat with all its ardor, and then, half exhausted, dove into a long and cool tunnel to reach the other "face" of the steep hill.

Four Ottoman artillery officers have their habitat there. Three of them were observing through as many "scissors" glasses; the fourth was in telephonic communication with Weber Pasha's headquarters.

After the usual coffee and cigarettes, one of the officers offered to do a little shooting for me—with a field battery. I wish to state that this is customary, that it is some slight compensation we get for the risks we run, and that usually this sort of fire is quite as harmless as the fire we receive in return.

Seventy-five-millimeter ammunition is not expensive, moreover. Nowadays, it is turned out like rolls by the baker.

The battery blazed away for quite a while. The result of the fire need not be recorded. It was *nil*.

July 19th.

The Allies must have discovered something in the deep ravine in which these headquarters are located. Bright and early this morning one of the Allied ships took the site under fire from Erenkoi Bay, with the result that I spent much of my time in the grotto.

The grotto is a great advantage of this place. It has obviated the construction of bomb-proofs. When the shells come the staff repairs to the large hole worn into the lime rock by the little brook,

Shavan, which comes from the hills of the Bairamli Dagh.

It is cool there and cozy. Over the brink of the grotto hang the branches of several old willows. Ferns stand on the moss-covered ledges. The brook comes over the top ledge in a thin trickle now, but there is enough water to feed the sandy-bottomed pool. The place is good enough, but woe to those in it if ever a shell enters.

Had a nasty experience this noon. Feeling the necessity of a little siesta after lunch, my colleague and I strolled up the ravine in search of a place where peace and quiet might be had. We soon found what we were looking for. A willow-tree supplied the shade, and soft white sand the couch.

I had fallen asleep in no time, and had slept about half an hour when I was rudely wakened by a detonation so nearby that I rose to my knees like a jumping-jack. Then I ducked to let an avalanche of small rocks and earth pass over me.

When the cloud of dust and smoke passed away I saw several horses near us stagger about. Two of them fell as I saw them. A man reeled and then shot headlong into the road. Two men lay prone. Six horses were on the ground.

What had happened? Shell, I thought. But just then I heard above me the hum of an aero motor.

Two aeroplanes stood directly over us, swinging about in circles. There was no doubt now that the Allies had discovered something in the ravine. Possibly they knew that Weber Pasha's headquarters were in or near the grotto.

Another acro bomb shot to the ground. It fell further away. Four more came and did no damage. The seventh fell close to the grotto, and the eighth hit a small wagon-park.

The bag: two men killed, four wounded; eight horses killed, three wounded.

The first bomb had struck a stable in which a small detachment of Ottoman field-gendarmes kept their horses.

Discussion of the operations of the Allies with Turkish and German staff-officers leads me to believe that the undertaking of the British and French has the following objectives:

SOUTHERN TERRAIN.

The Allied troops landed at and near Sid-il-Bahr have for their primary task the taking of the Atchi Baba Mountain and adjacent hills, so that heavy artillery brought into position there can silence the following Dardanelles coast defense-works: In Tepeh, Erenkoi, Dardanos, Anadolu, Hamidieh, Tchemenlik, and Fort Medjidieh of the Kilid-il-Bahr establishment.

The heavy artillery so stationed would also keep the mobile howitzer batteries of the Turks in check, in addition to facilitating progress of the Allied infantry along the peninsula.

Unless the Allied infantry is able to reach this objective the campaign must fail.

ARIBURNU TERRAIN.

The objective of the British operations at Ari-

burnu is in all respects similar to the objective
pursued from Sid-il-Bahr.

The British troops are to gain possession of the
Kodjatchemen Dagh. Heavy artillery is then to
be stationed on the various crests of the little range
to assist in the silencing of the works Anadolu
Hamidieh and Tchemenlik, and take under their fire,
as its main task, the works of Kilid-il-Bahr, Medjidieh on the Bay of Maidos, Nagara, and one or two
other smaller emplacements along the Maidos Bay.

Artillery so stationed would command the entire
Bay of Maidos, and would also control to a large
extent the waters north of that point, including the
beach of Akbash.

Unless the Kodjatchemen Dagh is taken the
general plan of the Allies to take Constantinople
by forcing the Dardanelles cannot be carried out.
For a land operation against the Ottoman capital
the troops landed on Gallipoli are not strong enough.

Résumé.

Reliable figures concerning the strength of the
Allied troops cannot be obtained. The force at
Sid-il-Bahr is estimated at 110,000 British and
British colored troops, and 70,000 French and
French colonial troops.

The Ariburnu force is for the greater number
composed of Australian and New Zealand con-
tingents, Anzacs, estimated at 90,000.

Little progress has been made by the Allied
forces. The ground they hold was largely gained
during the first four days after disembarkation.
But little heavy and light field artillery has been

emplaced so far, the Allied forces depending upon the supporting fleet for most of their artillery assistance.

The trenches are now so close together that the fire of the naval pieces becomes dangerous to the Allied infantry. As a result of this the fire superiority of the Allies in their dreaded heavy calibers is rapidly decreasing. The Turkish approaches to the southern terrain lying mostly in deep valleys and ravines, the British artillery, on land and sea, has not been able to interfere seriously with the supply system of the Turks. This is true in a measure of the Ariburnu terrain, with the difference that near the actual front transporting can be carried on at night only.

YALOVA, *July 21st.*

Cabled my service to-day that the Allies can not carry out the program outlined above, for the reason that the Turk is willing to put up a stout defense, and that the lack in supplies, felt so much by the Turks, is discounted by the terrain difficulties the Allies would have to overcome before the two vital parts of their program can be carried into execution.

In a mail story I predicted that the Allies, in the event of the operation extending into the winter months, would be obliged to withdraw from the peninsula.

July 22d.

"So Maidos is down!" cried F. Swing, with sorrow in his voice. "I wonder what has become of the red-headed one?"

313

"Nothing at all left of her street," I replied, sympathetically. "No doubt she cleared out with the rest."

"Have you heard that the prettiest girl on the entire peninsula, a denizen of yon city, was killed by the bomb of an Allied aviator?" asked my friend, dolefully.

"No; that is news to me," I replied.

"You see I have not been idle while you were away. I have nursed my poor bones back into shape, moreover."

We tried a poem on that happy event, but it wouldn't work.

July 23d.

This is Turkish Independence Day. F. Swing and I decided to celebrate it by making up our minds to return to Pera and Stamboul. We have found that the censor here, Major Prigge, is really too busy with other things to bother with the thousands of words of mail copy we must get off—and then war correspondents are not like Indians. All the good ones are alive.

This place is really all right. We will say that much for it. But with bombardments at any moment, with aero bombs for breakfast, lunch, and dinner, with flies in clouds so thick that you must drink your coffee and eat your meal under a mosquito net, and with the major so busy, with telegraph tools so heavy, with *Les Petits Champs* so far away, and with the rue Bairam yearning for us, we must really go

So we are off to-morrow with the *Maggie Mac-*

gregor, as she was known before the Turks painted on her, in red, the words, "Gül-il-Bahr," which means "Rose of the Sea" or something like that.

Liman von Sanders Pasha gave us a farewell interview. He said that he could hold Gallipoli if only Constantinople would give him more ammunition.

"What I need is ammunition, ammunition, ammunition, and then more ammunition!" he said. The old fire-eater cares not a hang for military secrets.

"I have no military secrets here," he told me yesterday. "Why, with aeroplanes, and these Greeks around, the enemy knows more about our affairs than we do ourselves at times. I haven't even got enough telephone wire to go around. Secrets—the devil! This is a question of hard work and hard fighting, of ammunition—of ammunition which I can't get, of ammunition which I must have."

So the old man was really very nice to us. They say—everybody says—he is a grouch of the worst type. I think that at times he is. But who wouldn't be a grouch with so large a contract on his hands and so little to do it with?

X

SOME OTHER TURKISH VIEWPOINTS

THE Ottoman Empire is in many respects an anachronism, a concrete form of inconsistency—an absurd institution. A minority governs. Minorities govern badly always.

With the races in the empire the reader is now familiar. I have pointed out to what extent they differ in everything that makes up mental endowment. The 22,000,000 speak four languages and each language has several dialects, with the result that French is the medium of inter-racial intercourse. There can be no easy meeting of the mind, therefore. And that is even true among the Turkish classes. The common people speak a form of crude Turkish, while the educated classes have a speech of their own, full of Persian and Arabic terms, which the masses do not understand.

KARABIAGH, *July 25th.*
The *Rose of the Sea* would never sail anywhere except on the Dardanelles, and then only in wartime. Even her skipper, an old tar, an Arab—strange combination—admits that. She can make eight knots an hour with the wind blowing over

her stern and the boilers steam-tight. Otherwise she makes seven—as she has been doing all day.

We are picking up a cargo of sheep and passengers. The *Rose*, etc., came down the straits with a cargo of shells and that sort of thing. She will not be a ship of war going back, so that F. Swing will once more have a chance of going to Rodosto, or maybe Panderma, in a rowboat.

To elude the British submarines, the skipper intends steaming to the east and north of the Marmora islands, in which case we would pull our rowboat into Panderma, should some British submarine commander take it into his head to wait for us on that route.

F. Swing and I had first installed ourselves on the lower aft deck. We retreated from there because the Turks and their wives insisted that we eat some of their butter—the stuff they call *gi* in India. Can't describe it any other way, though I might say that *gi* is butter melted in the pan after it has become very, very rancid. Then, too, one of the young Turkish ladies had to nurse her baby. We thought that our presence might not promote that very necessary undertaking. So we did what gentlemen will do under such circumstances—we meandered.

Found a place on the captain's bridge. The captain speaks English fairly well, having at one time or another sailed a dahabiyah, or maybe a Cook's steamer, on the Nile.

On the bridge we also met several passengers—the Calliondji family of Dardanelles, nice people whom the war has robbed of house and home.

317

They are going to Constantinople to live with some relatives. Father is, or rather was, a wine merchant *en gros*. Mother is a real motherly person, very proud of her daughters Elena and Theano.

To this family F. Swing and I seemed big people. Mr. Calliondji came to us and asked us if we could help him land in Constantinople, he having heard that the Ottoman government did not permit refugees to come to the capital any more. We thereupon informed him that no regulation of the sort was known to us, but that it was not out of the question that such a decision had been reached while we had been on Gallipoli. We promised to do our best.

Turkey is indeed a strange country. Its people do not seem to belong together.

Mr. Calliondji desired that his daughters and wife should have a better place for the night than seemed available at that moment—any old part of the deck. So he asked me to intercede with "my friend," not F. Swing, but the skipper of the *Rose of the Sea*.

"May I ask, Mr. Calliondji, why you do not ask the captain yourself?" I inquired.

"Well, it is this way. I can't talk English, and he can't talk French!"

"What's the matter with your Turkish?" I asked.

"I don't speak Turkish," replied Mr. Calliondji, in a matter-of-fact tone.

"Don't speak Turkish, and you were born at Dardanelles?"

318

"Not at Dardanelles, but at Lapsaki," replied Mr. Calliondji, to keep the record straight.

"Born in Turkey, then," I remarked. "All right. Come along!"

But the skipper of the *Rose*, etc., has nothing but the chart-room for himself. He calls it a chart-room. Chances are that he hasn't a single sheet of paper aboard.

Met the commandant here to-day. He gave us permission to have a bath in the sea if we went far away from the town. I feared at first that he thought we might pollute the water. But I learned later that he had the proprieties of Karabiagh in mind.

Well, we hadn't forgotten them. To see that nothing would happen to us the commandant sent a policeman along—who sat on the beach while F. Swing and I gamboled in the water.

Then a citizen of Karabiagh asked for the honor of having us as guests for dinner. We accepted —as we always do. Had pilaff, and *shish-kebab*, and Turkish sweetmeats at a table. Nobody offered to feed us *alla Turca*. The ladies of the household were in their rooms while the feast was going on.

In the afternoon we walked through the fields about the town. Toward sunset I introduced F. Swing to a new dish—*yaourt* and cucumbers—a sort of cucumber salad with sour milk containing little bugs that make you live long. In the case of Swing the bugs do not seem to have been very much on their job. At any rate, he complained of not feeling very well when we boarded the

21   319

Rose, etc., in an attempt to get through the submarine zone at night-time.

This is another Sunday. I always seem to travel on Sundays.

PERA, *July 26th*.

The *Rose of the Sea* managed to crawl to the Galata quay this noon. No submarines were seen, though once we crossed, in the glassy sea, a trail of oil that looked very suspicious to the Arab skipper, who, by the way, has sworn me eternal friendship. He says that my job is too dangerous and that I better come with him as first mate. I'll think it over.

The passengers were greatly exercised over the trail of oily eyes in all colors of the rainbow. F. Swing was sure that a submarine had passed. Everybody felt relieved, however, when they noticed what efficient counter-measures the Turks had under way—*mahonies*, each armed with a field-piece, but ostensibly out fishing. A tarpaulin had been hung over the gun. The idea was to let a British submarine come in close and then—bang!

It took a great deal of trusting to luck to get that fleet under way. The thing looks absurd, but the sea, and all that pertains to it, in war or peace, is not my bailiwick.

The Calliondji family—by the way they have relatives in Chicago—remained much perturbed all the way up. They finally landed in Galata without the slightest trouble. But they appreciated very much our interest in their case. Hoped they would meet us again.

F. Swing and I took an *araba* to our lodgings. It wasn't I who said that Constantinople had never looked her best so much as to-day. But I agreed with my friend.

July 31st.

Well, F. Swing is gone—gone to complete his study of the Balkans. I miss him much. There is no longer anybody to get mad at me, to scold and fume and fret, to grumble about the food, to complain of the heat, to make appointments which he doesn't keep to the minute (as I do mine), to do any one of a thousand other things that will try a fellow's patience—and still I would take all these things from F. Swing and love him more than before.

It is a sad season, anyway. The sirocco blows, and when this south wind, saturated with the humidity of the Mediterranean, goes over the city most people have either a headache or feel at odds with life.

Meanwhile I continue my study of Turkey, more especially Constantinople. The more I look into this thing, the more I become convinced that all Turkey is a mesalliance. Turk, Greek, Armenian, and Arab live on the footing of cat and dog. The strife going on between them permits none to give his better qualities a chance.

Just now I am much interested in the Greek side of this strange life. At the risk of being damned by the Turks and Germans, I have cultivated relations with some Greek *Perotes*. These people have a good many fine traits, despite all

321

claims to the contrary. It is another demonstration of the fact that no race is wholly bad.

The Calliondji family called on Swing and me two days after our arrival. F. Swing and I were in our rooms when the *sommelier d'étage* announced condescendingly that a family, evidently Greeks, were waiting for us in the *salon*. F. Swing believes in being fashionable, so the callers had to wait until he had thrown himself into his *redingote*.

They had come to thank us for our efforts in their behalf, said the Calliondjis. We protested that while we were glad to see them, we could under no circumstances connect their visit with anything we had done for them.

Theano was the spokeswoman. She speaks French very well, while the other members of the family do not.

Even if we had not been able to assist the family, it had been our intention to do so, and that was enough. We were to come to the house and have tea.

F. Swing did not have the time to keep this appointment, but I had. So to-day I went to the rue Gran' Capitan, as they call the street.

It was a pleasant event. Madame Calliondji served tea and introduced me to the youngest member in the family—a baby whom we had overlooked on the trip from Lapsaki to Pera. Elena had to make a visit somewhere a little later. The baby grew unruly and his mother had to put him to bed, so that in the end the tea was an affair between Theano and myself. We had more tea, more pastry, some Turkish candy *rahatlokum*—

alias "delight"—and then Theano sprinkled some *eau de Cologne* into my handkerchief so that wiping my face with it might be a pleasant exercise, as she said. How hot Pera can be!

We chatted about Dardanelles. It appears that the little girl and her family went through the bombardment of March 7th, but then left for Lapsaki.

"I have written a little novel," she said, "also some poems. I am sorry that you can't read them. They are in Greek. I have translated three or four of the poems into French—poor French, I think, but would you care to see them?"

I was astonished, to say the least. Theano is about seventeen years old, has never been farther than Pera in her life, and she had written a novel! The poems I could understand. All girls write poems, I think.

"I would like to see the poems—very much so," I said. "Also the novel. Though I may not be able to read it. I would like to see the book, anyway. A novel, you know, is quite an ambitious undertaking."

Theano left the room, soon to return with two volumes in her hand.

The poems were gentle things about spring, I gathered. Even the translation into Levantine French had considerable merit. The little stanzas breathed poetic appreciation of the beautiful in nature. A clean and sound sentimentality ran through the lines. I read them aloud. Theano listened attentively with a smile on her face.

"There was so little to occupy me at home that

I thought I would pass my time that way," she said, modestly. "I know those poems are not very good. Still they are the best I can do."

"Who published them?" I asked.

"Somebody in Dardanelles," smiled the girl. "And do you know that they had quite a sale?"

"And the novel?" I asked, looking over the book, which was printed on good paper and in a very fine Greek type.

"It was published by the same printer," replied the girl. "Of course, my father had to subsidize the firm for that. But the book, contrary to my expectations, has sold. This is a copy of the third edition. You can buy it on the Gran' rue."

"And the subject of the novel—the argument, the story, the plot?"

Theano smiled. "It is a love-story, of course," she replied. "What else could I write about?"

"Doesn't it take experience in love to write a love-story?" I asked.

Theano found the question very amusing. She laughed. "It doesn't seem to take experience," she said, lightly. "I have had none, anyway."

I took the liberty to doubt that in a teasing way. "In these parts the young ladies fall in love early, do they not?" I questioned. "Even in my country they do so at your age. It has been known that school-girls do fall in love."

"That may be," said Theano, earnestly. "But I haven't been in love. What I have written there is merely what I would like to have come true. But the things we want to have come true do not always turn out that way, do they?"

Copyright, by Underwood & Underwood

GREEK HOME ON THE BYZANTIAN WALL

Constantinople is *par excellence* the seat of the picturesque in urban features. There is hardly a lot without some romance attaching to it. The basement-rooms of this house are formed by vaults in which the Byzantians, ancestors of the Ottoman Greeks, stored military supplies.

Copyright, by Underwood & Underwood

STREET SCENE IN FYNDYKLY

Fyndykly is one of the poorer Turkish quarters of Constantinople. The Turk is an ardent lover of nature, a quality which often shows itself in the conversion by him of his narrow city lanes into wistaria bowers and vine arbors, as in this instance.

"Not always," I said. "But tell me what the story is—just the bare outlines."

"I won't do that now," said Theano, firmly. "Some other time; not to-day. Are you going back to the fighting soon?"

"In a week or so," I replied.

"Well, then, when you come back I hope I shall see you again!"

August 5th.

There is a big fire in Fyndykly to-night. Twelve hundred houses are down. The alleys to Galata, Pera, and Taxim are filled with the inhabitants of the district, trying to save the little they can. Some of them have already gone to housekeeping for the night in doorways and in the niches on the garden walls. About 8,000 people are homeless.

The flames find the wooden houses easy prey. They started somewhere at the bottom of the ravine-like site. Inside of an hour they had spread up the steep slopes, and now the gulch is a roaring furnace.

Above the steady roar of the conflagration ring the blatant tones of the fire-department horns. If the Turks were as good fire-fighters as they are blowers of fire-horns, the fire would have been in hand long ago. As it is, there is nothing to do till the fuel has been consumed—until the quarter is a heap of ashes, cinders, and calcined bones. Many people are perishing, it is said.

The flames rise heavenward in a steady sheet now. There is but little smoke. The heat of the summer has taken the last trace of moisture out of the lumber. From the sea of fire, which I am viewing from the roof of a house on the Gran' rue de Pera, come sheafs of sparks occasionally. Another house has collapsed.

The picture is a most fantastic one. That seen by Nero cannot excel it in magnitude and grandeur. The entire ravine is a seething furnace—in white heat, red, and yellow.

A little smoke will top a column of fire now and then like a purple coronet. Vapor rises from the boundary of the fire, which the fire-fighters have drawn under the supervision of German sailors, who were sent to save the German hospital, but who were soon in command of the affair from one end of the line to the other.

The streams of water are too thin to do much checking. They rise again in superheated steam that shows how hot the fire really is and how impotent are the jets of water played upon it.

Over the sea of flames floats a red mist of sparks. Pieces of highly combustible materials, sizzling and hissing like rockets, go through this mist. The shores of the fiery sea are formed by the stone and brick buildings near the top of the hills. The walls show red, like burnished copper, and the windows glisten like rubies.

From the streets and alleys comes the babble of a thousand voices. Fires are not rare in Constantinople. But this one is greater than any in the memory of living man. The long procession of pack-animals and Kurd *hamals*, who bring into safety whatever can be reached, go through the streets like funeral trains.

SOME OTHER TURKISH VIEWPOINTS

Three o'clock in the morning.

The fire has exhausted itself. The supply of dry wood is consumed. The wet walls further up stand unseared. I take my sketches and come home.

August 7th.

Had tea with Halideh Hannym to-day—over in the quiet house in Stamboul, *locale* of the school which Halideh Hannym maintains.

The direct purpose of the call was a meeting with the Sheik-ul-Islam, whom Halideh Hannym knows very well. But that matter was soon disposed of. So while we had tea we spoke of other things. We talked about the Gallipoli campaign, about my trip to Arabia, and about the Armenians.

"It's all too bad!" said Halideh Hannym. "I wish the government could find some way out of the situation. Now the poor things are being taken to Mesopotamia. The heat and the hardships will kill many of them. I have heard that there have been massacres. I can't believe it!"

I said nothing to that. I was unable to vouch for any of the many stories concerning the Armenian situation which I had heard. And my hostess felt the tragedy keenly.

We turned to other subjects. Halideh Hannym has introduced the study of physiology in her school. The colored charts of anatomy on the wall caused me to speak of that subject.

"I am trying to make the course of study as thoroughgoing as I can," said Halideh Hannym. "But it is hard work. Sometimes I grow discouraged. Then I take a run to Principo, to see my boy, or to Sultan Tepeh, to visit my father, and then I feel again equal to the struggle.

"The amount of work that must be done before we can get the education of the masses here under way cannot be appreciated by you. We are hampered even by our language. It is so full of Persian and Arabian terms that have no meaning to the common people. And then the system of letters we use, and the abuses of this calligraphy, add to our troubles. What do you expect from a medium of instruction that requires almost six years' study and practice before you can write it?"

I consoled the good woman as best I could.

She had written a new book—another novel. It dealt with the problems of the New Turkey— it spoke of a love that was subordinated to duty.

Halideh Hannym was not in her happiest mood, I could see. Her face had a drawn look. Her eyes were tired. She needed a rest.

I suggested a trip to Principo and its pines and cypresses.

"Yes, I will go there soon. I must see my boy. What would I do without him? It is he who keeps me going. Often I think: What is the use of all this? I would go to a place where the problems of my race could not reach me, where all the world would be dumb, where only the trees and flowers could speak to me."

Poor Halideh Hannym! As I looked at Stamboul beyond the trees in the garden, and saw the latticed windows and *shahnishins*, the proud mosque cupolas, the minarets, and the bland façades of the public buildings, behind which sat the most incompetent class of public servants one can find, I realized that Halideh Edib Hannym had set herself a large task.

The *shahnishin* would have to go before the Turkish public could gain an Occidental view of life. Those cupolas would have to listen to a shorter *Qua'raan* before the heavy hand of fatalism could be taken off Turkish throats, and the calls of the *muezzin* from the minarets would have to be limited to three before the faithful would have time enough to compete with their co-citizens of *giaour* beliefs.

Competent men would have to take charge of public affairs—not the competent agents of foreign governments and coupon-clippers, but competent Ottoman officials—men who would look upon their office not as the birthright of a conqueror race, but as a trust given them by a public needing and deserving their best efforts—all that was in them.

"When you come back I shall be at Sultan Tepeh," said Halideh Hannym, as we parted. "My father will be glad to meet you. Don't forget to come soon!"

August 9th.

Again the *muezzin* called from the gallery of the Ministry of War, and again the last notes of his call were swallowed by the crashing intonation of a military march.

"I am always glad to see you," said Enver Pasha. The landing of the Allies in Suvla Bay does not disturb me—does not disturb any of the men who assist me.

"Already we have the situation in hand. Though the Allies threw some 120,000 men in there, and we had but a battalion on the site at that moment, we are now again masters of the situation.

"I am confident that we will be able to hold them. No new military problem has been added to our burden. It is a question of more men. We have the men. I have 200,000 men to spare even to-day, after taking care of the Anafarta developments. I am not disturbed.

"It would have been different had the Allies landed at some other point.

"No, I can't name that. But you know the map. As it is, we have nothing to fear—will never have anything to fear from what the Allies may do on Gallipoli or at the Dardanelles. In the end we will defeat them.

" It is too much line of communication for them. The climate does not favor them. Our men are holding their own, though defending their ground with their naked breasts. We must hold out. We must prevent the Allies from getting to Constantinople. It would be our end if they did. We must prevent that end. We must win!"

Thus spoke Enver Pasha, Ottoman Minister of War, and Vice-Generalissimo of the Ottoman army. His handsome young face—he is thirty-six—was tense with fervor. His brown eyes snapped. His well-shaped lips were firm. His torso was erect, his fist had come down on the top of his desk.

I surveyed this enthusiast, and wondered how

his responsible office and his great youth could be reconciled. I knew how he had come to that office. But the mere facts gave no index to the man's character, to the great strength of will he had shown—a will that would send any man to swing from a tripod in the morning if he dared question it.

"My work has not been easy," said Enver Pasha. "At times it has come near overwhelming me. But somehow I always seem to keep up with the many demands made upon me by the office.

"I live very temperately; that may be what saves me. I do not lose time in worrying, nor am I long in making a decision. I have found that the first judgment one arrives at is the best. To consider a thing too long means procrastination. You become tired of the subject in the end; you neglect it, and it is never done.

"I try to do to-day what I would have to do to-morrow. Once I dismissed — cashiered — five thousand officers in that manner—a question of only a few minutes' thought.

"That step has made the Ottoman army what it is to-day. I have not the slightest use for the incompetent, the unfit, the weak, the hesitating, the evaders, the shirkers, the pleasure-seekers. I am obliged to thrust them out of my way, and so far, I am glad to say, I have not lacked the courage to do that.

"That is the only policy which will again make of Turkey, of the Ottoman Empire, what it ought to be. We must show those who hate us that we do not fear them. We must show those who think

331

little of us that we do not care a rap for their opinions. We must show the leaders in the West that we are their equals—in war as in peace.

"How can we do that unless we select a road upon which we may travel, and then stick to that road, no matter how long and dusty it may be? Turkey in order to remain Turkey must work, must improve itself, and right now it must fight, with the naked breast and a rock in the hand, as our men are doing on Gallipoli."

An ambitious program, I thought. Could it be carried out? That I doubted. Were the Turks somewhere by themselves the chances would be better. For such an undertaking there is only one basis—government by the consent of the governed. The Ottoman Empire has anything but that.

I asked Enver Pasha some questions concerning the Armenian situation. He showed no enthusiasm. He was doing his best to settle that affair. Just what he meant by his best I did not learn.

I left him with permission to go again to Gallipoli.

The Armenians are going through hell again. I have heard that some have been burned alive —at the stake. Massacres are said to continue; deportations are going on as before, despite all efforts made by neutral diplomatists to put an end to that shocking phase of barbarity. So long as the Armenians are in a town, life at least is secure. It is out in the open, in the waste places, that the worst comes to pass.

I understand that thousands have perished while being taken from one place to another. How they perish I have not heard, but I can imagine it—

lack of food and shelter, hardship, exhaustion, disease, and massacre.

Several attempts I have made to get out a story on the Armenian outrages have failed, of course. My efforts to do my duty have prejudiced the Turkish censors against me. Finally, I tried to get the German embassy to forward my copy to Berlin by means of its diplomatic courier. No such luck, of course. There were regrets that my request could not be considered. To forward my despatches would be a violation of diplomatic privilege. I suppose that is one way of putting it. Meanwhile, the story gets out anyway.

August 16th.

It is Ramasan—the month of fasting during the daylight hours; the month of feasting at night.

Through the acacias of *Les Petits Champs* peep the lighted minarets—the wreaths of little lamps on the gallery whence the *muezzin's* voice is heard. The day has been hot. From the gravel at my feet rises the heat that has been stored there, despite the shade of the acacias, under whose green roof I am a steady guest. The Golden Horn lies in purple drowsiness. The war-ships on it show their familiar banks of lighted port-holes.

I watch *Les Petits Champs des Morts* as I eat my supper. It is a restful place, restful not only to those who lie at the roots of the cypresses, but restful also to those who view it in the proper spirit. The gravestones have the appearance of *stèles* of dull silver in the faint moonlight. The grass reminds me of a carpet done in olive green

333

and Roman umber. Cypresses and gravestones and their shadows are the fitting pattern in this *tapis funèbre*—black and silver.

Through the cemetery, along one of the steep paths, comes a figure in black—one of Lady Falkland's rivals. The "man who was killed" appears, and then the two go over the path the woman had come. A common meeting in an uncommon place.

More guests come. Soon the serene stillness of the garden is broken by the clatter of dishes, the tinkle of glass, and the ringing of silverware. The conversation grows louder. Corks begin to pop. The pouring of the wine is heard. The smell of tasty dishes floats over the terrace. There are laughter and jest. What does it matter that the enemy is at the door and knocking in a manner that may not be misunderstood?

The concert begins. I stay a little longer.

A German *artiste* in a green dress sings a mediocre song with a worse voice, lacking even the rudiments of a training. Poor thing! They applaud, for all that. I applaud. She has done her best for the fifteen francs she gets per day.

A dancer appears. She is an Armenian. Every movement is grace, every gesture art, every look in her eyes temptation. It may be that Eve was an Armenian. I don't know. At any rate, we all applaud.

Chansonettes. The singer is a Greek, a slim Levantine with a reputation that reaches from here to Persia and back. Her French is not the best I have heard, but there is no difficulty in understanding what she means. Right now the lady is the "friend" of a pasha. That accounts for her marvelous costume and the diamonds—the two items which have placed her so well along on the program.

A Rumanian dancer appears. Her chief attraction is her odalisque beauty. An Ottoman surgeon of Jewish race shot himself because he lost her to a German aviator—a surgeon, of all people, committing suicide for a woman!

An Austrian ballad-singer is next on the program. She is one of the still waters that run deep. Demurely she steps to the front, bows, watches the orchestra leader, and then sings. Her songs are not bad, but in *Les Petits Champs* they would have never given her that place on the program were it not that a certain secretary of the K.k. Östreichisch-Ungarisch embassy had insisted on her getting a good position on the list.

An Egyptian dancer—a real one. She dresses the part and dances it. Rameses would have added her to his staff of *artistes*. But Rameses is dead, and so we have the pleasure of seeing how they danced in ancient Egypt. A rich Armenian pays her dress bills and flowers.

The next number on the program is a Spanish dance. The daughter of Castile breaks from the wings in all the glory of her many flouncy petticoats, in all the splendor of her gorgeous shawl, with all the coquetry of her face.

She dances as only the Spanish can dance. Toward the end of the first part she is joined by her companion, a young, dusky Spaniard in a bull-fighter's costume.

22   335

The castanets now clatter in double time. The dancers swing back and forth in a lively *fandango*. The picture is perfect. The guests in the garden go wild. The salvos of clapping hands do not seem to come to an end. The dancer takes the man by the hand and leads him to the footlights. Some, no doubt, think that she is his wife or mistress—but I know better. There never was such love as this girl holds for a certain German count. And if you must know how I know, I will say that she told me. She says that I am almost a compatriot of hers, even if my Spanish is not above reproach.

As I go out of the garden the castanets are busy again. I turn around, catch a glimpse of iridescent black beads on black satin, of the reddest of red shawls; catch the grace of the dancers; and then pass on.

The night is hot. The windows are open. The night noise of Pera is unique in its way.

The rap of the iron-shod night stick of the watchman comes from the pavement like a note from a xylophone. In the distance sound the horns of the fire-fighters.

"*Simitchi! Simitchi!*" comes the hoarse voice of the bread-twist vender.

"*Dondurma! Dondurma vanilly!*" shouts the ice-cream man.

"*Sisde ne turlu dondurma wardyr?*" ("Have you no other kind of ice-cream?") asks the voice of a woman from across the narrow street.

"*Vanilly yalynis!*" ("Only vanilla!") replies the man.

SOME OTHER TURKISH VIEWPOINTS

The woman doesn't want vanilla.

In *Les Petits Champs* the entertainment goes on. By this time the *artistes*, who have appeared, are sitting with the guests, drinking champagne, not because they like it so much, but because it is expected of them. The management gives them five francs a bottle commission.

In the morning I attend the execution, by strangulation, on a tripod gallows, of some soldiers who turned upon their officers. Two of them I saw at Akbash. They were trussed up in rope like bales of rags.

On that occasion I almost made a fool of myself. One of the prisoners had said something to the *onbashi* (corporal) which that personage did not like. The prisoner was standing on his feet at the time. A mighty blow over the heart, delivered by the ham-fisted corporal, felled him.

It was the sort of blow that makes prize-fighters "groggy." Being tied hand and foot, elbow and knee, the man fell hard. But that did not appease the brutal non-com.

He began to kick the man on the ground with his heavy munition-boots—in the chest, abdomen, and head.

Before long the prostrate man's face became blue. He began to gasp; he seemed to breathe with the greatest difficulty. Suddenly a stream of blood gushed from mouth and nostrils.

That was a little too much for me. I began to shout at the corporal. To my own surprise, the man stopped kicking the prisoner and walked away.

Some soldiers then occupied themselves with the

poor wretch. When he had been brought into a sitting position the flow of blood ceased. Somebody handed the man a drink of water, and as an evidence of the remarkable stamina of the Anatolian Turk, for such the prisoner is, he seemed in fairly good shape shortly afterward.

I took the trouble to bring the case to the attention of the commandant, and he took the trouble to inform me that it was none of my business. I agreed with him on that score, but made a few remarks anent the brutality and the like which caused me to be ordered out of the presence of this mighty Osmanli.

What could the Armenians expect from such a brute of an officer?

XI

THE INFERNO OF SUVLA BAY

ON August 6th Sir Ian Hamilton landed in Suvla Bay, and at Ariburnu, his second expeditionary corps, consisting in part of the first Kitchener army.

Developments on Gallipoli had shown that the forces landed in April and the constant stream of reinforcements they required could not accomplish anything. A little terrain had been gained at the two fronts, but that did not in any way better the position of the Allied troops.

There was one great obstacle that could not be overcome. The Allied forces depended to a large extent upon the guns of their supporting ships. For direct fire upon the Turkish trenches, so long as these lay some distance from the Allies' trenches, the naval artillery was well suited. There was no danger in that event of shelling one's own men.

But conditions changed, as the Turks, fully aware of the factors involved, sapped themselves closer to the trenches of their enemies. As soon as the two lines were but a hundred feet or so apart, the British naval gunners ran the risk of sending shells into their own infantry's lines.

The deck of even a moored ship is not the best base from which to fire. The Ægean Sea is never quiet. These circumstances and the necessity of keeping the ships moving, to thwart the effort of submarines that might be near, hampered the British ship gunners very much, as I have often observed.

If direct artillery fire suffered from these handicaps, indirect fire was still worse. The British infantry had advanced everywhere as far as the topographical crests visible from the sea. Up to that point it could still count upon the support of the Allied fleet. But to go beyond it meant doing without that support, if not entirely, then at least to a great extent.

Thus it came that even in June the British and French had advanced as far as it was safe. There was higher ground in front of them, but that was being stubbornly defended by the Turks. Then, too, before any of this high ground could be taken considerable areas of terrain, below the topographical crests visible from the sea, had to be wrested from the Turks.

In the offensive of the last week of June the British at Sid-il-Bahr tried very hard to take this higher ground. On their left flank they succeeded in a measure. At other points, near the center, they failed, however. The heavy sacrifices made were in vain. Part of the British line was pushed into ground that could not be shelled directly from the sea. The Turks had little to fear in the position they now occupied. A counter offensive was ordered by Liman Pasha and the British had to fall back upon their old trenches.

These were the reasons why Sir Ian Hamilton brought a second expeditionary force to the peninsula.

By the middle of August it was clear, however, that the British in Suvla Bay were in exactly the position of the troops at Ariburnu and Sid-il-Bahr. The efforts of General Stopford to gain the crests of the Kodjatchemen Dagh were promising enough for a few days. Ultimately they failed for the reasons indicated. The campaign became a stalemate. The troops began to suffer more and more from disease, and supply problems multiplied as the number of German submarines grew larger. The lack of drinking-water was always a serious matter. It was decided, therefore, to withdraw the Allied troops from Gallipoli. Suvla Bay and Ariburnu were first evacuated, in December, and Sid-il-Bahr was abandoned in January.

What the conditions at Suvla Bay were is shown by some of my entries:

RODOSTO, *August 19th.*

I am *en route* for Akbash and the Anafartas. Just now I am on land. The Turkish torpedo-boat on which I am a passenger is part of a flotilla of armed vessels that convoys a supply-fleet of the Turks to Akbash. We cannot travel during the day, because there are four British submarines in the Marmora.

The commandant of Rodosto had to be called upon as a matter of courtesy. We began to speak of the British submarines.

"Those things are a pest," he said. "Getting

cheekier every day. Why, early this morning, just before your convoy came in, one of them was lying offshore here, sunning itself. The boat was out of range of my battery. Fired a shot to scare her crew. But they wouldn't scare, those fellows. I wonder how you managed to get through."

I explained that we had *barely* managed.

We were going down the west shore of the Marmora last night when it happened. The four steamers going to Akbash with supplies were keeping well in shore, so that they might need no protection on their starboard sides. A Turkish destroyer was heading the procession, while my torpedo-boat was first on the flank; then followed another torpedo-boat. The rear was brought up by some sort of an ancient ironclad.

All went well until about ten o'clock. The sea lay still in the moonlight. I was sitting aft on a deck-chair, tired, finally, of the many forward spirals we had cut into the glassy surface. The torpedo-boat's direct task was to keep the flank of the convoy protected by scouting in circles and keeping up with the transports at the same time— sort of looping manner of progress. It was tiresome to see land now on this, now on that, side; to see the moon now on port, now forward, then on starboard, and finally aft, and then to do it all over again.

All had gone well so far. Suddenly the report of a gun came from near the head of the convoy. Excitement followed immediately. Other shots followed. More commotion The convoy went farther inshore. The submarine got out of the way of the destroyer and my torpedo-boat—and just then the foremost of the transports grounded on a rock. More excitement, more trouble.

We all helped to tow the 3,000-tonner off—and about twelve o'clock we succeeded.

YALOVA, *August 20th.*

We left Rodosto, and arrived at Akbash without further submarine incident. But we reached Akbash just as the Allied air *escadrille* was coming over the bluff. They saw us coming and saved a few of their bombs for our decks. But the decks are small and the strait is wide. The bombs did no damage.

But Akbash looked different. When I left it last there was a single wreck in the shallow water along the beach—an old *mahonie*. Now four fairly large steamers show their hulls in the little cove. Two of them are locatable by the top trucks of their masts. The third is submerged to the roof of the deck-house, and the fourth sits on the beach on a slant that keeps her bow high and dry, and her stern under the water.

There was much activity at the base. The new troops in the peninsula have increased the traffic by forty per cent., and the Allied submarines and aviators and the Allied indirect fire have augmented the proportions of the task. So the Turkish major in charge is not in the best humor. He was barely civil.

Through the heat and dust to Yalova.

August 23d.

Just back from a trip to the Kodjatchemen

Dagh, where I spend the day in an artillery observation-station fifty feet underground. The Allied artillery causes little streams of soil to trickle through the beam-and-board ceiling of the station, but beyond that we had no untoward experience.

But I had one this morning that is worth recording.

We left headquarters at seven o'clock in charge of the German military attaché at Constantinople, Colonel von Lassow, who in his turn was in charge, so to speak, of a Turkish *onbashi* (corporal) who had sworn that he knew the route that would take us past Buyuk Anafarta, and then to the Kodjatchemen Dagh—a mountain which the British would like to have in their hands.

There was no trouble until we got to the cemetery of Buyük Anafarta. We had cleared two short exposed stretches of the road at a gallop. No shells. But instead of turning to the left behind a ridge which seemed the limit of the safety zone to me, the Turkish corporal went right ahead. Again we came into view of the British ships—full view, this time—and zow—brrrrrrrrrrr—plopp-plopp-plopp-plopp!

A large crater lay twenty feet ahead of us, when the smoke and dust cleared. It was a narrow shave, indeed. I thought my hair had been singed. But it wasn't. But there is a canary-colored tint on my face and hands that will stay there for some time to come.

After that the corporal admitted that he was not so much of a pathfinder as he had thought he was. Well, we forgave him. It is easy to forgive anything when you have just stepped back from the very gate of eternity.

A study of the Suvla Bay proved most uninteresting. The British lie along the base of the hill range. They had the crest of the Djonk Bahir in their hands until August 7th, when Colonel Kannengieser drove them off.

The purpose of the landing is the same as that of the operations at Ariburnu; to-day, in fact, Suvla Bay and Ariburnu are a single front.

ABOVE TÜRCHÜNKOI, *August 25th.*

Ariburnu being what it was when I was here before, and with the Kodjatchemen Dagh visited and the Anafarta sectors viewed, I thought I would have a peep at things in the Kizlar Dagh, especially the famous Kiretch Tepeh.

Willmers Bey is the commander here. He is unusually courteous—a German cavalry officer of breeding and means.

Getting here was no mean undertaking. First the dusty valley from Yalova to Kum Koi and Turchünkoi, and then the hot ascent of the Kaval Tepeh. But we accomplished all of this in a day and landed here dusty, dirty, and dry.

I wanted to see the Kiretch Tepeh. Willmers Bey thought that it would be best to do it at night. The approach was still exposed in part, he said, and the Allied torpedo-boats and destroyers in the Ægean Sea kept the shore under fire all day long.

Well, night did seem the best time!

Despite the heavy traveling done during the day,

I decided to go to the Kiretch Tepeh that very
night. At eleven we started.

It was frightfully hot and sultry. Not a breath
of air stirred. We entered the long communication-
trench which takes one over part of the exposed
field. The ditch was like an oven. All day long
the hot sun had beaten into it. Now it was radi-
ating its store of heat. The perspiration began to
run in streams.

Down, down, down! The Kaval Tepeh is fairly
high. Before long I was under the impression that
we had gone below the level of the Ægean Sea.
A glimpse of the water showed, however, that
we were still far above it.

Suvla Bay came into view. It was lighted up
like a big port by some forty men-of-war and
transports. The banks of lighted port-holes, the
lights on deck and in the masts, the lights on the
moving tenders and the smaller craft on patrol
about the herd, gave one the impression that a
large harbor lay before one's eyes instead of the
once lonesome waters of Suvla Bay.

And it seemed to be fête-day in this port. A
score of projectors was busy. The search-lights
lighted up the slopes of the vast amphitheater back
of Suvla Bay. For a while they would hold on a
certain point, and then would move on to some
other part, stop, and then move on again.

We watched the spectacle for quite a while.
Then the arc-carbons in the projectors, one by one,
turned red and ceased to glow.

Turkish supply details were passed. Many of the
men carried large copper kettles in and out of the

trenches. The men in the advance positions were getting their rations of cooked food.

Soon I was to wonder how the men in front could eat food of any sort.

We had reached the Kiretch Tepeh. On its eastern slope, and on the little plateau below, had occurred the stiff fighting of August 13th. The dead had been buried where they fell, so that now we stood among the large company graves in which "Anzac" and Ottoman had been laid to rest, regardless of race and creed.

The nature of the ground made good burial impossible. The hard limerock does not yield to pick and spade. The Turks had dug down as deep as they could, had heaped the bodies in the shallow trough, and then covered them up as best as they could.

Through the thin layer of earth and rock enveloping the bodies welled a stench that was the worst I had ever experienced. The night being sultry and hot, with not a breath of wind stirring, did not help matters.

To get to the top of the Kiretch Tepeh and view the advance position of the British, known to the Turks as the "Green Hill," we had to get across the plateau. I tried to wrap my organs of smell in a thick cloud of cigarette smoke. But nothing could overcome that odor—nothing could combat its fearful density and penetration.

It was dark now—not the dark of a black night, but the uncertain light that comes from dense ground vapors and a moon standing behind clouds. We could not use the electric torch, because that would have drawn fire— we were only 150 yards from the British line. As a result a soldier who accompanied us stuck one of his feet into a grave. We had to pull him out.

We scaled the Kiretch Tepeh on all-fours. The Turks were busy putting their trenches in order. It was hard work on this ground. The soil is nowhere more than six inches deep, and what little there is had to be carefully scraped together for the sandbagging that was to form the parapet of the shallow ditch.

"Green Ihll" lay quiet.

Over against the slopes of the Kodjatchemen Dagh an outpost fight developed. Rifles were used first, then hand-grenades. One of the Allied ships on the bay fired a few shots at a point we could not see—indirect map fire at some Turkish line of communication, I thought.

At two in the morning we made our way back to the top of Kaval Tepeh, site of the Willmers headquarters. I turned in with a violent headache, due to the combination of heat and stench.

This morning at six *réveillé*. Willmers Bey wanted to inspect parts of his sector and invited me to come along.

Again through the long communication-trench, with every bone in the body still aching from last night's exertions.

This time we drew fire from the Ægean—fifteen shells of 15-cms.

Well, nothing happened.

After that we took a bath in the Ægean under the very noses of the British. We left the little cove quick enough when a torpedo-boat came around the point and began to use a machine-gun on the water.

I am sorry for the poor devils who have to fight in that hell hole behind Suvla Bay, be they Turks or "Anzacs."

OFF LAPSAKI, ON THE DARDANELLES, *August 29th.*
I am the baggageless guest of Admiral Souchon, head of the Ottoman navy. That I am so quickly returning to Constantinople is the result of a telegram I received, saying that important orders awaited me at the American embassy. That I have no baggage is another story.

When the wire came I made up my mind that the quickest way back to Pera would be by means of a torpedo-boat lying off Dardanelles. I didn't know it was the flag-ship of the admiral. But the admiral has an American wife and consequently is friendly toward all Americans.

"Why, certainly! Come along!" he said, in that whole-hearted manner of his. "Glad to have you!"

The torpedo-boat left Dardanelles at 5 P.M. sharp. Twenty minutes later we were in Kilia Bay, taking aboard a sick officer—no less a person than Lieutenant Wellman of the *Emden,* who has been trying hard to throw an effective anti-submarine barrage across the strait near Cape Nagara.

Ten minutes later we were in the vortex of as hot a bombardment of Akbash as that much-tried place had ever seen. The fire of the British men-of-war over in the Ægean was indirect—and high.

Most of the shells landed in the strait we had to go through.

We hugged the Anatolian shore as closely as we dared, received the full impact of a waterspout thrown up by one of the shells, and then with every ounce of steam on cleared the danger zone. Akbash was still under fire when the sun had set.

"A narrow squeak," commented the admiral while we had supper in the dingy, hot, and stuffy cabin. "But we are all used to them now. It is a rare privilege to see another sunrise nowadays."

For the time being we were safe enough. Lieutenant Gerdts, another of the *Emden* officers, was on the bridge, and we were making speed of the sort that leaves little to do for the submarines.

Wellman was having much trouble with that submarine barrage, he said. Didn't have material enough nor material of the right sort. He had fumed and fretted under his handicaps until the fever had found him in a receptive state.

After supper we went on deck again. The breeze stood in the north and brought down a little of Russia's temperate climate, so much of it that by midnight the admiral urged one of his coats upon the baggageless passenger.

At two this morning something happened—the steering-gear of the torpedo-boat failed. For two hours thereafter we lay on the water motionless and the ready prey for any submarine that might come along.

Admiral Souchon grew impatient, and after that repairs proceeded at a better pace.

In Pera with the first light of dawn.

XII

CONCLUSION

THOUGH the Ottoman Empire is an agricultural state and a good producer of wheat, corn, and other cereals, want, and then famine, made their appearance when the country had been at war about six months.

The food shortage hit Constantinople first. Already in May the price of food began to soar. In July the first bread-lines were seen in the city, and in October great numbers of the poor had to go without wheat bread entirely.

For a state which had in the past depended upon agriculture almost wholly that was a remarkable condition of affairs.

The fact is that there was a great deal of wheat in the interior of Anatolia and Syria. But it could not be moved. Hundreds of thousands of tons of breadstuffs rotted on the farms for lack of proper storage.

The Anatolian and Syrian farmers had in the past disposed of their cereal crops quickly. The crop was harvested and within a few weeks the grain was sold and shipped. The question of proper storage had never troubled them and so

23 351

they were not able to meet this emergency. The Anatolian and Bagdad railroads were no better prepared for the situation. They and their feeding lines were given over largely to military transports.

These systems are single-tracked throughout, and there is nothing quite so unsatisfactory as a line of that sort when overburdened with traffic. The Ottoman forces in the Caucasus, in the Suez Desert, and in Mesopotamia needed all the tonnage the railroads could haul. The fact that there were still two breaks in the Bagdad Railroad did not improve conditions.

Much of the grain raised in Anatolia and Syria had in the past been shipped to Constantinople by water. Syria exported through the ports of Beirut, Alexandrette, Mersina, and Smyrna. To the latter also much of the breadstuffs produced in southern Anatolia were taken by the feeding lines of the Anatolian and Bagdad railroads.

This could no longer be done. The British and French ships in the Mediterranean were blockading the Ottoman coast in a most effective manner, and at the Dardanelles the barrier of steel of the Allied fleet was insurmountable.

The Turks had also maintained a lively wheat traffic on the Black Sea. Much of the grain produced in central and northern Anatolia had in the past gone to Constantinople from the ports along the Black Sea shore. The Russian fleet made that impossible now.

Thus it came to pass that Constantinople depended entirely upon western Anatolia for its supply of bread and other foods. Western Anatolia might have taken care of the needs of the capital had there been transportation. But that was not the case. As I have already stated, the railroads were overloaded with military traffic, and, while the rails could have carried more, there was not enough rolling stock.

The Constantinople population ate up what had been produced in Thrace and around the Sea of Marmora, and then began to fast.

Another factor made itself felt. Turkey had entered the war in November and had mobilized on a grand scale. Most of the able-bodied men were taken from the farms at a time when they should have plowed and sown. As elsewhere, the women tried to meet this condition. But they were not equal to it.

With the shortage of food came the food-shark. The toll he exacted was crushing. The government increased taxes until the population groaned under the load. Though the German government saw to it that the Ottoman government could raise loans in Berlin, the men in the ministries of Stamboul were still obliged to find a great deal of money at home.

I must attest that the loans and taxes taken up by the Turkish government for war purposes went far—farther, perhaps, than money has gone in any other country during the war. Enver Pasha was the man to have any war profiteer, who leached upon the government, taken out and hung without ado of any sort—without a trial, if he was satisfied that the man had stolen one of the few *livres turques* available for the work he so arduously prosecuted.

But Turkey has long been a poor country. The best of its sources of revenue have been hypothecated for years to the international management of the public debt institute. The income from a great deal of direct and indirect taxation had in the past been turned over to the *dette publique,* without so much as a percentage to the Ottoman government finding its way back again in Turkish public channels.

That this was so was largely the fault of the Abdul Hamidan régime. Abdul Hamid and his personally conducted government had the knack of spending money lavishly without asking where it came from. So long as even the slightest prospect of posterity could be taxed the former Sultan was the man to do it. The rate of interest being good, Abdul Hamid could always count on the co-operation of the crowd of international Shylocks that was interested in Turkey.

The Young Turk party undertook the revolution for the purpose of improving upon this state of affairs. In 1908 Abdul Hamid and his specious crowd of adherents were disposed of in a rather bloodless revolution, and with the coming to the throne of his brother, Mohammed Réchad Khan V, in April, 1909, a better era seemed to dawn for Turkey.

But the promising dawn did not last long. Before long violent squalls came. Bulgaria, Serbia, and Greece made war upon Turkey. Italy joined them later. Most of the Balkans was lost to the Slav

CONCLUSION

Allies, and Italy deprived Turkey of her last possessions in northern Africa.

I have met few Turks who did not look upon this loss of territory as a blessing in disguise. In fact, I have met many who were of the opinion that the Turks should surrender more, by giving the Arabs and Armenians their freedom.

With the Balkan and Italian wars over in 1912, the Young Turk government attempted to set its house in order. But that was not easy. The old régime was still strong, especially in the provinces. The reformers of the Party of Union and Progress, as the Young Turks style themselves officially, found a great deal of passive resistance. A good impulse might start in Stamboul, but there was no assurance that it would get very far in the provinces.

Nor was the Party of Union and Progress an aggregation of angels. It caused the assassination of one of its best men, Nazim Pasha, then Ottoman Minister of War. In January, 1913, he fell a victim of his own good intentions. Nazim Pasha was a liberal in the true sense of the word. One of his ideals was to run the government in such a manner that the non-Osmanli subjects of the empire would for once feel that they were partners in the state instead of mere chattels.

It has been said that Enver Pasha caused Nazim Pasha to be murdered. The many attempts I have made to run down this story have failed. The fact that Enver Pasha stepped into the shoes of the assassinated Young Turk leader cannot be considered conclusive evidence that Enver Pasha perpetrated this foul act.

355

The Young Turk government had its quota of thieves, of course. No attempt having ever been made in Turkey to get intelligence and efficiency into government officials and employees, the administration of public affairs remained very much what it had been under Abdul Hamid. There was the same incapacity, the same ineptness, the same indolence, the same lack of civic spirit.

As to the reasons why Turkey entered the European war I have said enough elsewhere. I have taken the word of Ottoman government officials for that.

That was the political background of Turkey.

I must say that the Young Turks had made a good many improvements in and about the capital. With the elimination of the pest of dogs in Constantinople came a better regard for public health. For the first time in the history of the city the streets were kept clean. The pavement was improved, and by 1915 Constantinople was cleaner than most American cities. The streets were flushed twice daily when it was necessary, and "white-wings" swept them during the day.

As the war broke out a survey for a modern sewerage system was being completed. The police department had been improved, and the attempt was being made to better the woefully inefficient fire department. Perhaps the greatest blessing of the change in government was that the plain man came near getting a square deal before the law. The old Moslem *kadi* had made room for a judge not uninclined to be just so long as he could afford it. Government and jurisprudence were still corrupt, as seen from the Occidental point of view, but for the East they were not bad at all.

As a foreigner in Constantinople I came now and then in contact with the police administration. I must say that I found the officials uniformly polite and willing to oblige. It must not be over-looked, however, that in the eyes of the Turkish official classes I was somewhat of a personage. One becomes that in Constantinople after one has had an audience with the Sultan and is acquainted with the ministers of the government. That, I suppose, would be the case in many other parts of the world.

But I had occasion also to watch the treatment by the police of the common classes of the city. So long as the person dealing with the police was polite good treatment was assured. It never pays to "rile" a Turk. To do that is an invitation to him to show his uglier traits, and these, unfortunate-ly, are all more or less related to brutality. But that is the East of it. Of the Turkish as of the Russian official it may be said:

"Grattez le Russe et trouvez le Tartar!"

Upon this flinty reality impinged soon the want of the population. It was not a pleasant spectacle. Some of the entries in my journal of those days would make pity-rousing reading.

The government being for the greater part in the hands of Turks, discrimination against non-Turks ensued. Stamboul and Scutari, the Turkish quarters of the city, always got the lion's share of the food. That was bad enough so far as the stomach was concerned. But the effect of it went much further.

Again it was shown that while the Greeks and Armenians might pay taxes, and do such work in the armies as their doubtful value as Ottoman soldiers permitted, they really had no place in the heart of the Ottoman government. They were still stepchildren to whom one threw the crusts, to whom, in the case of the Armenians, came all the abuse.

I have known hundreds of Greeks and Armenians whom this conduct of the government estranged. Together with their Turkish compatriots these people had hoped that Turkey would continue and that better days would come. But again it was made clear to them that they were *in* the empire, not *of* the empire.

Those were sad days in front of the bakeshops. The lines would form in the night, and often, when dawn came, only a few of the bread-liners would get the ration their tickets entitled them to. The bread of Constantinople in other days had been very good. It had formed at least fifty per cent. of the people's sustenance.

With a few olives added, a slice of *ekmek* made a meal. For a few paras one could get a glass of wine or a cup of coffee. These things and a few cigarettes were all that a large part of the population expected. In the summer one could get vegetables enough, and, when times were good, meat, generally mutton, could be had. But bread and olives were the food staples. It was now hard to get them.

More corn was eaten. For a time there was enough of this. But the supply of that also failed. Then came famine to Constantinople.

CONCLUSION

Prices had soared steadily ever since Turkey entered the war. In October, 1916, they were no longer to be reached. Bread now cost four times what it was before the war. Olives were hard to get at any price. Meat was five times what it had cost before. Sugar sold at eight medjidiehs the oka— about $3.50 an American pound.

Even coffee was hard to get. The government increased the taxes on tobacco. There was not a thing, in fact, that did not sell at four times the former price. Clothing, if it was cheap, cost three times what it had cost in 1914. Coal could no longer be had, and there were times when stove wood and charcoal even were hard to get, though there is still much forest within easy reach of Constantinople. Petroleum also gave out, and the tallow that would have made candles had to be eaten.

By that time conditions were very much the same throughout Central Europe. But in Germany and Austria-Hungary wages at least had also shown a tendency to go up. Not so in Turkey. Men and women continued to draw the meager wage they had earned for a decade, and the storekeepers were now taxed to an extent that left them little, despite the extortionate prices they were asking for their wares. The Turkish government was mobilizing the paras of the poor as elsewhere the Heller and the Pfennig were being mobilized. But the Turkish government did this in a more brutal manner. It simply took from the individual without giving him a chance to earn more. Instead of exploiting the labor of the man, it deprived him of the little he needed and expected.

The needs of the government being many and broad in scope, it was soon discovered that even the Turkish population could not be spared. The tax-collector called on all, and was adamantine with everybody.

The non-Turk population was soon bled white. A few of its members stood in well with the clique in Stamboul. They were spared. Especially was this the case with certain Greeks and *espaniole* Jews who acted as the minions in the economic blood-letting that was going on. A score or so grew rich, and there is no reason for the assumption that their masters in the Ottoman government escaped with clean hands, Enver Pasha excepted.

It got to be the turn of the Turkish population. There was by that time not a single Turkish household in the empire that did not have all of its able-bodied men of military age at the front or in the barracks. What fighting there was done in the Caucasus and in Mesopotamia was done by Turks. The Ottoman Greek is of no value as a soldier, and the Armenian was no longer trusted The former was employed in the sanitary service and on the lines of communication; the latter built roads, dug trenches, and acted as beast of burden. That meant that the Turkish population lost all the blood on the battle-fields.

I knew the family of a Turkish major who used to hold forth as an artillery observation officer in the bomb-proof in the crown of Atchi Baba. The man had taken a liking to me and did the very un-Moslem thing of introducing me to his "household." He was getting the munificent pay of sixteen pounds Turkish a month, about $70. Private means there were none. His "household" consisted of a wife and five daughters.

Out of his pay the major kept enough to buy the cheapest of cigarettes—*sixièmes*. Now and then he had to have a uniform and a pair of boots. There were a few other things absolutely needed, and there were mess expenses.

Before the war that $70 had gone much further, and the major had found the time to do some sort of clerical work at night. Now, however, things were different.

To get a reasonable amount of food for her children the wife sold and pawned everything she could spare. At one time the family of the major had been better off, and the house, which he still owned, contained many things of value, such as fine rugs, articles of beaten copper, engraved brasses, good vases, and some jewelry.

The major's heart almost broke when he had to part with these things. But, rather than have the family go hungry, he ordered his wife to sell them. But she got little for them. Just then everybody was in the market with articles of that sort. There were thousands of families in Constantinople who had to sell and pawn rugs, copper, vases, laces, jewelry, and the like.

The dealers knew this and were not likely to pay good prices, for that reason. They, too, found it hard to get cash. Nobody bought. So it happened in the end that the fine rugs and carpets were combed into shoddy fiber, and that the brasses and copper utensils were converted into ammunition. The only thing that brought a good price at all was gold. But with that only the uninformed and desperate parted.

In the end the major sold his house. Real estate was not in keen demand just then. There is no doubt that the money brought by the sale did not last very long. When I saw the major last he was much depressed.

"I am disgusted with life, *mon cher capitaine!*" he said. "I have been willing to give my own life for my country. But I cannot reconcile myself to the fact that my family is suffering from want, almost because of what I am doing. What will happen to my dependents in case I should be carried off? The small pension they will get will not keep them in bread nowadays. Is that all the government can do for the men in the field?"

For the first time in the history of the Osmanli race its women began to work for their living. At first this went no further than the making of laces and embroideries at home. But that did not pay. Material was high in price and the market was not good. In the end no buyers of that sort of thing could be found at all.

Before the sphere of woman labor could be extended, many old customs and prejudices had to be thrown down. The Sheik-ul-Islam—head of the Mohammedan religion next to the Sultan-Caliphe—was a man of liberal mind. He let it be understood that these were extraordinary times and that many of the rules of seclusion would have to be cast aside. For the time being, at any rate, women would have to take care of themselves as best they might.

But at first the opportunities were few. Turkey is the land of home industry and small shops. The field of manufacture is very small, moreover, and just then it was impossible to get the raw materials that were needed.

The government, however, had realized that something would have to be done to employ the women. There was much muttering in the army. Officers and men were in an ugly mood. They wanted their women folk better provided for.

Some German economic experts were sent for, and under their direction the organization of woman labor was undertaken. First of all the greater production of food was taken in hand. For that purpose many of the Turkish city women were sent to the farms in western Anatolia and in Thrace. That helped quite a bit. A further alleviation was effected by removing from all industries men who were doing work that could be done by women. Again German efficiency and thoroughness came to the assistance of the Turks. In the winter of 1917 the situation was well in hand.

It is altogether unlikely that the Turkish woman will ever again return to the state that was hers before the war. She has tasted the sweets of self-reliance, as have her sisters in Central Europe, and it will take but little effort on her part to make her emancipation complete.

But these measures of relief always benefited the Turks more than others. It was a case of "nativism." Little attention was given the non-Moslem population.

Though the Levantine Greeks have the reputation of being able to take care of themselves, they no longer had the opportunity to do that as well as formerly. True, they were given the crumbs and crusts and they did much with them, but these would not go around. The Armenians were still worse off. Their sharpness in trade was of no value now. The government might think twice before it put a Greek food-shark in jail. In the case of an Armenian no such consideration was shown. When it came to menial labor there were the Kurds, who as *hamals* (carriers) have long been an institution of the Ottoman Empire.

Greek and Armenian women had in the past worked themselves round - shouldered and blind making lace and doing needlework. They were getting on an average two dollars a week for this when the war broke out. The younger women lived with their families, and the older ones with relatives. Often they would club together and then live four or five in a small flat or house.

Life had little good in store for them even then, but now it held nothing at all. A population in want does not buy laces and embroideries.

So the same old thing came to pass. Before long the streets of Pera were overrun with soliciting females. It ceased to be a rare thing to have mothers cast about for a man of means to take care of their daughters. Secret agencies for this purpose sprang into existence. The business soon set up regular standards and prices. The young and pretty were disposed of privately; the others sold themselves in public.

But they had a peculiar person in charge of the police of Constantinople—one Bedri Bey. The chief was in some respects as un-Eastern as he well could be. He wanted no soliciting on the streets. He even went so far as to raid hotels, and houses that had no license for their trade. The police station of the Galata Serai in Pera was each night full of women who had been taken from the street, especially the Gran' rue de Pera. They were fined in a merciless manner twice, and then they went to jail—that is, if they had no certificate of inspection. Since many of the women were not professionals at all, but had been driven to this step by utter want, the revenues of the Galata Serai police station were good just then.

I used to wonder how these women managed to pay the heavy fines. That they were able to pay them caused me to believe that the hard-luck stories they told were inventions. If a woman could still pay a fine of at least five Turkish pounds there was no good reason why she should solicit.

One day, however, I managed to get permission for the inspection of some of the jails about Constantinople. After I had seen them I decided that there was still a greater extreme than that which had driven the women on the street. And then we must not forget that in the East, where once it was the practice of young women to earn their dowries in this manner, they have their own notions about such things.

Virtue there is a luxury, not a necessity, as it is regarded in the Occident.

I had occasion one day to discuss this with Bedri Bey in Le Petit Club, of which we both were members.

I discovered that he was interested in the matter from a purely hygienic angle. He wanted these women to undergo inspection. Later I learned that the man was much better than that viewpoint would indicate.

He scotched the "white slave" traffic of Constantinople, and to do so he even invaded so sacred a precinct as the Russian consulate in the capital. Quite boldly, he one day arrested several of the employees of the consulate on a charge of traffic in women, and, what is more, he sent them to the worst jail in Turkey. Racial antipathy may have had something to do with that. At any rate, it was Bedri Bey who broke the back of the trade in flesh in Constantinople.

Bedri Bey regretted that I had never seen a certain quarter in Galata before he cleaned it up. But I had heard of the quarter. I understand that the worst in Cairo and Port Saïd was no circumstance to it.

Into the houses and hovels of that quarter were sold girls from all over adjacent Europe. Most of them came from Rumania, and the trade was entirely in the hands of Russians and Greek Levantines.

Veritable boatloads of young women were dumped into this modern Moloch—to amuse the very dregs of humanity, the wharf-rats and Kurd *hamals* of

Constantinople. As a little starter in cleaning out this place Bedri Bey caused the arrest and conviction of some three hundred men and women who were connected with the traffic.

Most of these were subjects of other countries—Russia, Rumania, Greece, Italy, and Austria. Not a few were of that peculiar dual-citizenship which makes a European born in Turkey a citizen of the country with whose consulate the birth is registered.

That these people should appeal to their respective consular officials for protection I can understand. But I must marvel at the hardihood of a government which in such cases would interfere with the operation of the law, even if it be merely an Ottoman law.

The consuls who demanded the release of any of the traffickers met the wrong man in Bedri Bey. He went out of his way to be unobliging. The traders in flesh were held and sentenced and the provisions of the capitulations were disregarded by the Ottoman government for the first time. The capitulations have since then been abolished.

On the whole, the effect of the war has not been so disastrous to the population in Constantinople as it was elsewhere in the countries of the Central Powers group. There was not so much to pull down in Turkey. Those who fell did not fall so far.

Life in the East is still primitive in the case of the majority. Want and famine did not bring much mental anguish. There was refinement in Constantinople, of course. But those whom it blessed were comparatively few in number and

24

generally they were able to weather the storm—out in the country, if in no other manner.

There was little privation at any time in the Ottoman provinces—the vilayets. Transportation was no problem out there. The breadstuffs that could not be sold could at least be consumed. When in Constantinople good wheat flour was already a rare article the little watermills in the Taurus and Amanus mountains were still producing the best in that line.

Thirty miles away from the larger towns living was but little dearer than it had been before the war. Many things could no longer be had, of course. For the first time within the memory of those living was there no coffee. The scarcity of sugar bothered nobody out there. In Anatolia and Syria much honey is produced.

Even such towns as Smyrna and Damascus were never greatly affected by the shortage of food. The same is true of Aleppo, Adana, and Tarsus. So long as one was willing to put up with the bill of fare of the country there was no need for going hungry. But there is little I can say for the cooking of the Near East. Some of the dishes are palatable enough—or they would be if there was no mutton tallow in them.

I believe that the peoples of the Ottoman Empire have suffered less from the food shortage than any other in the Old World. Want was acute and chronic only in Constantinople and its vicinity. But what the population was spared in that respect was certainly exacted in the heavy tolls in lives. The losses of the Turks on Gallipoli, in Mesopotamia, and in the Caucasus were large. They came at a time when the wounds inflicted by the Balkan War were not yet healed. How many Armenians perished is hard to say. The Greeks, however, suffered no losses of that sort.

If Turkey, so far as the Osmanli are concerned, has to-day a million fit young men she must consider herself very fortunate. War has bled the race white and one must agree with Halideh Edib Hannym's view that the future of her people rests with its women.

Of the Turkish races the women are the better element. The men have been ruined by the position of their race—that of a conqueror who subscribes to the fallacy that might is right.

That seems a little illogical at first. It might be so in any other case. But it is not in this.

What the Turk has been in the past to Armenian, Greek, Syrian, Kurd, Arab, the Balkan Slavs, and the Bulgar, not to mention all the others, he has also been toward his own women. He managed to hold them all in subjection.

Favors he has shown to all of them, but they were still favors. That those over whom he lorded it had rights has not often occurred to the Turk. He will go out of his way to oblige, but is hard to convince that not all the things he gives away are peculiarly his own.

The Turkish woman has developed an odd sort of class spirit. Turkey is the one country in which men and women are in separate camps mentally. In the past the Turkish woman has associated with no other men than those of her family—benign tyrants. Of the great outside world she knows only the women. In the course of a life she might meet thousands of women, but always the same men: Her father, brothers, husband, and sons.

Small wonder, then, that Turkey is a dual-world, a world in which men and women do not think at all alike.

The mental capacity of the Turk is too great, even if ill-directed and misapplied, to permit the women of the race to deteriorate mentally under the system of seclusion that has been adhered to in the past. Mental vigor and humility have been the heirloom of the daughters of the race.

The meeting of these two qualities has produced in the Turkish woman a fine sort of rationalism—a rationalism which is devoid of that grossness it takes on when tainted with materialism.

It may seem trifling to mention here that no Turkish woman will touch money so long as she can avoid it. There is a rule among these people that money intended for a woman is placed where she can take it after the giver is gone. That and similar customs have fostered in the Turkish woman, and preserved to the race as a whole, a degree of unselfishness and honesty which is not only hard to match in the East, but which contains also whatever promises the future has in store for the Turk.

The mind of the Turanian may run to conquest and oppression, but avarice is foreign to it. The Turk is a spendthrift; he is improvident, slovenly, self-indulgent, obstinate, and egotistical.

His woman is the very opposite. And in being that she has saved from obliteration the qualities of the "four hundred tents of Osmanli" who pitched their camp in 1175 within sight of the Byzantian frontier post of Dorylæum with the avowed intention that they would found an empire by destroying one.

They did that and conquered much of Europe besides.

Whether the Turkish woman will have the chance to resuscitate the good in her race, or whether the star of the Osmanli has set forever, is one of the questions which the Great War will decide.

THE END

Breinigsville, PA USA
31 October 2010
248406BV00003B/30/P

9 781176 635548